First Edition: 2016
Second Edition: 2020

ISBN 13: 978-1-7344198-7-0

Beyond The Fray Publishing, a division of Beyond The Fray, LLC, San
Diego, CA

www.beyondthefraypublishing.com

BEYOND THE FRAY

Publishing

SOMEWHERE IN THE SKIES

A Human Approach to the UFO Phenomenon

RYAN SPRAGUE

BEYOND THE FRAY

Publishing

CONTENTS

For the truth seekers, and those who support them along the way

---

In memory of Stanton T. Friedman

"There's an itch in my mind, but I can only find it occasionally. It's like rummaging through a box of ancient refuse and incomprehensible knick-knacks and suddenly feeling the two-pronged bite of a snake between your fingers; you recoil, shrinking, but your curiosity is irreversibly piqued. You want to empty the box in to the light of day, regardless of the danger, or maybe even because of it."

— Mac Tonnies,
Post Human Blues, Vol. 2, (2005–2006)

ACKNOWLEDGMENTS

To Peter Robbins. You taught me to never fear being wrong, especially in this complex and unforgiving topic. Our work together has only begun, and with each passing coffee we share, one more question is arguably answered... I think.

To my loving partner and editor, Jane Palomera Moore. You've taught me the difference between reliance and resilience in writing both editions of this book. You are my very own paradigm shift. You had me at, "What's up with UFOs over nuclear sites?"

To Susan Sprague, Douglas Sprague, and Kristi Sprague. You have never once swayed me from this bizarre and often ridiculed topic. As my unflinchingly understanding family, you have kept both open minds and open hearts through all of my endeavors inside and out of the UFO whirlwind. I am more appreciative of you than you'll ever know. I love you all to the moon and back.

Thank you also to MJ Banias, Greg Bishop, Mike Clelland, Curt Collins, Jeremy Corbell, Cheryl Carter, Cheryl Costa, Mike Damante, Kevin Day, Richard Dolan, Robbie Graham, John Greenewald Jr, Micah Hanks, Brent Hand, Ben Hansen, Jim Harold, Ben Hurle, Bryce Johnson, Leslie Kean, Paul Kimball,

Dennis Koch, Jane Kyle, Rob Kristoffersen, Erica Lukes, Jennifer Marshall, Michael McMillian, Christopher O'Brien, Jim Perry, Nick Pope, Nick Redfern, Nick Roesler, Alejandro Rojas, Miguel Romero, Chris Rutkowski, Aaron Sagers, Andrew Sanford, Lee Speigel, Jennifer Stein, Cookie Stringfellow, Amy Shira Teitel, John Tenney, Frederik Uldall, Gary Voorhis, Frank Warren, David Weatherly, Nick Westemeyer, and Bryce Zabel for your continued support in all my endeavors.

To Jason McClellan, Maureen Elsberry, and Shane Hurd of *Rogue Planet*. I consider you not only colleagues but close friends. You have been there for me many times in and out of the UFO arena, and have given me words of wisdom that have propelled me forward when I was ready to give up. And my immense gratitude to Shannon LeGro for inspiring me to create the *Somewhere in the Skies* podcast. You've taught me everything I know. My immense gratitude to both you and G. Michael Hopf for taking a chance on me at Beyond the Fray Publishing. This is for the entire "Frayzie" family!

And lastly, to those I had the absolute pleasure, honor, and rare opportunity to interview in the pages of this book, you are unquestionably its driving force, and you bravely lay at the heart of these deeply mysterious and perplexing phenomena. As you actively search for answers, perhaps that search will slowly evolve into theories that will one day become solid, hard facts. But until then, know we support your journey the best way we know how, with open minds, open hearts, and a need as human beings to question where we were, where we are, and where we are heading in this most mysterious universe we call home.

INTRODUCTION (2020)

Well, a lot has happened since the 2016 release of *Somewhere in the Skies: A Human Approach to an Alien Phenomenon*. And while the world begins to rebuild after a global crisis, we find ourselves in a position to question many things as communities, nations, and perhaps most importantly, as human beings. And one of the most enduring questions in this life is whether or not we are alone in the universe. We have asked this question from the beginning of time when chariots of the "gods" were said to have visited us then; now, saucers of the "gods" continue their visitations. But somewhere in between the cracks of uncertainty and mystery, we find the UFO phenomenon intrinsically linked with the extraterrestrial question. And this became apparent in late 2017 when the UFO issue gained mainstream attention like never before.

It may not have felt like it to most, but under the surface of overwhelming information bombarding our eyes, ears, and minds at a constant rate, a story broke that would alter the entire conversation on a topic once pushed to the furthest corners of the fringe: UFOs. And here we are today, talking about these aerial phenomena at the dinner table, over coffee with co-workers, and even with our most skeptical of friends and colleagues.

On December 16, 2017, a bombshell article released through the *New York Times* shot across the world with the headline *Glowing Auras and 'Black Money': The Pentagon's Mysterious U.F.O. Program*. It was co-written by Helene Cooper, Pentagon correspondent, and investigative journalists Leslie Kean and Ralph Blumenthal. Through astonishing admissions by the Pentagon and even the Secret UFO program's director, Luis Elizondo, we learned that the United States had been officially investigating UFOs. The highly classified and black-budget program known as AATIP (Advanced Aerospace Threat Identification Program) looked into various military-witnessed UFO encounters. Through the program, several official videos were investigated and eventually disseminated to the public through the *New York Times* online article.

Perhaps just as interesting as the UFO program itself was the announcement of a new company founded by former Blink-182 front man Tom DeLonge. As an avid UFO enthusiast, DeLonge worked his way into closed-door meetings with military and intelligence officials to propose a rollout of information pertaining to military technology advancement and, yes... UFOs. And born from these meetings DeLonge created To the Stars Academy of Arts and Science. The organization presently boasts ambitious projects in three distinct areas: science, aerospace, and entertainment. The controversial team behind the company includes not only former members of intelligence agencies and advanced development programs, but the former director of the AATIP program itself, Luis Elizondo. Elizondo had worked for the Office of the Undersecretary of Defense for Intelligence and also as a special agent for US Army Counterintelligence. Tired of the lack of interest by the inner workings of his department and a lack of transparency regarding the findings of the program, Elizondo resigned and teamed up with Tom DeLonge.

To date, To the Stars Academy of Arts and Science has been responsible for major mainstream media coverage of the UFO topic and has assisted in pushing the US Navy to change their protocols for reporting UFOs. The company also works directly with the US Army to analyze and implement highly anomalous materials said to have been recovered from UFOs. It's a lot to digest, and in order to continue their work, DeLonge created an entertainment sector that has already cranked out several fiction and nonfiction books pertaining to UFOs, an investigative television series on the History Channel, and several documentaries and feature films currently in development. It's undeniable that they have made waves in the intelligence communities, the military, and public perception of the UFO issue through mainstream news coverage and through their own multimedia layout.

With mounting pressure due to the work by To the Stars Academy of Arts and Science in obtaining the three Navy UFO videos, and their continued efforts to work with military branches on deciphering these mysterious objects and their capabilities, Luis Elizondo was able to assist several pilots and observers of the Navy encounters in several meetings with members of Congress to explain what they'd experienced and why UFO reporting protocol needed to change. And while the contents of these meetings would remain classified, one senator in particular did comment briefly on one of these meetings. On June 19, 2019, Senator Mark Warner, vice chairman of the Senate Intelligence Committee, stated the following to the press: "If naval pilots are running into unexplained interference in the air, that's a safety concern I believe we need to get to the bottom of."

This meeting with Warner put the US Navy in the limelight, and they had no choice but to officially announce new protocols for pilots and ground crews to report UFO sightings and encounters. In an official statement to *Politico*, a Navy spokesperson said the following: "The Navy is updating and formalizing the process by which reports of any such suspected incursions can be made to the cognizant authorities. These kinds of incursions can be both a security risk and pose a safety hazard for both Navy and Air Force aviation. For safety and security concerns, the Navy and the USAF takes these reports very seriously and investigates each and every report."

Most recently, the Senate Intelligence Committee made good on their word to look further into the UFO issue. It was announced in mid-June 2020 that the Office of Naval Intelligence actually had what was known as a "UFO Task Force." Initiated by Senator Marco Rubio, a bill was created requesting the director of National Intelligence and the Secretary of Defense create a comprehensive, unclassified report concerning unidentified aerial phenomena. If the law passes, we may see what many consider a specter of Project Blue Book, nothing but a publicity stunt for the US government to control the narrative of the UFO issue in the United States. Or perhaps it could be a major move toward more transparency by the US government. Either way, UFOs are more popular than ever.

With this renewed interest in UFOs, I thought this would be an opportune time to drop in on many of those whom I'd originally interviewed for the first edition of this book. While the mainstream media and To the Stars Academy focused on a narrative of threat when it came to UFOs, I wanted to remind people of the hundreds of individuals from across the globe who continue to witness UFOs themselves. And once again, I aimed to put the microscope on them and examine how these events affected their lives both then and now. Speaking of which, you'll hear from one of the individuals who was the very first to track the now famous "Tic Tac UFO" and is responsible for sending the intercept, ushering in one of the most important UFO events in modern history. This is a brand-new chapter titled "It was Raining UFOs."

Since the 2016 publication of this book, I created a podcast under the same title, *Somewhere in the Skies*. The weekly podcast features interviews with researchers of UFO phenomena, scientists and academics, case histories and audio documentaries. But most importantly, it features the witnesses and experiencers of UFO phenomena. Within the confines of the podcast, you'll find a series called *Witness Accounts*. This is literally a continuation of the book in audio form, where witnesses recount their incredible experiences and how those experiences impacted their lives. To date, the podcast has hit #1 in its categories on several podcast platforms, and remains in the top 20 of its categories as of early 2020. I stress this only to show the undeniable interest, hunger, and curiosity of the global audience for pursuit of the UFO topic and related phenomena. The witness accounts episodes of the podcast remain the most popular in the show's history. And I believe this to be for one reason: we love stories. We love to see through another's eyes and in another's shoes. What would we do if we were faced with the unknown like they were? In this way, we reflect on our own lives and find common ground.

In deciding to revisit many of the stories in this book, I reached out to those who had told them. And while some were happy to contribute, some were happy to never revisit their experiences again. I can understand why. For some, it was a traumatic experience. For others, it was deeply personal and powerful. Whether they chose to embrace the experience or reject it was completely up to them, and no matter their choice, it was the right one for them.

You will also find another new chapter, "Somewhere in Our Strange Skies," wherein I present three UFO cases that have never been published in detail to the extent of which you'll soon read. Each moves us forward in both legitimacy of a real phenomenon, the impact it had during and after the event, and how it contributes to the growing fascination with the UFO subject. One of these cases involves an ongoing investigation (by myself and various other independent researchers) of a multi-witness UFO event over Lake Superior in Michigan. It's a developing story and a case I am honored to bring to the page.

For those more science-oriented readers, you'll notice significant updates to chapter 7, "A Phantom War." In this chapter, I interviewed various scientists and members of certain organizations interested in, and even exploring and investigating the UFO topic in some capacity. Some faded into obscurity. Some morphed and changed. And some are continuing their efforts in exciting new ways. But perhaps even more exciting is that the list only grew. You will discover, as I did, that while many cower from the scientific exploration of UFOs for fear of ridicule, or simply because they await funding, there are those who truly put their money where their mouth is: they are creating, developing, and implementing exciting new technologies and endeavoring to find answers through science and investigation.

The point of this book was (and remains) to show the impact UFO events have had on the lives of those who experienced them. And in doing so, I realized that as time progressed, people's memories of experience change. Their outlook on the experience itself changes. And perhaps most importantly, they learn and grow from the experience. In relation to learning and growing, you may notice a term used sporadically throughout the book that you may not be familiar with. In some instances, the term *UFO* has been replaced with *UAP*. *UAP* stands for *unidentified aerial phenomena*. This term is growing in popularity, as it opens the possibility that we are not just dealing with solid flying objects in our skies, but all different types of phenomena. These terms can be used interchangeably most times, and you'll see several interviewees choosing to use it throughout the course of this book.

If this is your second time reading this book, I hope you'll appreciate the updates throughout and enjoy the new chapters as well. And for those reading the book for the very first time, you have the rare opportunity to step into the eyes, minds, and hearts of these people for the very first time like I once did. And I think you'll see a fuller picture of their personal journeys as time has given them a larger scope in which to view their experiences.

In his book *The Eighth Tower*, author John Keel stated, "If you could look far enough into the empty sky, you would be able to see the back of your own head." I think this speaks volumes in terms of what I originally set out to do with this book back in 2016. The goal remains the same today: to focus on the observer. The further we search for answers somewhere in the skies, the more we ultimately learn about those around us and about ourselves. *We* are the UFO. *We* are the mystery, and *we* are the answer. Someway and somehow, no matter how hard and far we search, it will always come back to *us*. And perhaps that was part of the great cosmic plan since the dawn of time, and will continue to be part of the plan as we move forward into an uncertain future full of endless possibilities.

Ryan Sprague
New York, NY
June 27, 2020

1

THE CATALYST

Being the sole patron in a bar can be liberating. Then again, it can also be depressing. I embraced the former.

"What'll it be?" he asked.

"Bourbon. Neat."

Tyler, as I would soon learn his name, poured a generous dose of Kentucky goodness into a smudged glass. It was April 25, 2013, and I was one of few patrons in this dive bar on the Lower East Side, an area of Manhattan that I didn't frequent often. But this was a special occasion and I needed something to calm my nerves. Within the hour, I was to take part in an interview about UFOs. So it didn't hurt to have a small bit of inebriated confidence.

As I took my first sip, something caught my attention above the two-tiered shelf of liquor behind the bar. Hung rather haphazardly by a rusty nail was a billiards triangle rack. It had a smudged autograph on one side, presumably from a celebrity pool shark back when this bar actually had a table to play on. I stared up at the triangle, its shape reminding me quite vividly of how my entire interest in the UFO topic had all began.

It was 1995, and I was twelve years old. My parents and I were on a weekend getaway to the Saint Lawrence River, a lengthy

body of water situated snugly between upstate New York and its
northern neighbor of Canada. As I fished off a nearby dock at
our motel, hoping to catch every perch and sunfish the lake had
to offer, I noticed a reflection in the water of something in the
pitch black above. Naturally, my gaze veered upward. I spotted
three white lights in a distinct triangular formation. While I
could see no solid structure, the stars were blotted out behind
the formation. These lights, constant, yet pulsating, were
moving over the water in complete silence. I could then make
out a hazy red light in the center. It seemed to burn brighter
than the lights at each point. All I remember hearing was the
water hitting the dock in its natural rhythm. I could feel a low
vibration behind my ears, running down my neck and into my
chest. I watched in awe as this formation slowly moved north
toward the Canadian border. I called for my parents to come
take a look. When they finally did, all they saw was what they
assumed was an airplane fade out of sight. I knew differently.

This experience at such a young age terrified me. I became
obsessed, taking out book after book from the public library,
researching accounts of sightings, encounters, and even abductions. I would write essays to myself about them. It was clear
that whatever I saw that night stayed with me for years to come,
prompting me to finally seek out others who had found themselves tangled in a UFO web. I started to interview people in my
hometown. I compiled local reports. I was essentially paving my
way to finally branch out and begin writing for several alternative publications on the topic. And thus, my career as a UFO
journalist had ostensibly begun. And while most days consisted
of interviewing others, the proverbial pen (and camera) were
now being flipped onto me.

My colleague, Peter Robbins, and I were to be interviewed by
a research group out of Copenhagen, Denmark. Their focus: the
1980 Rendlesham Forest incident, which occurred in and around
a military base in rural East Anglia, England. Over three consec-
utive days, personnel on the base witnessed a craft of unknown

origin land in the forest that surrounded it. Witnesses also claimed that the craft had adversely affected nuclear ordnance stored in nearby bunkers. A strategic cover-up was set in motion days after the events, keeping the entire Rendlesham incident under wraps for years to follow. Robbins had co-written a British best-selling book about the this deeply controversial case.

My involvement in the case was peripheral, consisting specifically of a stage play I was developing at the time. The play would chronicle the ten-year journey it took Robbins and Warren to write the book. Robbins, also having grown up with a theater background, embraced my endeavor with open arms. It was a match made in ufological/theatrical heaven. And I was very excited to share my own thoughts on the case.

"Brings ya down here, man?" Tyler asked.

"Being interviewed for a Danish television show," I responded.

His ears perked. This clearly wasn't the answer he was expecting.

"What's the interview about?" he asked.

"An incident that occurred on a military base in England."

"Heavy. What happened?"

"About eighty personnel witnessed some... strange stuff."

He pressed on. "What was strange about it?"

I was cornered. I had no choice. What I said next would either make or break the conversation. I'd experienced this conundrum many times before, and I was ready to immediately be shrugged off.

"It was a UFO sighting."

You could hear a pin drop. Rather impressive for lower Manhattan.

"UFOs. That's, uh... that's..."

He was done. I went to take a sip from my glass when Tyler suddenly slapped his hand on the bar, a sharp echo bouncing off the empty brick walls, causing me to dribble the bourbon down the front of me.

"Fucking awesome!"

He proceeded to throw down a coaster next to my drink, quickly rounded the bar, and sat next to me.

"So are you like, a *ufologist* or something?"

I hadn't lost him after all.

"Journalist," I bit back. The term *ufology* had always rubbed me the wrong way. While it was indeed a topic of study, I never considered myself knowledgeable enough to stamp the "ologist" on my forehead. At least, not yet.

"Ever heard of the Phoenix Lights?" Tyler asked.

I had indeed. I had actually written extensively about the Phoenix Lights incident in past articles. The incident occurred on Thursday, March 13, 1997, in and around the areas of Phoenix, Arizona, and Sonora, Mexico. Hundreds of individuals witnessed various lights and V-shaped craft floating through the night skies. Their testimony was only strengthened when the Arizona governor at the time, Fife Symington, also came forward to say he'd witnessed the event. Not only had I written about these events, but I had personally spoken with half a dozen witnesses who were directly involved. Tyler would now make lucky number seven. He went on to describe his sighting in great detail, a rush of excitement consuming him. I watched his eyes shut tightly as he tried recalling street names, his arms flailing like helpless ribbons taped to a desk fan. His wingspan was impressive as he went on to describe the enormity of a craft, once again in a V-shaped formation, that hung silently in the Arizona sky that night. Every word seemed like a confession. Something he had pushed down so deep for so long. He began to sweat as he fell further into his own memory, living out every moment in great detail.

I couldn't help but revel in this situation. I had walked into a random bar in a random neighborhood on a random day that a random bartender happened to be working, and this happens. In his incidental questioning of why I was there, Tyler had opened the floodgates to something he most likely hadn't spoken of in years, if ever. He had sparked a conversation that many had before but rarely admit to: experiencing something beyond his control. Beyond his concept of reality. Whatever happened in Arizona that night touched the lives of thousands of people. And each and every one of those people had stories to tell.

Tyler told me to stop by the bar any time and we'd discuss his sighting in greater detail. But for now, I had to make my way to my appointment. And as I left the bar that day, warm and fuzzy from the bourbon sloshing around in my empty stomach, I headed toward my destination, invigorated by the serendipitous encounter that had just occurred. I walked toward the location of the interview to meet our interviewer, Frederik Uldall, and his wife, Ditte. Peter was already there, donning his usual brown leather jacket and Indiana Jones–like hat. He smiled brightly, conversing with Frederik. After a few hugs and handshakes, we headed upstairs to begin.

As Frederik prepared the camera, I looked over at Peter. He was making small talk with Ditte, who was playing gracious host for the day. Peter let out a sincere laugh that stood out to me. And for a brief moment, I thought to myself of how challenging it must have been to spend ten years of his life on a single book project. The passion, blind faith, and sheer determination to bring to light not only a case he felt deserved it, but the fact that he had placed the UFO phenomenon prominently in front of so many people who had never thought twice about it.

I wanted that. I wanted something that I could bring to the table that would make people think. And in that moment, as I sat in my chair, feeling like I still had so much to learn, I knew I wanted to write this book. I wanted to write it for Peter. For Tyler. And for the hundreds of people I have corresponded with throughout the years who all have stories to tell, but weren't quite sure if anyone would listen. I hope, in some small way, that this book is evidence that there are those who will listen. Who will relate. Who will think. And perhaps will feel compelled to come forward with their own experience.

Perhaps, reflecting back on that moment as Frederik pressed record on the camera, I didn't quite know how crucial it was for these stories to be told. Not for some grand revelation or epiphany of sorts. But for closure. For those who have experienced something they cannot explain and feel as though they were alone. So many others have had similar experiences, each more bizarre than the last. And perhaps they'd find closure in knowing that most would empathize the best way they know how: by listening, reading, and acknowledging that something far more complex is happening than just lights in the sky.

After about an hour or so of on-camera conversation about Rendlesham and various other UFO-related topics, Frederik stopped recording. He shied away from the camera, staring straight at the floor. He shook his head. With a nervous laugh and a sharp Danish accent, he reacted simply with, "Unbelievable."

And it was. Most of it. With each passing story, it never got easier to just *believe*. In fact, it was the complete opposite. As I ventured further and further down the rabbit hole of mystery, I would meet many different people on the way. Some would become close friends. Others would remain on the periphery, happy to tell their story, but going no further. And some would leave lasting impressions on my journalistic and personal life. And it began where most UFO sightings often did. With lights in the sky.

2

DANCING IN THE NIGHT SKY

It Seemed to Be Following Me

In the suburbs of Sydney, Australia, Damien John Nott spent his summer days hanging out with friends, as any nine-year-old would. He was a skateboarder, scraping his knees on the neighborhood pavement as he and his friends passed the hours away.

It was 1988. The sun had just set as the night sky began to dominate. Damien noticed that he was late for dinner. Fearing his mother would be upset, he began a hasty trek home, skateboarding up and down the winding streets of his neighborhood, focusing on the quickest route. As he rounded a corner, his attention impulsively shot from the gravel below to the skies above. He noticed a glowing red sphere of light, about the size of a basketball, playfully hanging over his head. As he continued skateboarding, the ball of light spun and danced above him. "It seemed to be following me," Damien remembered. When he stopped, the light stopped. When he continued down the street, the light trailed only a few feet away. He watched it for several moments and noticed that whatever it was, it made no sound.

"It gave me an eerie feeling. As if it were watching me. I felt that it knew I was watching *it* as well," Damien told me. The orb continued to mimic his movements, becoming much more attuned. "This happened for about two minutes before I made it to a park that ran between the back of a series of homes." Damien began to feel imminent threat amid his intrigue. This clearly wasn't any type of airplane he had grown to see traveling through the Australian skies, nor would any aircraft be hovering that low to the ground. Damien grew anxious and decided that whatever games this object was playing were not as innocent as he may have first thought. "That's when I grabbed my skateboard under my arm and ran home as fast as I could without looking back."

Damien arrived home, immediately telling his mother of what had just occurred. She explained to him that it was probably just an airplane or perhaps his overactive imagination. But Damien, knowing full well that this was anything but, would never forget that day. And the orb phenomenon would not forget about him either, returning to visit him almost two and a half years later.

In 1990, Damien was on a weekend visit to his father's house. It was summer yet again when he found himself camping in the backyard with his two stepbrothers. The sky faded into darkness and a lovely array of stars appeared. The three boys lay on their backs, staring up at the starry display before them. It was within moments that Damien noticed a bright, burning red sphere coming closer. Although this orb seemed to be much more aggressive and powerful, a sense of familiarity connected Damien to the object immediately. And as his heart began to race, he took minor comfort in knowing that he wasn't the only one seeing it this time. His two stepbrothers looked on as the object made sudden ninety-degree turns, moving at incredibly high speeds. "My brothers and I watched this orb for about three minutes while it performed amazing maneuvers, as if putting on a show for us."

What made this different from Damien's previous encounter was the addition of a blue spherical light that appeared and began to almost chase the red orb. Within moments, yet another spherical light, this one giving off a yellowish tint, began to chase the blue light. It was becoming apparent, in Damien's opinion, that whatever these lights were, they knew the boys were watching. "The aerial acrobatics went on for roughly ten to fifteen minutes as my brothers and I watched in amazement," Damien continued to tell me, but then, "All three objects then took off at very high speeds in the same direction and completely disappeared from view within a fraction of a second."

The boys, scared and excited, went in to tell their parents what had happened. Figuring boys will be boys, their father shrugged it off. It would be decades later in 2012 that he would have his very own UFO sighting in Dunedoo, Central Western Australia. He soon left behind his skeptical views, admitting to Damien that he now believed the boys had truly seen something anomalous that night in 1990.

Although these two experiences were amazing in scope, the orb-like objects still were not done with Damien. The orbs returned time and time again, even up until 2012, when Damien would contact investigators from the New South Wales UFO Research Group. Upon arrival to his home, the investigators immediately witnessed the orbs. Intrigued, the president of the organization, Mariana Flynn, decided to spend two nights at Damien's home to investigate further. Within the span of these two days, she had no fewer than nine separate UFO sightings. During this time, a journalist for the *Sun Herald*, a major publication in Sydney, came to report on the sightings, and witnessed two orbs playfully following one another over the house. Clearly, between Damien's initial sighting as a child and those which continue today, something fascinating was shaping itself around not only his property, but he himself. Whatever these orbs were, they found a deep connection to this seemingly normal individual. And they weren't about to let up.

Because of the consistency and corroboration of Damien's

experiences, I needed to learn just exactly what he thought of all this. Why was it happening to him? And what did he truly believe it to be? Whatever it was, it was clearly affecting him on a physical level. His health seemed to deteriorate not from the experience itself, but from the anxiety of it possibly happening again. "I would spend hours at night anticipating their return. Many nights, I wouldn't sleep. I lost a lot of weight. Some nights, I would wake up at 3 a.m. to go outside. There, I'd witness glowing balls of light hanging low over the backyard. Other nights, I would have the glowing balls of light come close to my window and illuminate my room. I lived in a constant state of fear mixed with wonderment and anxiety."

Anxiety proved a dangerous game as Damien found himself feeling distant from those around him because of these experiences. But whatever the orbs were, one thing was certain: his life was changing. Evolving. "I now find myself acutely aware of my surroundings, and more keen to people's intentions." Damien would begin to meet others who had similar experiences with UFOs. And he soon learned that his feelings of bafflement and anxiety were similar to many others'. "In a way, I've become more empathetic and have gained a better understanding of others who have had similar experiences. I feel a deep connection with them."

Empathy is something rare in its human form. The fact that these experiences were opening up Damien's mind and heart gave me cause to dig a bit deeper. What did he feel was most important about these orbs? What, if anything, had the orbs taught him? He'd continue, "I have a deeper understanding that we are not alone in the universe. Something very special is happening to this planet. Due to the reports I gave to local media, I've met many people who have had similar experiences, so I don't feel as alone as I have done most of my life. I've made some great friends and I feel like I've finally found my true family." This stood out to me as being an integral part of not only Damien's experiences, but the experiences of many. There is a connection among those who have witnessed UFOs. Not only is it something of wonder and awe, but it brings with it a personal responsibility to uncover the mystery behind its purpose.

Damien looked further into the phenomenon, digesting every UFO case he could get his hands on. While some may find this obsessive, Damien saw it as opportunity. Through his newfound friendships and personal research into the topic, he began to see the phenomenon in a whole new light. The fear and anxiety began to dissipate, and his mind was open to the possibility that whatever was happening, it was happening for a reason. "I feel like I have a mission. That mission is to share with people what I have seen, and what I capture through film and photographs. No matter the fear they once instilled in me, the orbs, in all their chilling accuracy, are quite beautiful."

So perhaps the orbs had sought Damien out. But why? What made him different from the majority of people who have never and will never have an orb sighting? "With most of the UFOs that I see, I feel a certain connection and comfort, knowing that they mean no harm. Sometimes when they pass overhead, stop for a short time, and continue their journey, I feel sadness and wish they would take me with them. In a way, they have become closer than my own family. As to why they seem to follow me around, I can only guess. What I do know is that I don't think I'm special. But I *do* think I'm different. From what I've seen and experienced, it has reaffirmed in me the knowing that what I'm doing is what I'm meant to be doing. I do believe that there are other realities, and for some reason, at this time on Earth, they are showing themselves in a big way for a big reason."

So what was that reason? "Honestly, I can only speculate," he admitted. "I've always been a person with the courage and conviction to stand up for what I believe in and not back down to anyone or anything. At the same time, I've tried to keep an open, yet logical and skeptical mind with regards to what I see, because I know that this route can make many people doubt their own sanity. I feel that special times are ahead for the human race. We are at the precipice of something truly amazing and paradigm-shifting."

Clearly, a lifetime of sightings left a lasting impression on Damien. And he continues to search for answers. But just like most who have experienced the unknown, he remains content in knowing that he has built lifelong friendships through these orbs that enigmatically dance around his existence. But perhaps even more importantly, it was no longer a struggle with belief. It was validation. His life, just like so many others', was unique, important, and integral to whatever may lie ahead in the cosmic agenda.

Looking for Something That We Already Learned

Joe Kiernan was an entrepreneur. Between him and his wife, Cindi, they had successfully started three businesses in their hometown of North Myrtle Beach, a coastal resort city in South Carolina. Wanting to ensure the financial security of their two daughters, Joe and his wife dabbled in businesses that ranged from construction and textiles to fine art research. They lived a stable and modest life in a town that bustled with tourists in some seasons and was calmly serene in others. But it was in December of 2012 that Joe would go from a simple resident to the life-altering role of a tourist in his own backyard.

It was December 6 when Joe returned home from a long day at work. It was just getting dark outside. Joe was about to head inside when he happened to glance up at the sky. There, directly above him, dangled a cluster of orange orbs pulsating before his eyes. His first inclination was to brush it off as the familiar stars of the night, or perhaps a plane was flying overhead with its lights caught in a mist. But the closer Joe looked, the more he realized this wasn't something as simple as a plane, nor a string of stars. These bright balls of light were completely stationary and silent. There was no sound from a plane, nor the distance of a star to assure him that this was mere misidentification. Still, the options were endless as to what exactly it could be. Joe, being a rational person, shook off the experience as something out of the ordinary and didn't think too much of it. Until it happened again the following night.

In almost the same exact spot, the orbs had returned, only pulsating more strongly. Joe knew he needed others to witness this, reassuring him that this wasn't just a figment of his imagination. Soon, his wife and a close friend came outside to witness the orbs themselves. It became apparent that this was anything but a trick of the eye. Camera in tow, the three headed further into the wooded area of Joe's land to investigate further. There, they watched for hours as these strange objects seemed to be bouncing around in the night sky. They noticed a solid white orb off in the distance and then another trailing not far behind. These three orbs were rotating around one another, an almost choreographed pattern playing out before the trio of witnesses. Soon, all three orbs converged and then darted off into the sky, disappearing.

The three witnesses began their trek back to the house, full of excitement and uncertainty as to what had just occurred. They intended to upload the memory card and charge the batteries of the camera just in case the orbs returned and they could get a better angle on them. But just as they reached the side door to the house, a tremendous roar filled the atmosphere, vibrating and shaking the very foundation of the house. The three ran to the backyard where a large pond sat in the middle of Joe's land. There, about thirty feet above the pond's surface, the orbs hung silently yet again. They were now glowing a bright blue and pink. Joe's eyes then shot higher up, where he witnessed a staggering six fighter jets in tight formation. Seeing jets in the area wasn't a rarity. However, being that it was dark at this point, it struck Joe as odd that absolutely no light came from the jets. Joe and company were only able to make out that these were jets because they were unusually low.

The orbs began to ascend as if taking off towards the east. It seemed as though the jets were actually pursuing these objects. Joe assumed that the jets had turned off all their lights to remain elusive, save the thunderous roar of their engines. The orbs soon made a sharp turn westward, jets in tow. One more sharp turn eastward led the orbs toward the ocean nearby. The jets once again followed. Joe, Cindi, and their friend stood there, speechless. The night's activity seemed to finally come to a startling conclusion as they headed inside.

The following day, Joe contacted the state director of the Mutual UFO Network (MUFON) to report the amazing sighting. MUFON contacted Shaw Air Force Base to see if they'd had any jets in the sky that night. Perhaps, if they did, they could shed some light on the orb sighting as well. Base commander Officer Sexton informed MUFON that no jets had been in the sky in the entire state of South Carolina that night. As for the orbs, Officer Sexton wouldn't comment on the sighting.

Joe wasn't going to give up that easily. He did a bit more digging and was able to obtain a document through the Myrtle Beach International Airport. This document, created by Moody Air Force Base in Georgia, issued that jets were to be deployed, no lights, within a twenty-mile radius of the area. Frustrated with conflicting stories between Officer Sexton and the Myrtle Beach Airport, Joe decided that the best course of action was to not push any further and to instead focus on his own life and the well-being of his family.

While Joe tried to put the events behind him, there was no denying that it had affected him greatly. When asked how, he spoke first on his work in art history. "It was not long after when I was finally able to put the last pieces of a puzzle together in several works of art that I had been researching for quite some time. These works, having been over five hundred years old, had deeply hidden messages within them. I had been trained in perspective at a very young age, but since my experience, I have now been completely opened up to different perceptions within the art I research. I now see everything in a geometric way.

Shapes and numbers mostly. I can now see the relative nature within everything."

This seems to be a common occurrence among those who have experienced the UFO phenomenon. Whether they be artists themselves or have no artistic abilities whatsoever, the experience somehow triggers new ideas and aspirations within the experiencer. Could this be a mere coincidence? Or could the phenomenon literally be opening parts of the brain that were once closed off? In Joe's case, he claimed that his experience had "given me the courage to follow certain truths and passions that I had put on hold for so many selfish reasons. It was an awakening, in a sense. A new perspective. And as wonderful as it has been, I can also tell you about the negatives as well." Joe adds that there is a lot of ridicule in coming forward with an experience such as his. "People are good at that; they criticize and ridicule what they can't understand. When truths are revealed in this so-called awakening I have had, what was once enjoyable now seems pointless and you begin to miss what used to be pleasure for passing time." It could be summed up rather eloquently by Joe himself, who states, "We are all looking for something that we already learned, have taught, and have discovered. We have forgotten our way. But it isn't entirely lost. The answer will be found, heard, and accepted. And as I continue to search for answers from within, I can honestly say that I feel that I will see the big reveal in my lifetime."

I Banked My Plane Left and Headed Straight for It

Gary Travis is a business owner in North Carolina. He is also a trained pilot with over thirty-eight years of experience flying. So when he stared up into the sky from the deck of his home one night, he was completely shaken when even his expertise couldn't explain what he was seeing.

It was 2011. The sun was just beginning to set when Gary noticed a bright orange light coming in from the south over the ocean. His first assumption was that it was aircraft lights as a plane was heading in for a landing at Ocean Isle Beach Airport. He turned to talk to a friend, and when he looked back, the light was gone. He brushed it off, but only moments later, another orange light appeared in the same area. The orange color did catch Gary off guard, as most aircraft lights were usually white. He thought to himself that it was indeed strange, but didn't think much of it. The orange lights would not escape his memory for long, as they returned a few weeks later.

It was approximately 9 p.m. when Gary's daughter came running into the house, claiming that there were "funny lights over the ocean." This was when he and his daughter headed outside and observed several orange orbs over the water, spinning around one another. Soon, Gary's son joined in and watched as the strange lights continued their display. The event lasted for about three minutes before disappearing in the blink of an eye.

Perhaps the most dramatic of Gary's continued encounters with these orbs came in October of 2011 while he was piloting his personal aircraft. As he was coming in for a landing near the airport, he spotted an all-too-familiar orange orb off in the distance. As his continued intrigue in these mysterious lights was now at an all-time high, Gary decided that this would be his best chance to get closer to one of these objects. "I banked my plane left and headed straight for it," Gary told me. He glided toward the object when the following thought brushed past his mind: "I briefly recalled reading stories of people's car engines and radios malfunctioning in the presence of UFOs. I thought that this would be a bad thing to happen to my plane over the ocean. But I was compelled to take advantage of my first chance to get closer to the object." As he approached the orb, it suddenly shimmered brightly and vanished completely out of sight. Gary headed in for a landing, feeling somewhat defeated, but still in complete awe of this cycle of orange orb sightings.

Drawn to the ocean yet again, Gary grabbed a camcorder

and headed to his deck to record a full moon that was rising over the water. The moon, however, would be overshadowed by our scene-stealing friends soon enough. The orbs were back, and in full force. Within a twenty-minute span, over a dozen orbs began to appear over the water. But this time, Gary was ready to record the event as it unfolded. He was able to capture a twenty-two-second clip of four orbs as they appeared. With this, Gary now had proof of his ongoing interactions with these mysterious spheres of light. He sent the video to a local news station, and within days the video went viral, people from all over the world commenting on how amazing the dozen orbs were.

Although Gary's sightings may not have affected him in as profound a way as Joe's did, he does admit that by coming forward with what he has seen, many friends, family, and neighbors have also come forward with experiences they have had with the orbs and other sightings in the area.

Gary, being a man of few words, opened up quite eloquently as he left me with his final thoughts. "Expect many more reports of UFOs and keep an open mind. I do believe that the majority of sightings are explainable. But even so, there is mounting evidence that we are not alone." And while Gary believes that he was just in the right place and the right time during this strange pattern of sightings, the sighting definitely left him feeling a certain way. "I have been left with a complete sense of awe and wonder." But did he want to know the truth behind what he'd seen? His answer left me hopeful. "The truth can only be a positive thing."

The Mysteries of the Orbs

Orbs can be a tricky bunch. When we look at the orb phenomenon in the context of paranormal studies, we are often led to hazy photos with small balls of light littered throughout. This phenomenon is usually chalked up to retroflection from particles within a camera lens. But how can these orbs explain glowing balls of light in the sky? Some may brush it off to what we know as ball lightning. This can be created when two strokes of lightning collide. Typically, one stroke travels from cloud to ground, and the other stroke travels from ground to cloud. When convergence occurs, if correctly polarized, the energy can wrap around itself to create a spherical shape. The only problem with this theory, in the context of the incidents above, is that these balls of lightning will almost always disappear immediately. Both Joe and Gary witnessed these orbs at a constant rate. The orbs also appeared to be spinning around one another, under some sort of intelligent control.

Whatever may be responsible for the orbs that both witnesses were exposed to, it was most likely not any type of ball lightning. Other possibilities have ranged from electromagnetic anomalies to flares being dropped from the jets that Joe, his wife, and friend witnessed shortly after the orbs were seen. But if they were flares, why were there no jets the first night Joe witnessed the orbs? This was also true for Gary's sighting, as no other aircraft was tracked visually in the area that day. We must remain open to the possibility that a prosaic answer could be responsible for these sightings, but they remain, to this day, unexplained.

One thing is certain when it comes to the orbs in both Australia and in the Carolinas: they continue to be reported almost on a weekly basis. Damien, who considers himself an avid sky-watcher, will spend hours with his telescope searching the skies. But, unlike most who give up and never spot even the slightest of aerial anomalies, Damien is able to capture some of the most stunning objects both through the lens of the telescope and even through both video and photographic captures.

As for the Carolina orbs, witnesses across the bordering states are reporting these mysterious spherical objects even up to the day both editions of this book were published. Joe continues to monitor them on a web camera he has set up in his backyard, uploading videos of them at a constant rate. Gary also continues to witness these orbs both from the ground and in the air.

These experiences have opened up the artistic eyes of one man, while leaving a pilot of thirty-eight years open to the possibility that the UFO phenomenon is quite real and has been peeking from behind the clouds ever since he began his career as a pilot. It took a string of mysterious events to change his entire outlook on the existence of a nonhuman intelligence visiting the planet. And this opening could be exactly what the phenomena wanted from each of these witnesses all along.

3

WHY ME?

I knew there would be those who simply shrugged off Damien's, Joe's, and Gary's sightings as misidentifications. I encountered this dilemma time and time again in mainstream news coverage of such events. So all I could do is move forward and search for the most credible accounts that I could. This led me to Chris, Kevin, Larry, and Scott. All four of these men had served in the United States military in one capacity or the other. And while this doesn't lend them more credibility than the typical civilian witness, it does bear acknowledgment. The attention to detail, analysis, and assessment of a situation ingrained into these men are what set them apart from most. They are trained to focus. They may even possess some knowledge of the technology being used with advanced aircraft. But what happens when that focus is shaken to the core?

It Didn't Move and I Didn't Move

He had always been rather reserved. Nine years in the Navy could do that to a man. If it didn't need to be said, it wasn't. But as Chris Bilecki recalled that warm summer night, I could tell that whatever had happened to him, it was big.

It was 1972, and he was almost three years into his service. He was making his way from Syracuse, New York, to Pensacola, Florida. The drive was filled with excitement, as he would soon be training at the Naval Communications Center, a small detour that would soon solidify the next two years of his life on new assignment. After Florida, a job as a cryptologic technician awaited him in Virginia. The future looked bright as his Plymouth Duster coasted down Route 95, somewhere on the brink of Fayetteville, North Carolina.

It was around 2:30 a.m. as the car barreled down the empty road. It was pitch black outside. The radio blared as he enjoyed the solitude of the road. He took intermittent sips and smokes from his Pepsi and cigarette. Just as he exhaled out the window, the radio inside the car completely cut out. Chris adjusted the dial, but nothing came through. As he looked up in front of him, he could no longer see his headlights on the road. They had completely cut out.

What the fuck? he thought to himself. The car came crawling to a stop. *This is a brand-new car! What the hell could be wrong with it?*

Just as he was about to attempt turning over the ignition, he noticed a bright light reflecting in his rearview mirror. A sense of relief rushed over him. Hopefully the passerby could be of some assistance. As the light moved closer, Chris noticed that it seemed to be gradually ascending. The road around him was completely flat, so whatever this was, it didn't appear to be the headlights of an approaching vehicle. Chris peered closer into the rearview mirror, searching for a source of the light. Suddenly, it disappeared completely from sight.

Is it gone? he thought to himself.

The radio burst with loud static as the power to his car suddenly revived. Chris jumped in his seat, noticing that the light wasn't gone. He could see it burning brightly through his passenger-side window, now visible in an empty field about two hundred feet or so away.

"Holy crap," Chris blurted out to himself. He watched as the light just hovered over the field, pulsating luminously.

"I wasn't about to get out of my car for a better look, and I wasn't about to sit there," Chris recalled to me. There seemed to be only one solution.

Chris hit the gas pedal, speeding away as fast as he possibly could. "I must have hit a hundred miles per hour, but that damn light followed just as fast as I proceeded," he told me. "My curiosity got the best of me, so I slowed down and came to a stop." It was at this moment that the light also came to a screeching halt, hovering above. Instead of hitting the gas again, Chris gathered the courage to get out of the car this time. He stumbled around the car and walked to the edge of the road, staring up at the light. But as he focused on the center of it, he noticed an interesting shape. Chris described it as "sort of like a fried egg, from a cross-sectional view. It had a darker shape at the bottom and a brighter dome-like top." Chris watched, completely in awe, as the object hung silently in the air. "It didn't move, and I didn't move," he told me. Here he was, on the edge of an empty road, staring up at something that for all intents and purposes shouldn't be there. But it remained bright and steady. Slowly, he got back in the car and started to drive away. The moment he accelerated, the object started following again on his right. This was no longer a game. Whatever it was, he was beginning to feel immensely afraid. "This is too spooky," he said to himself. Suddenly, it blinked out and was gone. Chris' eyes scanned his passenger-side view for any sign of the object, but saw nothing. Just as he fixed his eyes back on the road, the car stalled again. It was back.

"I looked in my rearview mirror, and there it was again," Chris remembered.

The intensity of light in his mirror brightened. He closed his eyes and gripped the steering wheel tightly. "Please go away. Please just go away," he kept repeating to himself. After a moment, he opened his eyes and looked in the mirror. The light blinked once and completely disappeared.

He loosened his grip on the steering wheel, took a deep breath, and slumped down into the driver's seat. *What the hell just happened?* he asked himself. After calming himself down, Chris drove on, not stopping once before arriving in Florida. He simply couldn't stop thinking about the event. "I was sweating, my hands were shaking, and I needed a drink," he told me. *Should I report this? Who the hell would believe me?* he remembered thinking. "I didn't even check in when I got to the training center. I went directly to the base club and had a couple drinks, trying to settle back into reality."

Chris was hesitant to bring up the entire event with anyone in Florida. After all, he was new to the area and this sector of the Navy. Why take any chance of being ridiculed? He began to inquire whether his fellow students at the training center had ever had similar experiences. After confiding in several people who claimed their own unusual experiences with the UFO phenomenon, Chris felt some relief in knowing that he wasn't the only one. After explaining his sighting, many others also came forward with their own experiences with UFOs. He eventually recalled the experience to his family and friends back home in Syracuse. His story was met with skepticism, however, so he decided to keep it to himself for years. But the events of that night never truly left him. "I still think about it every time I take a solo trip in my car."

Chris had witnessed something undeniable and incredible. He would experience several other incredible events in his life as time progressed. "I had a life-after-death experience on the operating table during a carotid artery surgery some years back. Also, when I was younger, I had a car accident while in Italy. According to many who witnessed the accident, they all agreed that there was almost no way I should have survived. But I did. There was one other time when a religious medal I had hanging over my sun visor in my vehicle fell on the ground near my feet. I pulled the car over to pick it up. If I had continued on the road at that moment at the speed I was going, I would have been part of a severe car accident that occurred only a short stretch ahead."

While these occurrences could all be attributed to sheer chance, Chris believes a greater hand was at work. And the event on that night in 1972 left a lasting impression that only deepened his belief in the unknown. When I asked him what he had taken most from this and the many life-altering experiences he'd endured throughout his life, he told me, "Why me? I have no answer. Then again, why do some die while I seem to have escaped death several times? I truly don't know. But I have grown to embrace the unknown and keep an open mind. I have grown to truly believe we should never take anything for granted. And we should never dismiss anyone's beliefs just because they may differ from our own. There appears to be some sort of plan. What it might be, I do not know, but I have been given these chances for a purpose."

Whatever it was that followed Chris on that lonely, dark road was a mystery. While lights in the sky are common, this particular light seemed to have characteristics of intelligent control, as it blinked in and out of Chris' sight, followed him several times, and stopped on a dime when he did. This would make anyone believe that something otherworldly had occurred. Chris would end our conversation by stating the following: "I had always believed that we may not be alone. But I never expected to have proof. This event was proof enough for me." But for a man of few words, Chris left me with a rather lighthearted response that I didn't expect. One that left me smiling through the intrigue of his story: "I just wish I had something stronger than Pepsi in the car that night!"

It Was Beautiful

During his time at Fort Benning, Georgia with 3rd Battalion, 75th Ranger Regiment and 1st Battalion, 29th Infantry, he'd risen in the ranks. Being part of a special operations regiment, his training consisted of direct action, airfield seizure, airborne and air assaults, reconnaissance, and personnel recovery. He was also trained to adapt and think on his feet in any given situation. He also bore witness to some of the most highly advanced and elusive aircraft the military had to offer. But nothing would prepare Kevin Burnes for what he saw in the Florida skies one autumn night in 1997. Whatever it was, it would throw all of his training into a new perspective of otherworldly proportions.

Kevin's mother had been in town for the weekend. As Sunday drew to a close in Panama City Beach, they celebrated with a heavy dinner of pork chops, potatoes, and greens. The sun had just set, leaving a beautiful clear sky above. It was about 9:30 p.m. when his mother retired to his bedroom, leaving Kevin to pull the couch out in the living room to sleep on for the night. He turned on the TV and soon drifted off to sleep.

Harsh static from the television awoke him around 2:30 a.m. He tried a few channels, but soon realized the cable had gone out. He decided to go outside to check the cable box. He turned the corner to find the cable box on the side of the apartment building and began fidgeting with it. Just as he did so, he saw a bright light reflecting off the side of the building. He turned around to see, off in the distance, a brilliant green light off to the west, heading east toward him. His first inclination was that it could possibly be a plane making an emergency landing on the nearby beach. He started to head back to the apartment, but felt a sudden urge to look once again for the light. To his surprise, it was now much closer and much, much bigger. "It was tracking parallel to the beach and looked to be about one hundred fifty to three hundred feet high. It was staying on a straight path," Kevin told me. "It was moving very slow. And absolutely no sound seemed to be coming from it. My heart started racing."

His curiosity was piqued. He started to slowly move down the edge of the sidewalk toward the beach to get a better look. He stood awestruck as he stared out over the water. "From my vantage point, it looked to be right over the beach or just off of it, maybe one thousand five hundred feet or so from my position. It was a perfect green orb about the size of the moon." Kevin watched as the orb-like object hovered in the air, pulsating. "On the very front of the orb, it was white hot, like it was pushing against the atmosphere. There were these gas-like tails floating behind it. It was almost translucent. It almost looked like some sort of force field. I deduced that it was not a meteor or comet, because I'd seen those all my life." Kevin felt a sudden rush of adrenaline surge through him as the orb burned brighter. "All I could hear was the blood rushing in my eardrums." Kevin was completely transfixed by the orb. "It was beautiful."

He broke his daze, running into the apartment to wake up his mother. Was he going crazy? He wanted confirmation that he wasn't the only one seeing this mystifying ball of green light floating over the water. "God bless her, she allowed me to drag her outside to witness this thing for herself," Kevin admitted. He pointed skyward as she peered upward, half asleep. Her eyes widened.

"Oh Jesus," she said.

They both stared up at the orb as it seemed to travel away from them into the distance. It was getting smaller and smaller as it slowly floated away. After several moments, it brightened to a blinding degree. Suddenly, it shot straight up into the air and completely disappeared. The two of them stood in silence, not quite sure how to react. Soon, Kevin helped his mother back inside, asking her what she thought they had just witnessed. "I have no idea," she replied, clearly affected by the sighting, but more than ready to fall back asleep. Kevin saw his mother off to bed and returned to the couch that night, unable to rest.

Whatever it was they had seen had shaken him to the core. He wanted to know if this had anything to do with the nearby Coast Guard or naval station. "I phoned both to inquire if they had seen it or tracked it. I got the usual and condescending 'this guy probably wears a tinfoil hat' attitude, and they left me hanging, for sure." Kevin finally fell asleep that night, though not easily. His mind raced with questions that only multiplied when he reported to work the next day at a nearby golf course. He relayed his experience to a co-worker, who immediately laughed him off. "I felt like no one believed me. I had this world-changing experience and it was like it never even happened. I decided to just stick to my work, and didn't talk about it anymore."

However, that would change when the same co-worker spoke to him three days later. As he approached Kevin, he was as white as a ghost. "Holy shit, man," the co-worker began. "You know that green thing you were telling me about?"

Kevin nodded.

"Over eight hundred people reported it."

Kevin stopped his work, looking at the co-worker in disbelief.

"It's all over the news."

Finally, Kevin had vindication that the event had actually happened. The green orb had been seen by hundreds of people. "They said it was some sort of atmospheric anomaly or something," the co-worker added. But Kevin knew deep down that what he saw that night was more than just a natural phenomenon. This object, whatever it had been, seemed, just like Chris' story above, to be under some sort of intelligent control. "I know what I saw, and it was definitely advanced technology. Whether it be military or extraterrestrial, I can't say. But it changed my life forever."

How exactly it changed Kevin was the answer I sought most. So I pressed him on this. His words mirrored those of Chris: "I wondered, why me?" He speculated, "Maybe I was chosen to see it. Makes it seem a little more special." Kevin would continue to elaborate on just exactly how the event had altered his life. "It gave me a real go-for-it attitude. I dropped everything I had in Florida in 2013 to move to Nashville, Tennessee, to pursue a career in acting, film, and television." He soon began working for the hit ABC television series, *Nashville*, in several different departments, including being featured on the show. "It's working out pretty well so far," he told me.

So what exactly was it that Kevin saw that night? He refused to believe it was an atmospheric anomaly, but if it was the case that this object was in fact under some sort of intelligent control, who or what was that intelligence? "I can't be completely sure. What I do know for sure is that I became really at peace after that event. If it was extraterrestrial, I knew the answer. I knew they were real. And I really don't care if anyone believes me or not. On the flip side, if it was military, well, we are just badass!"

What Kevin and his mother witnessed that night made him sit and reflect on where he was in his life, and just exactly what was out there. His career path spanned military, maintenance, and now the world of show business. And when asked what he hoped for most, he told me, "I hope we someday get hard evidence from these UFO sightings. I also hope we will have disclosure." But most importantly, Kevin wished for something far more ambitious than life elsewhere. "An Oscar would be really nice!"

A Diamond In the Sky

Larry Gessner had spent over fourteen years in the United States Air Force, working his way up from a weapons technician bomb loader to master instructor, teaching the entire weapons system on the B-52 bomber to fighter pilots and other technicians. After his extensive service, he spent the next eight years on the police force, rising through the ranks once again to sheriff in Sheridan County, North Dakota. He'd always been quite familiar with the aircraft flying in our skies, whether highly advanced military or strictly commercial. But it was in late 2003 that he and his wife would witness something over their hometown of McClusky that defied every convention he'd grown to know and accept.

It was July 10, a quiet summer night casting a calm blanket over McClusky. The sky was dark and clear, making the spiraling remnants of smoke billowing from his wife's cigarette all the more distinct. She finished up the last few puffs, ready to head inside from the porch. Larry was inside, settling in for the night. Back outside, his wife stared up into the sky, admiring the cluster of stars that hung overhead. Suddenly, as Larry began to doze off inside, she began yelling for him in a panic.

"Larry, come out here! Come outside! Now!"

Law enforcement mode kicked in. Larry hopped to his feet, assuming that perhaps an intruder was on their property and that she may be in trouble. As he made his way out to the back deck of their home, he watched as she frantically pointed upward to the southeast.

"Do you see that?" she asked.

Larry squinted up at what he assumed was just a simple star hanging loose from Orion's Belt. But as he continued watching, he could see the light beginning to break away from the constellation, rapidly making a descent. "At first, I thought it may be an aircraft that was traveling at an unusually high altitude, but as it came closer, it just stopped, and these lights came on. Red and green. What was most unusual was that the lights were going vertically." The light began to move again, eventually descending directly overhead of Larry and his wife. "I'd say it was approximately eight hundred feet or so in the air." Although it was still rather high up, Larry could make out a solid structure to the lights. "That's when I realized that it was a ship of some kind," he told me.

Larry's gaze could not be broken from the craft. "When something like this happens, it catches you by surprise and your brain becomes occupied with trying to make sense of something you believe can't be." He stood in awe, taking in as much as he possibly could. "It was diamond shaped," he recalled. "Somewhere in the range of a hundred feet long and two hundred feet wide. There were two rows of windows on the front edge, facing us. My eyes were glued to those windows, hoping that I would be able to see who was inside. The only detail that I could make out was a structural support partition that was made out of what I believe to be metal. I say this because of my extensive experience with aircraft. The structural supports in aircraft are flat beams that have holes purposely crafted in them to reduce weight."

The red and green lights glimmered from the diamond, making it even harder for Larry or his wife to make out much more detail to it. But those windows held his gaze. Would he be able to make out some sort of pilot? And if so, would he even want to know who, or what, was inside the craft's interior? That was when Larry noticed one other very interesting attribute to the mysterious diamond that floated above him. "I could hear a thrust sound coming from it. It did not sound heavy or forceful enough to keep a ship of this size moving in the air above us at such a slow speed, yet there it was, floating there in front of us."

As they stood silent, watching the diamond glide overhead, Larry took notice that it was now making its way over a nearby house, which happened to be that of his deputy at the police station. As his wife ran around to the front of the house to follow the craft, Larry ran inside to call his colleague. His fingers shook in excitement as he dialed. Outside, his wife relayed what was happening, the object continuing its slow glide. Inside, the answering machine picked up. Larry started to explain to the deputy that there was a UFO over his house, but just as he mentioned it, his wife yelled from outside, "It's gone, Larry! It's gone!"

Larry put down the phone and ran outside. His wife was now staring at the empty void in the sky where the diamond had been. "My wife told me that the diamond had stopped, a white light came on in the tail point, and it shot straight up at a tremendous speed. She told me that the moment I said the word UFO over the phone, that was the exact moment it disappeared out of sight." Both Larry and his wife headed inside, completely at odds with how to proceed. They sat and talked about just exactly what they'd observed, and Larry again launched into law enforcement mode, writing out a detailed report about what had happened. He'd eventually send this report to the Mutual UFO Network for further investigation. "I would also show the report to everyone I knew. That was until I got pulled into the North Dakota Bureau of Criminal Investigation office and was told to be quiet about this. They were afraid that it would affect my testimony in drug cases or any kind of testimony I would have to provide."

The event itself came to a dramatic end that night, leaving many more questions than answers. This left Larry and his wife lying in bed that night, too excited and scared to sleep. They had witnessed something truly extraordinary. But it would be some time before Larry himself would truly feel the impact of the diamond in the sky.

Almost two years passed. Larry was outside his home, admiring the sky, when a familiar sound hit his ears. Suddenly, memories of the diamond-shaped craft rushed back to him. His eyes scanned the horizon, frantically searching for its sudden return. But he saw nothing. That was when he realized that the sound, strikingly similar to what he remembered hearing the night of the event, was coming from a rooftop of a nearby home. It was specifically coming from an air-exchange system. "This is when I realized that the thrust sound I heard coming from the craft that night wasn't a part of its propulsion, which I believe was completely silent, but the sound was in fact an air exchange." Why, I asked Larry, would the craft need an air-exchange unit? He answered, "Whatever manned that craft either needed to turn our air into something else to breathe, or they needed oxygen inside the craft because they were perhaps human."

Whether human or something else, Larry followed orders from his superiors and didn't talk about the event until 2006, when he was forced to resign from law enforcement. "I contracted a mysterious illness that drastically affected my work. My auto-immune system started attacking itself, and it took two years for the doctors to figure it out. I resigned as sheriff and it was obvious that my health was not in good shape. I figured now was as good a time as any to speak about the event since I was no longer under threat from my job." While Larry wasn't going so far as to speculate that the event had anything to do with contracting the illness, he did say the following about the potential capabilities of the craft he'd seen: "Whatever it was, it could hear the phone call I had made that night to my deputy. The moment I said 'UFO' into the phone, according to my wife at the time, it completely disappeared out of sight. The next morning, my phone lines were completely dead, as if the intelligence behind that craft didn't want me to contact anyone about what I had seen."

This event left a lasting impression on Larry. But just exactly what was that impression? "I witnessed technology that I can't explain. I now know that it exists, and I think it would advance us tremendously if we could implement it. Maybe it is too much for us right now. Either that craft was piloted by an intelligent being from some other part of the universe, or we are flying these craft and have that kind of technology. One thing I know is that whoever was flying it, they took a huge risk of being detected. So perhaps it is time for us to know."

No matter what may be behind the technology Larry witnessed, I still wanted to press him just a bit further. Just as with Chris and Kevin before him, I wondered if Larry felt any special connection to the event. Why were he and his wife the sole witnesses to this event? "I have asked myself many times, what are the odds that I would be lucky enough to have this sighting. Who knows? Perhaps it will eventually prepare me for something bigger."

While awe and wonder may have been the primary reactions to the event as it happened, it was obvious that Larry took the possibilities of the technology he witnessed far more to heart than the actual intelligence behind it. Whatever it was that he saw, its ability to accelerate, stop, and disappear at such tremendous speeds challenged every aspect of conventional aircraft that Larry could possibly think of. Perhaps it could be summed up best with Larry's own optimism: "I want the world to be a better place. I want everyone to come together and request the technology be released to the world in a responsible fashion. I strongly feel that if we knew the truth behind what I saw that night, and what so many others have witnessed, it could truly change our thinking in many ways. We could advance as a planet. We could find new ways to educate people. And then, and only then could we finally excel as a unified race."

A little over four years had passed since I had last spoken to Larry. We'd chatted on and off again throughout the years, but something happened in 2019 that put his story front and center for the entire world to see. He was interviewed by Luis Elizondo, the former head of AATIP, the Pentagon's once secret UFO program. Larry explained the very sighting he'd originally come forward with in this book. Larry had agreed to speak with Elizondo for the History Channel television series *Unidentified: Inside America's UFO Investigation*. In the episode, we got to see the exact location where Larry's sighting had occurred, and get a visual representation of the surrounding area. Having been following the work of Luis Elizondo, Tom DeLonge, and the endeavors of To the Stars Academy, Larry was excited not only to meet Elizondo in person, but to tell his story on a scale he'd never thought he would.

Upon Elizondo's arrival to meet him, Larry had this to say: "Opening my door and seeing him there was a very uplifting experience." Larry would walk Elizondo to the exact spot and describe the event just as he had in this book, at which point Elizondo sprang something on Larry that every UFO witness hopes to hear, but rarely does. Larry stated, "One of the first things that he said to me was that someone else had seen what I had seen. 'Did you know that someone else saw what you saw?' I said, 'No, I wasn't aware of that.' He was shaking his head up and down and saying, 'Yes, someone did!' He did not elaborate on it and I didn't ask. This floored me at first because no one else had come forward that I was aware of."

Though Elizondo would not divulge who this other witness was to Larry, Larry recalled another witness coming forward to him personally and in confidence that it would not be made public. "The only other person who came forward about a month later was a nineteen-year-old who saw it shoot straight up and out of sight. His father let me know about a month after it happened. The only way that information could have reached Elizondo would have been if it was shared via phone conversation and intercepted through someone listening."

Could AATIP have actually been looking into Larry's incident long before this television program, or even the writing of the 2016 edition of this book where Larry first went public? It's quite possible, but perhaps even more revelatory was a conversation Larry had with Elizondo before he left. Elizondo proposed that the location where Larry had the sighting was in close proximity to Minot Air Force Base and several nuclear installations. "Knowing that missile silos were disabled during UFO events, and seeing that these were in the path of this craft I'd witnessed, it gave him concern."

Could Larry have seen a top-secret military craft? He remains open to the possibility, but also can't deny that the craft's structure, maneuvers, and acceleration remained much more advanced than anything he could have imagined from US technology. Between the fact that Elizondo knew of another witness and the nuclear connection to this case, Larry was now under the impression that whatever he saw that night was possibly being tracked. "Knowing that the craft stopped and shot straight up at the moment that I said 'UFO' to my deputy on the phone always made me think that whoever was on that thing had caught that conversation. For me that will always be more than a coincidence. I think Elizondo was letting me know that the US government is capable of tracking them. It probably is still classified and that is why he did not say any more about it."

Having now met a former member of a highly secretive Pentagon UFO program, I wanted to know how Larry felt about the meeting. Had it bolstered his case in a positive way? "I really enjoyed the conversations I had with him during the time he was here. I genuinely believe that he took his job at AATIP very seriously and continues to dedicate himself to finding the answers to help provide not only the proof, but help us provide a defense if they turn out to be a positive threat."

I asked Larry what he wanted readers to take away from his experience, and any advice he would give to those who have witnessed something truly incredible in our skies. He told me, "When I was being interviewed and we returned to the location of the sighting, I suddenly remembered that I could tell that the hull of the craft was thick by looking at the window that I had been looking at. So the moral here is always return to the place where the sighting occurred. You may remember details that you had placed in your subconscious mind." The last thing Larry would leave me with was truly inspiring, making his journey and all of ours that much more real. "I want readers to know that I have always been a levelheaded guy, and I would not say I saw something unless I saw it. I look forward to a time where memories can be shown somehow, and then others can see what I have seen. I want to believe that before I pass from this world, I get the full story of that craft and what it was doing. Let's find out what they *all* are doing."

No One Said a Word About What Just Happened

Twenty years of his life had been given to the US Coastguard as a radioman 1st class and cryptographer. Eighteen of those involved top-secret clearance for many projects, some of which still remain classified. Today, Scott Santa is enjoying his retirement after fifteen years of employment with the US Postal Service. He was a dedicated individual and a stand-up citizen who lived what many would consider an ordinary life. But in 1974, something occurred in his hometown of Cuyahoga Falls, Ohio, that would leave him feeling anything but ordinary.

It was a mild August evening when Scott, having just finished his second year of college, decided to join a friend for a night of movies at the Ascot Triple Drive-In theater. There wasn't a single cloud in the sky as the stars began to appear. They pulled the car into the back of the parking lot. Scott left the car and headed past a small playground littered with children. The children watched as cartoons played from the movie screen. Refreshments were in order, and as Scott headed back with popcorn and drinks in hand, he noticed that the children's collective gaze was no longer fixated on the movie screen, but something above it.

"Do you see that?" Scott asked his friend.

"Yeah. What the hell is that?" he replied.

They both watched as just above the movie screen, a large chevron-shaped object coasted over the screen and began advancing toward the lot. "It was incredibly slow," Scott recalled. "It seemed to float rather than fly." He would go on to describe the object in greater detail. "It was black. It had no lights and was silent. It was enormous and blotted out the stars in the sky. From wing to wing it overlapped the drive-in enclosure."

Scott's friend joined him outside the car. They stared upward at the object as it proceeded in a straight line over the other cars. At this point, Scott noticed that almost everyone in the parking lot was now outside their individual vehicles. Some were pointing up at the object as others frantically looked around at one another, a sense of confusion and unease setting in. The object continued to float over the parking lot, and just as it was almost directly over Scott's head, all the lights at the drive-in, including the movie screen itself, suddenly went black.

At this time, many of the people in the parking lot got back into their cars, attempting to leave. But none of their cars would start. Scott noticed people were now becoming very scared, but there wasn't any panic. Just the terrified looks on people's faces. The feeling soon became quite mutual for Scott, as the chevron-shaped object was now directly overhead. "I could feel that something wasn't quite right. The air was very heavy and I could see and actually feel that the air around us was shimmering, like you see on top of asphalt or cement on a hot day." The object was much lower now as it floated above the parking lot. "If I could have reached down and picked up a larger piece of the gravel, I could have thrown it and hit this thing. That's how close it appeared."

The object hovered for about ten minutes or so as the entire parking lot of people stood frozen, staring upward at it. "Everyone seemed to be in a funk," Scott recalled. "I only took my eyes off of it a couple of times to get a quick look at what other people were doing." The object began to travel from west to east. "It headed toward a vast field of undeveloped real estate behind the drive-in." That is when the air around Scott lost its heaviness and things seemed to return to normal. "All of the lights flicked back on and the movie started again. Just like that, like a switch had been flipped." Scott continued to watch the object as it floated in a straight line off into the distance before completely disappearing from sight. "It was incredible," Scott remarked.

The night's strange events seemed to be over. But Scott soon realized that far weirder things were to come. "I got back in my car, almost robotic-like, and completely forgot all about what I had just witnessed." The movie began to play, and Scott and his friend sat silent, watching as if nothing had happened. Apparently, so had everyone else in the parking lot. "No one, and I mean nobody was running around asking questions or doing anything but watching the movie." Scott had to use the restroom at one point and remembered waiting in line, and everyone just stood silent. "No one said a word about what just happened." Scott returned to the car, finished watching the movie, and he and his friend soon left the drive-in. They didn't speak the entire ride home, and Scott dropped him off, headed home, and went to sleep that night remembering almost nothing of the dramatic event that had occurred. It was as if he'd suffered some sort of immediate amnesia. It wouldn't be until several years later that seeing a book in a local bookstore on UFOs triggered something, and memories of the chevron-shaped object hit him like a ton of bricks.

Scott's account was compelling to say the least. Here we had a case where many people apparently witnessed this massive object floating overhead, and after its disappearance, no one spoke of it. One would assume that mass panic would have ensued, and that everyone would have caused a frenzy. Yet something kept everyone there, motionless. Why, in Scott's opinion, did he believe that he and the others reacted this way? "I do not recall this incident with any fear whatsoever. I do have the feeling of something awe-inspiring, but not fear inducing at all." The fact that Scott had to recall the incident without fully remembering it happening, this sense of almost blacking out was also rather curious. "It was a complete hole in memory of leaving the drive-in, or what, if anything, I did for some time of which I am unable to account for."

Scott would admit that he'd lost touch with his friend who had been there that night. Frustrated with being unable to corroborate the event, he didn't speak of it often. "I told no one, but not by a conscious decision to do so. I have no idea why. One would think that after such an experience that I would have, at the least, spoken to my family, but I didn't do that until many years later." And while Scott's wife and children believed him, they simply couldn't make sense of the event just as much as he himself couldn't. It was the odd reaction that night and the feeling of missing time that haunted him. But even through that struggle to make sense of it, Scott remained optimistic about the event as a whole. "It was definitely a positive, awe-inspiring encounter. But having that time gap," he admitted, "is a disturbing issue, as well as my nonaction or immediate shut-down on recall."

So what was it that Scott saw that night? Could it have been some sort of man-made aircraft traveling a bit too close to the ground? Or could it have been something more? "The object was either an off-world craft, or it was from here. Being that this took place in 1974 and the effects that occurred, I have to think that what I saw was possibly alien in nature." These were bold assertions indeed, but assertions that Scott and so many others have contemplated after such an extraordinary event. "Reality, as presented to the masses, is not what it seems. We do not know as much as we think we know," Scott added. And given his exten-sive career and clearances, I couldn't help but believe him.

One of the most intriguing things about Scott's sighting was how blatant the craft was in terms of being seen by him and everyone at the drive-in that night. I wanted to know if Scott thought that this was all by chance. "I believe I just happened to be in the right place at the right time when this craft floated over us." But he was quick to play devil's advocate. "Or we possibly could have been a target of opportunity." Could that opportunity be, whether made-made or nonhuman, to observe how witnesses would react to such a dramatic and seemingly threat-ening invasion on their night out at the movies? One could only wonder. And as Scott continued to piece together the events of that night, including trying to reconnect with his friend who also saw it, all I could do is wonder myself.

Since the release of the 2016 book, Scott and I had grown close. We conversed almost on a weekly basis. As a fellow UFO book collector, we often bragged about what editions of vintage UFO books and magazines we had obtained throughout the years. In fact, Scott had graciously gifted me some of the most rare books I'd ever come across. And though our conversations always started with books, they always circled back to that night at the drive-in. Without ever pressing the issue, Scott would inform me of small snippets of memory that would rush back. "You showing the interest that you did in my sighting really forced me to look back and formulate or try to structure my recollections about it in a way that I really hadn't ever done before," Scott commented. "With every UFO book I read, my experience is always hovering in my mind as I read, contrasting and comparing it to my own. It's always there."

And the other thing that was omnipresent in Scott's mind, and my own, was the fact that nobody was reacting in a panicked way to what was occurring that night at the drive-in. And as we played over those moments in the story, Scott was beginning to remember small bits of detail. Not so much about the craft itself, but how it felt during and after the event. "I was in no way frightened or scared. Just awestruck," Scott explained. "My mouth open and practically unable to register anything else, my eyes were just glued to that craft. Strangely, I don't remember there being any panic at all, as if a 'calm' button had been pushed. It was at this moment that I experienced the 'scan.'" But what exactly was this scan, and what did Scott think it was? "I don't remember thinking of it as a scan right at that moment—I really had no idea what was happening. I think this may have been the 'calming' thing that kind of sedated everyone to some degree. I remember ears popping and feeling like the air was sucked out of the immediate surroundings. To compound all that was happening, there was utter stillness and no sound whatsoever. I still felt no fear. Merely awesomeness throughout."

Years had passed since he first described the entire series of events, but I was curious if in that time gaps had been filled in of what happened directly after the event. As Scott recalled, nobody reacted to what had just happened. It was as if it were all a dream. But it wasn't. The last thing Scott remembered was going to the restroom, and usually being a very personable and gregarious individual, he expected to be making conversation with everyone about the craft over the parking lot. Nothing. "I still have no memory after returning to the car. I don't remember leaving, don't remember driving home. It's a black hole. Nothing."

With dozens of people having been there that night, the burden of proof had been firmly planted on Scott's shoulders for a long time. His hope was always that someone would connect with him about it, come forward and say that they were also there that night and remember something. Anything. "Not one person had contacted me. I just thought there would be more inquiry after being exposed to such a wide multitude of people in your book."

This was of course a hope for me as well. After the 2016 release, I received many emails from readers who either reported similar sightings as those in the book, or felt compelled to reach out to those featured in hopes of learning more. And every time I started reading the emails, I hoped it would be in reference to one of the most stunning UFO cases I'd ever come across, and that was Scott's. But nothing. I even used Scott's case in a lecture I would give at conferences, and still, nobody ever came forward. I was beginning to lose hope, and so was Scott. This UFO sighting seemed to be his and his alone.

Then an email came to me in October of 2019.

Usually, I would take a quick glance at spam emails just in case before doing a mass purge. As I scanned the emails that day, one in particular caught my eye. It was an email submission to my website. The subject line read "Drive-in movie theater UFO." I immediately clicked on it and read the following:

I read your book during a camping trip last month and I almost dropped it after reading the story about the man at the drive-in theater! I grew up in Summit County, not too far from that drive-in. I remember one night in the summer I was in the backyard smoking a cigarette with my sister, and she noticed something above our house and moving over the backyard. And I swear to you it looked exactly like what the man in your book described. It was very big and pitch black. My sister freaked out and ran inside, but I watched it until it went out of sight. The only difference from what the man saw was that we could see a few white lights on each end of the thing, pointing down at the ground. The light beams were going in a motion like they were searching for something. We thought maybe it was some sort of blimp or helicopter, but it had no propellers and was silent. I remember it to this day, but when I talk to my sister, she denies it ever happened. Anyway, I thought I'd share this with you because it was so close to where he saw this and where we saw what we did. I know it was the same year because my sister graduated high school that year. Again, she denies we saw it, or she just doesn't remember it, like the man in the book. Either way, if he wants to talk to me about it, you can give him my email. I just want him to know I think I saw the same thing. I think.

Thanks,

Cynthia

THE WOMAN who sent this email agreed to let me publish it in its entirety if I didn't use her last name, which I honored. My hope is that after connecting her with Scott and others reading this email, perhaps more people from the greater Ohio area will come forward to bolster this incredible event seen by Scott and perhaps Cynthia. Perhaps the memories of other possible witnesses will be triggered like Scott's had been when seeing a UFO book cover some years later. Maybe, just like Cynthia, someone will pick up this book, read Scott's story, and can start piecing this enigmatic puzzle together. Sometimes all it takes is a word, an image, or a chance reading of a story to change everything. And for Scott, I hope that change will come with a better understanding of what truly happened that day at the drive-in theater.

4

THROUGH A WINDOW DARKLY

It Was Just Gone

She plugged her phone into the car radio. Her fiancé, Phil, turned the volume up, and both of them began singing along to the first song that popped on. The sun had just set in Staples, a small suburb in Minnesota. As the car headed down Warner Road, Jennifer Lundell cracked the passenger-side window open to blow the smoke from her cigarette. It would be a leisurely twenty-minute drive to their friend's house, one they had made many times before. But on March 17, 2015, a small detour would alter the couple's plans and transform the night into one that Jennifer wouldn't soon forget. As the smoke from her cigarette billowed out the crack in the window, something in the night sky took its place.

"What the hell is that?" she found herself blurting out.

She could see a very large, circular light hanging over a nearby field. "It was much brighter than a star and appeared to be much closer," she recalled. "It was moving very slowly." From behind the single light, Jennifer could now see two other lights, equal in size and distance from one another. Phil's attention veered to the passenger window. Both of them squinted, the light almost too bright to bear. After a moment, the object hovered directly above their vehicle. "It was about a hundred feet up or so, and it was huge. I'd say about the size of a football field." The three lights together formed a triangular shape. The sky and stars behind could no longer be seen, Jennifer deducing that this was in fact a solid object. "It was almost in the shape of a V, but not so distinct. More like a boomerang." The lights of the craft reflected off its dark chrome exterior.

Having grown up on this road and traveled it daily, Jennifer knew the area well. She figured that she would have seen this extremely bright object traveling either from behind her or in front. "It was almost as if it just appeared out of nowhere. From the size of it and the brightness, I feel I would have seen it come into view." She continued watching as the object moved slowly upward and away. By this time, Phil had turned off the music, and as they slowly coasted down the road, they both rolled their windows down to see if they could hear anything. Continuing to watch the object drift through the sky, they sat in the car in complete silence. The object above was silent as well. "There was absolutely no sound, no wind, nothing. It was so large, and yet so quiet," Jennifer told me. She also noticed something interesting about the lights on the craft. "We didn't even see the light hit the ground, which was strange to us because they were so big and bright, yet they didn't light up the ground anywhere."

Just as Jennifer and Phil had begun to process the object, something else soon came into sight. Phil noticed another light coming in from the distance in the field. As it got closer, they thought that maybe it was some sort of plane tailing the object. "This is where it starts to get a little tricky," Jennifer went on to tell me. "The lights of the plane were different than most planes. It also didn't make any noise, just like this other object. Maybe it was some type of military craft." Whatever it was, it began to follow the boomerang object as it drifted further into the distance. What happened next left Jennifer shaken. "I literally watched the craft disappear. It wasn't in a poof or a flash. It was just gone. Like it had never even been there in the first place."

Jennifer and Phil remained silent in the car. "I was shocked. Scrambled," she remembered. "I knew I had just seen a UFO. Something from another world." Soon, Jennifer and Phil arrived at their friend's home. Jennifer began to tell the friend about the object, and just as Phil tried to stop her, fearing ridicule, the friend finished Jennifer's sentence for her, describing a strikingly similar object. It was clear that whatever had visited them wasn't some sort of hallucination or misinterpretation. This boomerang-shaped object had made itself known to the very friend that Jennifer and Phil had gone to see. The three conversed for hours, trying to come up with any reason for having seen what they did.

It was clear that the experience had left Jennifer scared, but what she told me next sparked my curiosity. "I also felt a little bit blessed." I wanted to know just exactly what she meant by this. "I feel like I am one of few to experience something like this. For my entire life, I have rested on my back, stared up at the stars, and wondered what was out there, waiting for a sign. And I had it. For me, it was confirmation."

So if this event confirmed her beliefs in some sort of alien phenomenon, what did it want? Why had the occupants made their craft so obvious to her? To this she answered, "I don't know. I really don't. Maybe it was just passing by. I wonder sometimes if my experiences in my life led me to be one of these people who gets to be aware of these things." But what did she actually think these "things" were? "For about three years now, I have been extremely aware of life and things around me, above me, and everywhere. I am lucky enough to see the world from a different angle than I ever have before. I am beginning to think it was some type of extraterrestrial-related gift from that night to begin with. In fact, I am starting to hope it was. Some type of spiritual awakening."

Many whom I've interviewed in the writing of this book

would, in one way or another, describe the very same thing: a spiritual experience. Something just beyond the physical realm had struck them as they stared into the sky, trying so desperately to process the mysterious phenomenon before them. This seemed to be the case with Jennifer, as she continued describing how the event had altered her beliefs. "It has completely changed my beliefs and who I am at the core." But just exactly what did this event spark in her? "I will never stop searching or expanding my knowledge. It has really jump-started a whole new venue of information for me, because I am now researching and learning about all things around these topics. It's made me a little more eager to learn more about what it could all be or mean, but I know I won't know those answers in this lifetime."

So why her? Why had this craft entered her life for a brief moment in time and then completely vanished in the blink of an eye? "Maybe they know I am a friend," she answered. "And I'm not afraid. As a child, I always looked up into the sky and wondered. Now I had confirmation. It seems that in ancient times, everyone always looked to the skies. Worshipped them. And I think these other beings knew that. Cared more about us then. No one ever looks up anymore. Humanity is selfish and busy. Confused. Not united in anything. I don't think, whatever or whoever they are, that they value that very much. Perhaps that is why it seems that these things don't happen as often anymore."

Jennifer and Phil had experienced something that night that was as fantastic as it was inscrutable. While that can leave many disturbed or obsessed with finding answers, Jennifer remained calm and collected. Even in the face of something so profound, she knew that life would go on as it always had. It was merely enhanced. "It's all real," she told me. "Don't be afraid. Just be open-minded. And don't expect yourself to understand it. Just embrace it."

Her words comforted me. Though adrenaline, shock, wonder, and fear had overcome her that night in the car,

Jennifer knew deep down that this had happened for a reason. And even if that reason hadn't been revealed yet, she felt a small sense of satisfaction. Vindication. "I am going to continue to learn and try to discover ideas of what I may have seen that night. It has only made me more excited to do so. There's a lifetime of knowledge out there, and even more lifetimes' worth of wonders to which we as humans will never know the answers. That, more than anything, will keep me busy."

The boomerang craft had clearly left a lasting impression on Jennifer that night. But it would be several months later when I would hear from another witness about a similar experience with an almost identical craft. Only this time, it wasn't a singular object. It was an entire fleet that invaded the skies over North Carolina.

People Aren't Ready for Them

Nothing screams routine like a weekly trip to the local grocery store. As Linda Tuckman pulled out of the driveway with her husband, the two debated essentials versus guilty pleasures. It was approximately 6:30 p.m. on January 16, 2014, when the evening sky began to blend nicely with the uphill road. Just outside the city of Durham, the friendly debate continued between the two while their Toyota Corolla crested a gradual hill on its way toward the grocery store. Linda found herself staring out the passenger-side window. Suddenly, something in the distance caught her attention. There, in a curved pattern, sat five stationary lights, beaming bright.

"What in the world is that?" Linda asked her husband, Brian.

He pulled his eyes from the road for a brief moment, looking in the direction where Linda was now pointing.

"The radio tower?" he assumed, his eyes quickly returning to the road ahead. Linda squinted, trying to get a better look as the car barreled onward.

She shook her head, knowing that it just couldn't be. "The

radio tower is in the other direction," she responded. As they turned a corner, the view of the lights ranged into Brian's driver-side window.

"That's pretty weird," he remarked, his curiosity now piqued. They both realized that the lights weren't stationary, but seemed to be descending and moving with the car as it continued forward.

"What is it? What is it?" Linda kept repeating, excitement and unease brimming over. They soon lost the lights in a strip of trees. As they continued looking, the trees gave way to the sky once more. There, the lights returned. Only now, they were much larger, brighter, and looming closer.

"It's right near us!" Linda observed. Brian gripped the steering wheel, not sure if he should stop or continue driving. Linda soon rolled down her window to stare up at what she could now discern as six separate objects, triangular in shape, drawing closer. "I was in awe," she recalled to me. "They were ships. With a bright light on each wing and a red light in the middle. I could see the outline of the bottom of them. They were black. Metal. Very sleek. I could hear a dull vibration coming from them."

Continuing to follow the objects as best they could, Linda and Brian pulled into the grocery store parking lot, hoping that others were seeing the event play out just as they had. They parked the car and Wendy quickly got out. "They were still there," she remembered. "But they began moving slowly back in the direction that we had come from."

Linda tried to get the attention of others in the parking lot to no avail. Uneasy already, she decided to confide solely in her husband as they both watched the objects float away. At this point, Linda could no longer make out the outline of each craft, but the red light in the center of each one blinked once, in rapid succession until the craft and lights were almost out of sight. But one more thing struck Linda as the dramatic event seemed to come to a close. "A small helicopter or aircraft flew overhead in the direction of the ships. And then the aircraft and ships were completely out of sight."

The entire event, lasting only a brief car ride, had left Linda and Brian completely shaken. They hurriedly purchased their groceries, headed home, and hopped onto the computer to try to figure out if they could find any images of what they had seen. As they sifted through photos of stealth bombers, jets, and declassified aircraft, nothing seemed to match the size and slow maneuvers of this fleet of objects they had witnessed. They began searching for somewhere to report the sighting, which eventually led them to the National UFO Reporting Center (NUFORC). They filed a report with the organization and went to bed that night excited and scared for what they had seen. "Immediately following the experience, I felt nervous, wondering if we were being watched by whoever was flying these ships. But it really caused me to question whether anyone else had seen this that night or if they just appeared to my husband and me."

Similar to the previous witnesses of triangular craft, I wanted to know how this event had impacted Linda's beliefs. "I had never studied UFOs or thought about them until after my sighting. It seemed like a benign experience, but it has caused me to question everything I thought I knew about our reason for being on Earth. I normally would say I believe in a great creator who set this life in motion, but now who really knows what else is out there?"

So her beliefs had indeed been altered. How would this propel her forward in terms of what exactly she may have witnessed? "I have always sought deeper meaning in life. This experience makes me stop and think about what else is out there and what more I might learn. I would say that I am slightly more pessimistic about the religions and rituals we create for ourselves. Things seem to be merely human interpretations of reality."

With such a dramatic sighting, I was also curious as to

whether Linda would invite the phenomenon into her life again. Would this be some sort of primer to future sightings? Many witnesses have admitted to me that after their initial sighting, they would indeed watch the skies more closely, thus increasing the odds of at least seeing something out of the ordinary again. "I do wonder if I will see the ships again; however, if it only happens one time, I feel that I served the purpose 'they' asked me to. There may be things I do not yet know about that will be revealed to me, so I always stay open-minded."

Whatever these craft were, they had made Linda question many things. What exactly were they? Who were piloting this fleet of triangular craft? With ease, she admitted to me that whatever it was, it wasn't human. "I believe that I was being used as some sort of communication from another race. These craft were using some sort of highly intelligent technology. And although I'm open to this concept, I don't want to participate with whatever message they may be sending too much. I don't want to get caught up in it." I found this response extremely compelling. In the profundity of her experience, Linda was able to stay grounded amid her extraordinary experience. It wouldn't stop her from having to put clothes on her children's backs or go on with her everyday life. Her life hadn't stopped. Just like so many others who'd had similar experiences, her life had merely been altered.

So, with the possibility, and Linda's belief, that what she had seen was alien, did she perceive this supposed message from them as a positive one? If these were craft piloted by an alien race, were they here to invade? Destroy? "People aren't ready for them. Spiritually. They cling to religion as it is the only law that governs. I think for some people willing to try to open up to these triangular sightings, they would see that a lot could be learned about zero-point energy."

Zero-point energy. Many who have witnessed the triangular craft have reported absolutely no sound emanating from them. And they seem to float effortlessly, with no conventional explanation as to their propulsion. But what had drawn Linda to connect these craft with zero-point energy? From previous conversations, I'd learned that Linda worked for a corporation specializing in advanced energy. So she was anything but ignorant when it came to various types of energy fields. But I soon learned that after her sighting, she would go so far as to contact the prestigious Fetzer Institute, urging them to look further into the capabilities and benefits of exploring zero-point energy. She also admitted that is definitely something she never would have considered doing prior to seeing what possibly could have been a product of this type of energy. The Fetzer Institute was actually quite responsive to her suggestions, which Linda felt could potentially be a game-changer, and I looked forward to hearing progress on this front if and when it happens.

With her husband and children by her side, Linda continues to explore the alien presence in moderate doses, remaining grounded while also opening up to the world around her. And while something alien may have played a profound role in her moving forward, her remaining words would say it all: "This experience caused me to question everything that humans have created to make their lives make sense. I am struggling not to throw out the baby with the bathwater and to still create meaningful rituals for myself. It is more than okay to create a human experience that you can count on and to hold the balance. And even though you may know there is a lot more out there in this galaxy and beyond, all you can really count on is here in front of you."

The more sighting reports I came across, the more these triangular craft fascinated me. They hit all too close to home as I remembered my own sighting over the water that night in 1995. The accounts of how eerily silent they were struck me most. If an engine or filtering system couldn't be seen or heard, what sort of propulsion were these craft using? And according to both Jennifer and Linda, these sharp-angled craft were massive in size. How could they travel through the skies with such ease and not make any type of noise other than a faint or low humming? The more I looked into these triangular craft reports, it became clear that not only were they invading the skies between Minnesota and North Carolina, they were making themselves ominously at home on other continents as well.

5

SILENT SCREAMS

There Was No Reason for Us to Have Been Crying

Kieran Woodhouse spent a lot of time on the rugby field. It was a vast departure from his day job as a warehouse manager for a medical equipment company. In his hometown of Halesowen, in the West Midlands of England, he found both comfort and invigoration in rugby, a pastime he'd take part in with his younger brother, Cameron. But it was on the evening of April 10, 2013, that the invigoration became pure terror.

As Kieran and Cameron travelled home from Bromsgrove, a nearby town, they made small talk about the day's rugby training. It was a warm, clear night as they made their way through the empty roads. Something seemed to catch Kieran's eye in the distance. A bright light hung effortlessly in the sky. He shrugged it off at first, but it became brighter and seemed to be getting closer. As his brother continued the conversation, Kieran glanced toward the light. He suddenly slammed on the brakes of the car, not even bothering to check if any vehicles were directly behind him.

"What the hell is that!?" he yelled to his brother. Cameron leaned over to get a better look. Frozen in their seats, the brothers looked up to see the single bright light break into a pair that hovered over a distant field. "The lights were huge," Kieran added. "This gave me the impression that they were much closer than I had first thought." As both Kieran's and Cameron's eyes adjusted to the pitch-black sky, they could make out a shape that connected the two lights. It soon became clear that this was a solid object. With the two lights in the back, the shape ran sleekly to a front point, making a perfect triangle. "The craft was moving so slowly that If I had carried on driving, I'd have overtaken it." He turned off the engine and rolled down the window, curious as to what noise the craft was making. Perhaps propellers would be heard and could explain the slow movement of a hovering copter of some sort. No luck. Cameron was actually the first to point out that the craft was completely silent. Although moving extremely slowly, the craft was beginning to get away from them as it soon floated behind the tree line in the distance.

"It was at this moment that I should point out that my brother and I were absolutely petrified. We were visibly shaking and both crying," Kieran admitted. "It's something I'm not ashamed to admit, but at the same time, something I can't explain. There was no reason for us to have been crying, but we were, all the same."

Kieran and Cameron sat there, not sure how to proceed. Impulsively, Kieran, struggling with all his might due to his hands uncontrollably shaking, started the car, and slowly they began the trek home. It would be the quietest car ride of the brothers' lives. As they neared their hometown of Halesowen, hey both noticed a singular light that seemed to be hovering over the town. Whether it was connected somehow to the craft they had seen twenty minutes earlier, Kieran was not entirely sure. But there, in front of them, the light was slowly ascending toward the heavens, shrinking as it rose higher. "Because of the slow speed it was moving upwards, I believe the light was simply diminishing out of choice, not because it was getting further away. Finally, it disappeared completely."

Kieran had experienced something that many around the world have reported as black triangles. These craft seem to be sleek, glassy, and massive in size. They have sometimes been reported to stretch the length of a football field (or in this case, rugby pitch). They seem to float across the sky in a menacing yet silent manner, cruising at low altitudes over highways and cities. This has led many to believe that because of their somewhat routine nature, they may in fact be man-made experimental technology. Whether human or alien technology was behind the sighting of Kieran and Cameron, it had lasting effects far beyond a moment of shock and awe. Kieran, having had a keen interest in the topic of UFOs before that startling night, feared that many wouldn't believe him due to a possible bias in belief. Because of this, he told a few friends and family, but remained silent about the events, the threat of ridicule looming over his head like a dark cloud.

What struck me most was Kieran and Cameron's shared reaction to the incident. The sighting hit them so suddenly that it brought tears to their eyes. This could be based on many different things, yet the fact that both brothers had the same emotional release was curious at the very least. For both, it was a moment of pure vulnerability. With its presence, this triangular craft altered these men drastically. Many others who experience events like this report also having similar reactions during or after a sighting. And although the experience of Kieran and Cameron was alarming and potentially dangerous, it was also quite beautiful.

The phenomenon was speaking to Kieran whether he wanted it to or not. And after his sighting, he bravely took a step forward to begin listening. I asked Kieran what he took away from this experience, and he had this to offer: "After my sighting, I had this urge to look further and deeper into the UFO topic. Having previously brushed off many witness claims of UFOs, I now find myself, more than ever, completely open to any and everything." I then asked Kieran what or who he believes responsible for his sighting, and he added, "I ask myself this question almost on a daily basis. Was it governmental? Extraterrestrial? Something else completely? I struggle with this question every time I relive that night. Whatever or whoever it was, I have no doubt that this massive craft was most definitely under intelligent control and that my brother and I were meant to see it."

I was able to catch up with Kieran in early 2020, and I was curious if his thoughts about what he'd seen that day with his brother had changed at all. He firmly stated, "Absolutely not. If anything, it has only become more imprinted in my memory as time has gone on. Which is interesting because usually memories change or fade with time, but most definitely not for me." I was also curious about his brother's involvement and where he stood, since he was also such an integral part of this close encounter event. And while Kieran had embraced it fully, they occasionally would talk about it, but not in depth. "To be honest, he's not massively interested in all this like I have become."

Perhaps the biggest change in Kieran's life post-encounter was his headfirst dive in to the world of UFOs and the paranormal. "Since the sighting, it has opened up a world of synchronicity that has led me to where I currently am in my life: a paranormal researcher, published author and public speaker on the subject, and a podcast host. I genuinely believe this has all stemmed from my sighting in one way or another."

But it wasn't just an interest in reading, writing, and broadcasting his interest on the topic. It was full immersion in to the various realms of the unknown. "That sighting opened up something in me where I have had many experiences since then. I've since gone on countless paranormal investigations, sky watches, and close encounter investigations."

I was also curious, now that he was well integrated in to the UFO topic, if the current news of Navy encounters and a keen interest by the mainstream media in looking at the UFO topic had any bearing on his personal thoughts on disclosure. Would the world someday learn the truth, according to our world's governments, about the UFO reality and everything that stemmed from it? "I find the course of disclosure that seems to be underway very interesting," he remarked. "It seems they like to drop nuggets of truth when the media is distracted elsewhere. I think eventually full disclosure will happen, but I don't think it will be how we have always expected it to be."

While a grand disclosure of sorts may not happen in the ways we hope or expect, I did wonder if Kieran was any closer to his own disclosure on what he saw that day. Was it man-made, or was it something from another world? "I have never said that it was an alien craft. It could very well have been a government-made craft that was out being tested. I am absolutely certain of my description of the craft and the event itself, but what the actual craft was, I don't think I'll ever truly know."

So as Kieran continued to embrace the experience, what roads was he heading down in terms of researching these types of mysterious phenomena? "Part of my published work and speaking events revolve around trying to explain what paranormal activity is (including UFOs). This has led me down the path of many theories, but one I have stood by and used in my research is looking at where the paranormal fits in to the perception and nature of our reality. I am a strong believer that we are living in a holographic universe, vibrating on particular frequencies and co-existing with other paranormal phenomena who are all vibrating on alternate frequencies. As we can only see roughly 0.05% of the light spectrum, you have to question what is existing in the 99.95% that we cannot see or interact with. I will continue to research, theorize and present my evidence, as well as continuing with my investigations." While this was certainly an ambitious theory, it deserves just as much attention as any other when it comes to UFOs and beyond. "For me, one thing I have learned is that these types of things will always happen when least expected. 'A watched kettle never boils' is certainly true, in my opinion. When you are desperate for something to happen or manifest, it probably won't. It will wait until you least expect it. So never be too desperate for contact, as it will happen, if it is meant to."

Kieran, even though not expecting to see a UFO that day, still feels that while the event seemed random, he and his brother were meant to see it. This broaches a whole new level of the phenomenon. Targeting a certain witness or observer. And it seems to be much more prominent when dealing with these triangular craft. We will now take a look back to the year 1996, when another triangle floated its way through the skies and left one man completely altered in its wake.

On the Road to Area 51

Shawn Kevin Jason had always had an interest in just exactly what was going on in the Nevada deserts. He'd heard many stories about strange aircraft having been spotted around Groom Lake at the installation known only as Area 51. So he decided one night in 1996 to check it out for himself. Little did he know, he was about to get much more than his curiosity had bargained for.

It was approximately 9 p.m. on March 27 when Shawn was trudging through the remainder of his shift at a local pizza joint in Las Vegas. Deliveries were sparse that night, and he found himself picking up a broom to clean the kitchen in the hope that it would pass the time. As he continued sweeping the floor, a sudden rush of nausea overtook him. He paused, a not-so-subtle message brushing past his mind, telling him that he needed to head out to the desert. Something within him believed that this was urgent, and that it had to happen then and there. Just as he approached his boss to ask if he could leave early, she beat him to the punch, explaining that it was a very slow night and he could leave. Naturally, Shawn dropped the broom, punched out, and headed for his car.

He was soon on the road, heading out of Las Vegas and through the dusty terrain leading to a little place right on the edge of Groom Lake. This location, tucked deep into the desert, was better known by its now officially acknowledged name: Area 51. Whatever heightened intuition seemed to be leading Shawn, it was bringing him closer and closer to one of the most secretive and highly secure installations in the world. As he drove down a winding dirt road, he noticed that he wasn't the only vehicle heading toward the base. About a mile ahead of him, he could make out a set of stationary car lights. Assuming the car was broken down, he planned an impromptu pullover to see if there was any assistance he could provide. As he drew closer, however, he noticed that these lights weren't on the ground, but off in the distance. And they weren't from a vehicle, either. His second assumption was that perhaps it was a police helicopter on speeding patrol. But being this far out in the desert without sign of a single other car on the road made it highly unlikely. Curiosity now getting the better of him, Shawn hit the gas, speeding up to get closer to the lights. Within moments, he found himself directly underneath them, and they were quite a sight to behold.

"There were nine white lights in total. I could make out a large black triangle against the night sky," Shawn told me. "It was equilateral in shape with pointed corners. It was only about twenty feet off the ground. The front point of the triangle was directly over my head. Its rear extended across the road and many feet off into the desert. From the front point to the center of its rear, I would say the UFO was about thirty feet wide. The craft was low enough to the ground that my view of the horizon north of me was being blocked by it."

It was at this moment that Shawn began to question the reality of the situation, going so far as to pinch his own arm to make sure he felt it. He ended up pinching himself so hard that he drew blood. His sights shot back up to the sky where the triangular craft remained stationary. "The lights were perfectly round. The face of the lights appeared to be made of glass. They were flat or flush with the surface of the craft. Inside the lights was an inverted chrome-colored cone. From the center of the cone was a metal-looking wire, which extended out and then was wrapped in a large coil. The portion in which this wire was wrapped into the coil is what produced the light. The other parts of the wire were not putting out any light. On the inside face of the glass cover was a diffusion pattern that reminded me of diamond steel plates, but with longer and thinner diamonds. By any definition, what I was looking at can best be described as an incandescent light bulb."

Shawn wanted to get an even better look, so he reached for a pair of binoculars that he always kept in the car, but when he finally found them and turned back, the craft had completely disappeared from view. Frustrated, Shawn now scanned the skies and noticed, about a mile away, the triangular formation of lights yet again. It wasn't completely gone after all. Instead of driving closer, Shawn stayed idle, using the binoculars this time to try to get a better look at the craft. This is when he noticed that it wasn't actually black, but a charcoal color. It was moving at a steady pace but was drawing near a mountain. For a moment, he thought it was literally going to crash right into the rocky terrain. But as it reached the mountain, it seemed to almost climb the surface and float right over, completely disappearing out of sight yet again. Although this would be the end of the events that night, Shawn drove home with a wary eye on the skies above him.

What did Shawn believe was behind the craft he'd witnessed? "I'm almost certain that the UFO was of military origin and design," he responded. "I don't believe any aliens were involved. Just by the detail and circuiting involved with the lights on this thing, I have no doubt it was man-made."

With our previous witnesses in the UK having had a most

visceral and powerful reaction after their sighting, I asked Shawn how the experience made him feel immediately after his sighting occurred. Shawn's answer was anything but similar. "Anger. Shock. Astonishment. Wonder." Anger intrigued me most. I asked him to elaborate. "I was really angry with my government for covering up the reality of UFOs. As well, I had to come to terms with the fact that what I witnessed was most likely man-made." It seemed that Shawn wanted this to be alien in some way, not wanting to believe that the US military was in possession of something so advanced and refused to let the public know.

The anger only grew after Shawn made fellow co-workers aware of his sighting, hoping they would react respectfully, which some did. Others were a bit more intolerant, opening the ridicule floodgates wide. "I did deal with a case of discrimination while employed at a Fortune 20 company. While working as a computer network security analyst, I began having problems with my manager. Our team was spread out across the US, so we often had regular conference calls. During some of these calls, my manager would single me out as the butt of his jokes. Many times, these jokes dealt with aliens and UFOs. Given my manager's behavior in front of my peers, it wasn't long until some of them started doing the same. Of which, management condoned. I soon filed a discrimination case, and eventually those involved were given a soft slap on the wrist. Disenfranchised, the job only lasted a couple years after that as I got shuffled around."

Had Shawn regretted ever having told his peers about the experience? "I don't regret speaking up against something I felt was wrong." When asked what he felt was wrong, he said, "... these things are flying through our skies, sending fear through those who witness them. And then, they are in turn told they are crazy if they talk about it. And the government continues to turn a blind eye and suppress the truth. It's disgusting."

Although anger played a large role in the aftermath of Shawn's experience, there were several beacons of light that did

and continue to shine through. He admitted that in direct relation to the sighting, he progressively became much more aware
of what was both around him and above him. "It has definitely
risen my level of awareness and understanding." What exactly
Shawn was trying to understand was something I yearned for as
well. That awareness was bringing him closer to figuring out
what it was he saw in the desert that night, and it would also
bring him and me closer than I'd ever imagined.

In 2019, I had the opportunity to meet Shawn face-to-face in
Nevada. I was filming an episode of *Mysteries Decoded*, a television series I'd been working on with my investigative partner,
Jennifer Marshall. Jennifer was a top-notch investigator. Aside
from hunting UFOs with me, she was a Navy veteran with five
years of service, even spending time on the USS *Theodore
Roosevelt* Ship Security Defense Force team. After her time in
the Navy, she founded her own private investigation firm,
searching for missing persons, helping adopted people track
down their birth parents, and even investigating cases of stolen
valor. Suffice to say, hunting down leads on UFO cases was small
potatoes for Jennifer but something she'd always found of great
interest, especially when it came to military involvement with
UFOs. And the proximity of Shawn's sighting to Area 51
prompted our interest in revisiting his case. Our balance of
skepticism and open-mindedness meshed quite well when we
first investigated the most famous UFO event of all time, the
Roswell UFO crash of 1947. This would ultimately lead to
another investigation in to more current events within the UFO
world.

After news of the secret Pentagon UFO program, AATIP, had
broken, and numerous UFO videos surfaced of Navy run-ins
with UFOs, we decided to investigate these videos ourselves to
find connections between the maneuvers of these craft in the
videos and purported craft being witnessed, tested, and highly
guarded at Area 51 and the surrounding Nevada testing sites. We
went so far as to make our way to the gates of the secretive

installation ourselves. But not before meeting with Shawn and stepping foot on the exact location where he'd witnessed the triangular craft in 1996. Could his event have had any direct connections to Area 51 and the technology being displayed in the Navy videos? We were ready to ask these questions, no matter the outcome. And it started with Shawn.

It was a crystal-clear day when Jennifer and I made our way down Highway 93 in Nevada. Shawn had given us approximate coordinates to the location of his sighting. We arrived before him, surveying the area. Besides the occasional long-haul truck and speed demons whizzing past, I could only imagine Shawn driving down the desolate, dark road in the middle of the night. There was open space as far as the eye could see to the west and a sharp view of a mountain range miles away in the distance. Jennifer and I had revisited Shawn's story prior to coming out to the site, and as we stood there, imagining what it must have been like, Shawn arrived in a cloud of dust, pulling to the side of the road in his Fiat 500 Special Edition. The vehicle complimented his retro-style clothes and vanity license plate that simply read AREA 51. It was all just so strangely perfect meeting yet another witness who had related their incredible story in the pages of this book.

"So this was it? This is where it all happened?" I asked.

He took off his sunglasses and stared out over the western direction of the mountains. I could see the memories seeping onto his face, bringing him back to 1996 when the craft hung above him. He reiterated the string of events in such clarity and authenticity, never wavering or changing a single aspect of the event, solidifying for me how honest he was about what had happened. Shawn's original theory about the craft he'd seen that night was that it was a man-made craft. I wanted to know if that had changed at all since that night.

"No," he told me. "While a good number of researchers and spectators alike may disagree with my conclusion that it was man-made, that hasn't swayed my thoughts on the matter."

Jennifer and I had been looking at several of the Navy videos in great detail. And while some of the individuals involved with these more recent events have gone on record to state that what they witnessed could possibly be something from another world, Shawn stressed that we should be very cautious of immediately going to the extraterrestrial hypothesis when it comes to UFO sightings, especially with the military. In relation to the Pentagon revelations, he also told me, "The conversation is largely centered on aliens, still. That said, we have little insight into the potential terrestrial origins of some craft being reported. In this new era, officialdom continues to ignore and/or deny any possible connection with said craft. And as a result, the public will remain in the dark. My sighting stands in stark contrast to the status quo. Recent events haven't changed that."

With mainstream media outlets capitalizing on the alien meme and continuing to push the narrative of UFOs being a vehicle piloted by otherworldly visitors, Shawn expressed that the opposite can be just as intriguing. The possibility of earth-changing technology being developed here on our planet is exciting in itself. But the belief in an extraterrestrial presence will always overshadow the proclamations of the witness saying what they saw was anything but. Luckily, this didn't bother Shawn much. "What people take away from my experience will be determined by whether or not it supports their existing belief system. With that in mind, I have no interest in imploring others to believe me," he explained. "Had I not lived it, I would have difficulty with it myself."

And while Shawn's experience remained one of my favorite sightings to date, primarily because it was so similar to my own, I wanted to know how Jennifer felt about it, having met Shawn and having heard his story for the first time. How would this influence our investigation moving forward? "I hear a lot of witness accounts," she told me. "Most of them years after the fact. Memory is fallible. More and more research is being done on memory and how it works, and even if a person is being 100%

honest and truthful in what he or she recollects, the memory itself is still going to be less than factual. Over time, a memory becomes an amalgamation rather than a pure regurgitation of the event."

This resonated with me now, looking back at all the time that had passed since the original release of this book, more than I had realized back in the years of interviewing everyone in this book. While their experiences and recollections were extremely vivid and personal, from an objective standpoint, how accurate could their memories actually be? This was a struggle and needing analysis on a case-by-case basis. For Shawn, the detail from his recollections from 2016 to 2019 hadn't changed in the slightest. But, keeping in mind that the event itself had actually occurred almost twenty years prior to the publication of the 2016 edition of this book, what holes or gaps had been filled in by Shawn's memories? We'll never truly know. But it was comforting to hear Jennifer's observations of Shawn's testimony. "The silent nature of the craft is the most intriguing feature of his account," she explained. "Like Shawn, I found the structure of the lights to be the most interesting and unique feature—not something you would expect from something extraterrestrial."

Jennifer, being extremely grounded and objective in her approach with UFO investigations, presumed that the majority of those who believe in an extraterrestrial presence on our planet tend to believe that when they see a UFO, it's otherworldly. But upon learning that Shawn didn't feel that way about his sighting, she remarked that, "It surprised me, but actually made me appreciate his account even more. I think that Shawn saw something compelling that he couldn't explain that has stuck with him until this day. Whether the craft was military or extraterrestrial in nature is unknown, but it did make quite the impact on him."

We left that day appreciating how open and honest Shawn had been with us. He never claimed that this was an alien spacecraft, nor did he claim it was reverse-engineered alien technology integrated in to a man-made, top-secret project out at Area 51. He simply stated the facts as best he could from memory. And although, as Jennifer pointed out, those memories could falter at times, that goes for any scenario by any individual about any type of memory. But heading out on the dusty road that day, pursuing our leads on both the Area 51 angle and the videos we'd seen from the Navy, it became more and more clear that at the end of the day, we'll never truly know what Shawn saw. It was a moment in time he'll always have, and a moment in time when I got to finally meet face-to-face with yet another witness of the unexplained. As Jennifer and I continued our search for answers, heading out to the top-secret military instal- lation for a look, I watched in the rearview mirror as Shawn headed in the opposite direction, his vanity license plate shim- mering in the hot sun. No matter what he'd seen that night, that license plate said it all. This event had certainly impacted his life. And now, more than ever, it was impacting mine as well.

6

SOMEWHERE IN OUR STRANGE SKIES

Glowing Rocks Below Lead to Glowing Orbs Above

Erik tripped upon a discovery so unique that it would change his life. But it wasn't a UFO sighting. That was to come later. It was the summer of 2017 when Erik Rintamaki, a gem and mineral dealer, went out rock hunting on one of the beaches off Lake Superior in Michigan. Using an ultraviolet light, he noticed a strange glow he'd never seen before coming from certain rocks that had washed up. He gathered them up and would eventually have them analyzed at the Michigan Technological University and the Saskatoon University. They confirmed that these specific rocks were indeed the first of their kind in Michigan, and were what is known as syenite rocks that are rich in fluorescent sodalite. The discovery by Erik was published in several mineral and scientific journals, and he soon coined a specific name for this type of rock in Michigan: Yooperlites.

Word began to spread about these highly unique and luminescent rocks, and mineral and gem collectors began to flock to Michigan to study and collect their own. Found mostly on Lake Superior between Whitefish Point and on the Keweenaw Peninsula, Erik decided these were the areas where he'd start a touring business. With these tours, he would lead groups out to find Yooperlites themselves. And it was on one of these very tours that Erik, and several other tour group members, would make a discovery not on the ground, but in the skies over Lake Superior.

It was June 12, 2019, at about 1 a.m. when Erik was wrapping up a Yooperlite night picking tour at the Whitefish Point boat harbor beach. Accompanied by a woman from Wisconsin and a retired couple from Ann Arbor, they began to head south down the beach and to Erik's vehicle, as the wind had picked up and it was beginning to rain. "The four of us had a successful evening hunting Yooperlites, and then without warning, something happened that changed all of our lives forever," Erik told me. The tour members slowly made their way to the vehicle, continuing to search for Yooperlites along the way. As Erik analyzed a few of the rocks, the wife in the group grabbed his sleeve. "Erik... what are those lights behind us?" she asked, concerned. Erik, without even looking, assumed it was a ship on the water and told her as much. She shook her head aggressively. "That is not a ship. Erik... turn around."

As Erik took his sight off the rocks and scanned the water, he immediately knew it was not lights from a ship. "There were three bright orange balls of light hovering above the water directly above Whitefish Point and Lake Superior. These orb-like lights were in a formation that looked like an elongated triangle. Then a second after I turned to see them, the orbs then swapped positions with each other and then very quickly swapped back to their original positions. Then one of the three lights would fade out and a second later one of the other two lights would move to the position where the light that disappeared had been. The lights did this until only one light was left, and then another light would appear above or below the original light. This went on for a long time."

Erik was compelled to move closer to the water to get a better look, but one of the group members held him back, clearly scared of what was happening. They all stood in awe, watching the brilliant, almost choreographed dance of lights in the night sky. "We stood there in the pouring rain at 1 a.m., looking at the orbs and wondering, *What the hell are we looking at? Are they UFOs? Aliens?* None of us could believe what we were seeing."

After watching the orbs for about fifteen minutes, Erik broke out of a trance and realized he should be filming this display. He took out his phone and began recording. "I started taking video and standing on a rocky and sandy beach, in the rain, wind, and dark, trying to film orange orbs in the sky with a cell phone. It was no easy task. I filmed for about five minutes, when we noticed that a thousand-foot iron ore freighter named the *Spruce Glenn* from Canada was moving towards the orbs that were hovering above the shipping channel just out from Whitefish Point."

As this freighter moved closer to the orbs, Erik continued filming. The orbs suddenly went from two to one. This single orb was very low to the water and it almost seemed as though the ship was going to run right in to it. "The orb hovered just high enough for the ship to go right underneath. Unseen in the video is the fact that the deck of the ship could be seen lighting up to the naked eye as the ship passed underneath. We were all sure a collision was about to occur." Luckily, the ship passed safely under the orb. Seconds later, a second orb reappeared as the other faded out. "My phone was very critically low on space at this point, so I quit recording."

What happened next was perhaps the most concerning part of the entire incident. Suddenly, without warning, the single orb shot down the beach at breakneck speed, traveling directly toward Erik and the group. "As it came down the beach, you could see the wet rocks and water lighting up orange as it came close. Then it stopped and hovered about a hundred feet up at about a hundred yards away. We tried our best to make out any shape or ship, but with the rain and low cloud cover, it was too dark to tell if the orb was part of a structure of some kind."

While Erik was taking this all in, he noticed one of the women in the group had hidden behind a large boulder, clearly scared of what was happening. She began screaming at Erik that they had to leave. The other members looked very concerned. The orb began moving north back over the water as another reappeared next to it. Erik, not wanting to take his eyes off it, reluctantly decided it was time to leave. "So I got everyone in my truck, pulled the truck around to face directly towards the orbs. Then I decided to turn my truck's headlights on and off three times to see if it had any effect on the orbs." As Erik did this, one of the orbs faded out, and the other sped toward the beach again, stopped, and hovered the same height and distance again above Erik and the group. "When the orb came towards us again, the woman who hid behind the boulder freaked out and hit my arm and screamed for us to get out of there. So I put it in drive and left."

Erik drove about seven miles back to Paradise, a small township where he'd originally picked up the group members. As soon as he dropped off the members, he drove as fast as he could back to the harbor where the entire incident had taken place. "To my amazement, the orbs were still there!" he recalled. "I sat in my truck, alone, and watched the orbs for a while." Erik then remembered that he had a pair of binoculars in the truck, so he excitedly grabbed them to get a better look at the orbs. "I got out of the truck and headed toward the water. Through the binoculars, the orbs looked like someone with a giant sparkler in the sky. It almost looked like a plasma ball. I thought maybe it was me shaking from adrenaline, so I put the binoculars on the dash and looked through them while stabilized. And to my amazement they looked the same."

For the next forty minutes or so, Erik tried to play games

with the orbs, flashing his headlights on and off, attempting to obtain some sort of response by the orbs. They flickered sporadically, sometimes fading back in and out, but nothing like what had happened when the entire group was there. "I flashed my lights on and off, and unfortunately, the last remaining orb flickered out and disappeared. That was the last I saw of the orbs." Erik sat there for another forty minutes or so, waiting to see if they'd return. With no sign of the orbs, it seemed like this incredible event had finally come to a close. He pulled out from the harbor and headed home.

Upon returning home, Erik excitedly reviewed the camera footage he'd taken, questioning what he should do with it. "I toiled for a day or two wondering to myself whether or not to post it online for everyone to see. I did not want to be ridiculed or have this experience hurt my business. But after talking with my wife and sleeping on it for a few days, I made the decision to post it online. Within a few more days, my footage was picked up by the *New York Times* and then by some pretty popular YouTube channels and finally by the television series *Paranormal Caught On Camera*." Seeing as his video had ostensibly gone viral, Erik still feared that this would harm his reputation and business he'd built from the ground up. But as he soon realized, that couldn't have been further from the truth. "Being featured on television and online had the opposite effect that I had thought it would. It only helped my business. And still to this day, I have yet to receive any negativity from anyone at any time."

Many hoped to speak with the other witnesses that were there that night to back up the story that accompanied Erik's video. I had the rare opportunity to be connected with all three witnesses. And in three separate, private interviews, they recalled an almost identical experience to Erik's. The descriptions of the orbs, the behavior they displayed, the dramatic blinking in and out, zipping through the sky at incredible speeds, and even hurtling toward the witnesses and hovering almost directly above them. It was clear that all of these witnesses were genuine in their testimony, which only strengthened the account's credibility.

After all was said and done, I was curious, what did Erik believe them to be or represent? "Look, I've been picking stones on the shores of Lake Superior for forty-five years, and this was *the* one and only time I'd ever seen anything in the sky that I could not explain. I can't tell you what they were, but I can tell you what they were *not*. They were *not* drones, Chinese lanterns, Saint Elmo's Fire, or anything man-made. Whatever they were, they did seem to be intelligently controlled."

Erik went so far as to attempt finding other witnesses in different locations that may have seen the orbs that night. Maybe they would have a better idea of what had occurred. "My friends who were at Vermillion, six miles to the west, could see the lights that night, but from their vantage point, it looked to them that there was a giant bonfire on the beach. Another gentleman who owns a cabin a few hundred yards up the beach from us also witnessed the orbs that night, but did not have a camera and does not want to be named."

In one last attempt, Erik knew the exact ship that was out on the water that night, as it made the same trek often. Perhaps contacting them about their proximity to, and almost near-collision with, these lights could offer some sort of explanation. Erik told me, "I am friends with a 'boat nerd,' and she is friends with all the freighter captains. We emailed the captain of the *Spruce Glenn* and asked if we could see the deck footage from the ship from the time frame of my video. But instead of replying with a polite yes or no, the email bluntly stated: *We have nothing to report*."

It was clear something amazing took place over Whitefish Point that early morning. With multiple witness testimony, video footage, and an active investigation ongoing between several independent researchers, myself included, this remains one of the best documented UFO cases to happen in the last few years. As I eagerly await the opportunity to travel to Michigan to continue digging in to this case, Erik continues his Yooperlites tours out on the beaches near Whitefish Point, hoping that perhaps one day the orbs will return to shed more light on this most mysterious phenomenon dancing above the waters of Lake Superior.

Somewhere Above the Law

Tim McMillan currently resides in Spangdalem, Germany. After sixteen years, he retired from his roles as police lieutenant and investigator and moved overseas, where he now works as a freelance investigative journalist, mostly focusing on the defense and intelligence communities. His work has often included peripheral UFO discussion, which landed him several featured articles for *Popular Mechanics*, *VICE* news, and *The War Zone*. Tim's continued efforts to both clarify and report on the intelligence communities and their long history of involvement with the UFO issue has made him one of the most sought-after writers on the topic in the last few years. But how does someone like Tim first become interested in UFOs? Well, like a lot of people who find themselves deeply entrenched in the enigmatic topic, a UFO sighting of his own.

It was December of 2011 in Rincon, Georgia, a small town about twenty miles north of Savannah. Late in the evening, Tim finished watching a movie at a friend's home. "Her and I were standing in the front yard talking before I embarked on the forty-five-minute journey back to my home in Savannah. In coastal Georgia, only on the coldest of nights can you escape the usual blanket of humidity and get a chance to see really clear, beautiful, starry nights. This particular night happened to be especially cold, and I remember my friend and I were marveling at the night sky as we chatted." As they continued talking, their eyes scanned the dark skies above. Suddenly, beyond the stars and pitch black, something caught their attention. "Three very bright, perfectly circular lights suddenly appeared in the sky above us. The lights just appeared as if someone flipped on a switch and were about the size of a pea at arm's length—much larger than a star or navigation lights of an aircraft. They had a sort of antique yellow hue to them and were all in a perfectly straight line as if attached to each other or something else unseen."

To Tim, this was not a subtle "huh" moment of curiosity. It was, as he recalled, a stark "Holy shit! What is that!?" moment. They watched as the lights hung motionless for a little under a minute. Suddenly, the three lights just turned off. "Again, it was as if someone flipped a light switch and they didn't just fade or dim away." Tim and his friend looked at one another, but before they could say anything, the three lights suddenly reappeared in the same exact location as they had before. "However," Tim added, "this time there were two more lights, making a total of five bright bold whitish amber lights. All five lights were in a perfectly straight line, with the first three lights evenly spaced about a degree apart from each other. The two new lights were spaced about a degree apart from each other."

With Tim's analytical skills, he determined that the lights were at an elevation of about thirty degrees off the horizon. But what he noticed next would only amplify the sighting and what it could have been. "Once all five lights were visible, a massive rectangular shape behind the lights seemed to block out the ambient city lights on the horizon." So it seemed possible there was a solid structured craft of some sort that held these five lights. However, Tim was quick to point out, "I'm always cautious in stating as fact that there was indeed a rectangular shape the five lights were attached to. Essentially, with a background in cognitive psychology, I understand that our brains struggle to make sense of nonsensical stimuli and can cause incorrect perceptions such as pareidolia. Regardless, the five lights were absolutely certain."

Once again, the lights remained motionless and hung there

for a minute or so, and then all five flicked off. "My friend and I stood outside with eyes peeled to the skies, hoping it would reappear, for the next thirty minutes or so; however, they never did reappear." And with that, Tim headed home, not quite sure what to make of the event but knowing it was most definitely something out of the ordinary. He also added, "My friend was a ten-year police veteran at the time of our sighting. She still works in law enforcement and presently is a sergeant and supervisor with the Chatham County Police Department." Again, stressing that both had significant observation and reporting skills, the fact that they couldn't quite make sense of what they were seeing definitely added both credibility and mystery to the incident.

When Tim arrived home that night, he immediately hopped online. "I started researching anything and everything I could to figure out what it was I'd seen. After some searching, I stumbled upon MUFON's website for the first time. I remember being stunned at discovering someone had already reported seeing *exactly* the same thing we saw twenty minutes before our sighting." Their sighting, however, was, "in Statesboro, Georgia, which is about forty miles west of where we were. I still to this day don't know who that other person is that reported the sighting."

The biggest question skeptics often have when hearing a UFO witness account is, *Why didn't you take video or photos of it?* It's a fair question. Being that Tim's sighting did take place in the age of cell phones being accessible to almost everyone, I had to play devil's advocate and ask if the thought had crossed his mind or if he attempted to capture the aerial phenomenon. "I remember just being awestruck and wondering both aloud, and in my head, *What the fuck is that!?* Additionally, the only time in my life I've ever had an Android cell phone was during the time of my sighting. I hated that phone with the fire of a thousand suns because it always seemed to freeze up or not work at the most inopportune times—the sighting being just one of the times. I remember being pissed because I wanted to try and record what we were seeing, but my phone froze up and had to reboot. By the time it was finally ready to record, the entire sighting was over."

Tim remembered being fascinated by the event at the time. But what about after? What impact had this singular event had on him? "Afterwards, I began to wonder just how much that feeling of fascination that 'something' else might be out there actually had a significant impact on me. At the time of my sighting, I happened to be in one of those low points in life. My girlfriend of several years had just abruptly broken up with me and I'd had to move back in with my parents while I searched for a new apartment. I was a thirty-year-old police sergeant at the time, and I remember feeling a little lost with what direction my life was going in. However, when you're reminded about life's inherent mysteriousness, you suddenly realize there's more to life than what you see around you or what's going on in any given moment. Symbolically, my sighting later seemed like a little nudge that said, *Don't assume you've seen all there is to see or know all there is to know out there. You're fine… just keep going.* Ironically, months later, I'd end up meeting my wife and future mother of my children."

The impact of this event on Tim's life was a gradual but truly inspiring process of self-discovery and perseverance. And it would open an entirely new world for him in terms of applying his writing skills to the UFO topic. "Since my sighting, I became interested in the UFO subject. I spent the first seven years afterwards very quietly outside the 'UFO community,' but researching and interviewing people from my academic background in cognitive psychology. I'm still very interested in examining whether there's a nexus between the observed and observers in UFO sightings. Essentially, are people who see UFOs simply at the right place at the right time, or is there more personal reasons why these events occur? After taking early retirement and being frustrated at what I saw was the lack of good investigative journalism towards the UFO subject, I decided to use my law enforcement and investigations background to look into the topic and provide good, credible info to the public. I highly doubt any of that would have happened if it had not been for my initial sighting."

The event had changed Tim in many ways. And while that may be the most important part of the entire event, I was also curious if he had any theories on exactly what it was he saw that night with his friend. "I've always been very content with the unknown and perfectly comfortable in saying that I truly don't know what I saw. Now, the last six years before retirement, I was the night-shift lieutenant for my police department—working from 3 p.m. to 3 a.m. Surrounding my jurisdictional bubble was Fort Stewart, Hunter Army Airfield, the Georgia Air National Guard's 165th Airlift Wing, Gulf Stream Aerospace, and the Savannah/Hilton Head International Airport. Roughly a hundred miles south was Naval Nuclear Submarine Base Kings Bay, and less than thirty miles north was Marine Corps Air Station Beaufort. With years of operating during the hours most smart people are sleeping, and surrounded by military institutions or airports, I began to learn all of the normal flight paths and lanes that conventional aircraft in the area traveled. With Hunter Army Airfield being home to the 3rd Battalion, 160th Special Operations Aviation Regiment, during those long nights patrolling the mean streets, I frequently saw some pretty unique stuff in the sky. In some instances, I saw aerial objects that behaved or resembled unconventional aircraft. However, in each of these instances, though I couldn't identify what I was seeing, I always knew it was 'ours' because I knew the flight patterns of the environment around me. All of that said, what I saw in December of 2011 did *not* resemble anything I'd seen before or since. I simply do not have a prosaic explanation for it, but at the same time, it would be a huge leap for me to say that it was aliens. Instead, I just settle on the fact that I simply don't know."

And while Tim accepted that he may never truly know what

it was he saw that night in 2011, he realized that it wasn't about finding the answer. "I don't know if the *what* is really the most significant aspect of UFO sightings. Whether it's my sighting or in general, at its core, the only true consistency with the UFO phenomena is a steadfast commitment towards enigmatic and elusive displays that reject conventional norms and pragmatic understandings. As a good friend once said, 'It is as if the phenomenon uses our love of the chase as the main motivator to entice us.'"

Having written extensively on the developing stories of Navy UFO encounters, the Advanced Aerospace Threat Identification Program, and the intelligence communities' growing interest in UFOs, I was very curious to get Tim's thoughts on where he thought this was all heading when it comes to looking at the big picture of both UFO phenomena itself, and the official study of it. "For the first time since the closing of Project Blue Book, you have the US government actively discussing their interest and involvement in investigating UFOs. Discussions with people I know in the defense and intelligence community—people who are not known for being in the 'UFO world,' and have professional backgrounds in national security—tell me this is a real issue and these unidentified aerial phenomena, or UAP, do not comport with known capabilities in service or engineered development by US or foreign state and non-state actors. Congressional leadership has been briefed and US government is extremely confident that this is not adversary, primarily based on performance capabilities. Additionally, advances in classified sensor technologies have caused the detection of UAP to be an unavoidable issue for the US government."

So while independent researchers—some with highly extensive scientific, academic, and psychological backgrounds—continue to examine this topic through grassroots efforts and civilian-run organizations, where would the roads converge with the government and military study to these phenomena? For Tim, he admits, "Where we'll be a year, two years, or five years down the road when it comes to knowing more about UFOs, remains a mystery. For me, I'm very encouraged in how much the subject continues to evolve into a credible topic for legitimate discussion. I'm excited to see where it will continue to go."

A Phenomenon That Thrives On Mystery

Rob Kristoffersen hosts one of the most thoroughly researched, executed, and respected UFO podcasts available. He is a walking encyclopedia of UFO history and cases. In fact, he is one of the most requested guests to join me on the *Somewhere in the Skies* podcast on at least a monthly basis. And while we always enjoyed each other's digital company, and while I knew he would always make for a highly knowledgeable and entertaining guest, the respect I had for his research is what made him a true inspiration. And I was curious where that had all started for him. For many, myself included, it was a sighting or experience of some kind. For some, it was simply an interest or fascination with the topic. And as I soon learned, it was the former for Rob. And his sighting left me with very little doubt that it had inspired one of the most promising and up-and-coming UFO researchers to date.

It was June 15, 2015. At around 10:15 a.m., Rob was at work at a nursing home in the village of Tupper Lake, New York. A fellow co-worker, Dennis, asked him if he wanted to take a smoke break with him. "On breaks, we'd go to the edge of the property, because you can't technically smoke on the grounds. We were standing there for a couple of minutes. Dennis was smoking and we were just talking. Suddenly, I just had this urge to look up." As Rob's eyes shot up in to the clear, blue sky, he saw something odd that caught his attention. "There was this object floating in the sky. It was moving really slow, at what I would guess to be a low elevation. Maybe a thousand feet or so. It was the shape of an egg and quite large. From my vantage point, it looked to be the size of a small car, like a VW bug."

Rob continued staring up at the metallic-colored object, getting Dennis' attention and pointing toward it. They both looked on as the object floated in place. "At first, I wanted to take a photo of this object; then I remembered that I didn't have my phone on me. I'm not sure if Dennis had a phone by that time. He may have, but I can't remember. I know we never took a photo of the object." They watched the object from its side, as it moved parallel to them. "It continued to move towards us to almost directly above where we were standing." This is when the object stopped in midair , turned ninety degrees, and moved away from Rob and Dennis very slowly until it was out of sight.

While seeing a UFO would leave most people frantic, awed, or extremely excited, for Rob it almost seemed like a calm had rushed over him as he was seeing this egg-shaped object in the sky. "I remember having the urge at first to take a photo, but that feeling kind of melted away. There were other people about a hundred feet away, and I never felt the urge to call out to them to look. I was just calm, and then when the break was over, I went back to work like nothing had happened."

This idea of a sense of calmness would be a running theme in many of these cases, especially the event with Scott Santa at the drive-in theater. It is as if the moment is manipulated some-how. But for people like Scott, Rob, and a few others you'll read about soon, there's a sense of unexplainable calm that blankets what would usually be an intense situation. "It was like a curious apathy," Rob explained. "I was of course interested in what I was seeing, but I almost didn't care that I was seeing it. It's kind of hard to describe. Dennis and I would often hang out and talk about paranormal topics, so it was kind of weird that when we experienced something like this, we didn't react differently."

What was it that Rob believed he saw that morning in Tupper Lake? "I'm not entirely sure. Maybe it could have been a drone, but the object had no windows on it that I could see, and something that's egg-shaped doesn't seem very aerodynamic. I only saw it from two sides, so it's possible that it could have been a military craft of some kind, but there is a small bit of doubt in my mind. When I saw it, I'm sure I thought otherwise. There was a time when I thought anything like that would have been alien, but I like to maintain a healthy dose of skepticism."

While Rob may not know what it is he saw, how had it affected him? "Before this incident, I spent my time doing paranormal investigations. After it, I devoted my time to reading about UFOs and UFO-related phenomena. My library has a copy of *The UFO Experience* by J. Allen Hynek, and I remember checking it out quite a few times. After my interest was piqued, I started to develop a reputation for being well-versed in UFO lore, and I would often help other podcasts with topics and research. And then, in 2017, I started my own podcast called *Our Strange Skies*. And every day at work, I go back to the spot where Dennis and I had stood, looked up, and saw the craft, hoping to see something again. But I never have."

Some search until their dying day for that answer. Or at least something to make sense of it. Did Rob feel he needed an answer to what he saw? Would that answer ever truly come? "I often see people on social media talk about wanting answers to these strange incidents, and expecting someone to have them. This is a phenomenon that thrives on mystery, and knowing *us* more than we do *it*. And yet, many people feel connected to it. It's a very strange feeling and one that pushes me to read more and to talk to experiencers more."

So while Rob continued to dive deep into his own research and produce the *Our Strange Skies* podcast, it was clear he'd found the perfect medium to showcase his talents, knowledge, and curiosity. He concluded by reminding us, "There is a mystery here worth probing. A mystery that can be embraced by science and believers alike. In seventy-three years, it feels like we've gone nowhere. It's as if the group of people who find this topic fascinating are sitting in a car, they've turned the key to use the battery, the radio is on, but the car isn't running. Hell, we haven't even established what counts as evidence. I hope that the future deems this topic worthy of scientific rigor."

And as we'll see in the following chapter, that idea of a topic worthy of scientific rigor is an extremely complex and contentious issue. And one that excites, frustrates, and continues to mystify even the greatest scientific minds.

7

A PHANTOM WAR

It seemed impossible to me that the public, as a whole, ignored these phenomena happening all around them. With sightings occurring at an alarming rate, and the credibility of those involved only strengthening, there remained a towering wall between the serious study of these UFOs and the resistance from the mainstream scientific communities to carry out those studies. I tried desperately to track down scientists who'd be willing to speak freely about the topic in a serious manner. Even with a growing interest by everyday people in all walks of life, and headlines littering our news cycles, the scientific community remained on guard, seeing ufology more as an idea than an actual field of scientific study. Finding those who would attempt studying it was much easier said than done.

After decades of US government-funded projects involving scientists in countless fields, the conclusions drawn in studying UFO phenomena were almost always the same: they held no scientific basis. The phenomena could not be steadily monitored, measured, nor compared to any other science. And military and scientific investigation was unnecessary due to these phenomena posing no clear threat to the welfare of humankind. This conclusion seemed to satisfy the mainstream scientific communities, whose suspicion of the topic caused a trickle-down effect of ridicule for anyone who dedicated their time, intelligence, and reputation to studying the phenomena. This led to independent researchers refusing to accept this conclusion. Yet they had nowhere to turn to gather data and properly investigate the reports brought to them.

It was as if a thick line had been drawn between the natural sciences and the study of UFOs, the latter having very little to rely on other than witness testimony and scant evidence. The line became thicker, the cloud of ridicule looming ominously over anyone who considered crossing over to the other side. Science had ostensibly become the enemy in a phantom war between realists and dreamers. But when and how had that war of mistrust truly began? How could science so easily turn its back on what could potentially be one of the greatest discoveries of all time?

A Natural Ally

This brought me to the work of Greg Eghigian, a professor of Modern History at Penn State University. Eghigian had written extensively on this very topic in a paper entitled "Making UFOs make sense: Ufology, science, and the history of their mutual mistrust." The paper was featured in *Public Understanding of Science*, one of the leading journals in the social study of science.

So when did this mistrust really begin? Eghigian explained that it was "pretty much there from the beginning, from the late 1940s/early 1950s, when the first ufologists like Donald Keyhoe began publishing their work." So one can trace the mistrust back to what is considered the modern UFO era, which was ushered in by Kenneth Arnold's 1947 sighting over Mount Rainier (in which the term *flying saucer* was coined) and the controversial Roswell UFO crash of the same year. UFOs were making themselves at home over the skies of the United States. But the military was quick to stamp down these events as nothing more than misidentifications and test projects. Because of this, the scientific community followed suit, seeing no merit in investigating untestable phenomena.

So had the scientific community ever taken the topic of UFOs seriously? "It all depends on how one means the term 'science,'" Eghigian explained. "In general, I think it's safe to say that academic science—and here I mean academic institutions, organizations, leading researchers in the scientific community, and publication outlets—has never taken the topic altogether seriously." But Eghigian was quick to point out that there was a big difference between the physical and human sciences. "The academic physical sciences have categorically rejected many of the basic premises/conclusions of ufology. The human sciences, on the other hand, have shown a great deal of interest in the subject since around 1969, but researchers there have focused primarily on trying to analyze 'believers,' witnesses, and reporters of UFOs and aliens. In these cases, researchers have tended to treat the claims of the latter as sincere, but not as authentic."

So here we have a conundrum. Physical evidence of UFOs exists in one way or another. These objects appear and disappear via video, photographs, or even on radar. Yet the claims of those who have experienced encounters and abductions remain in the dark corners of pseudoscience. We are left wondering how science could even begin to appraise such claims and evidence, if any that is pertinent to this type of phenomenon actually exists. "It depends on how one means phenomenon," Eghigian was quick to point out. "As a historian, I treat UFO and alien contact phenomena as 'social facts.' They have constituted genuine personal experiences with significant social, cultural, political, and institutional effects and impacts. These impacts and effects can and should be recognized and studied from the perspective of historical and social analysis." This is where the study of human science comes into play. However, if the physical sciences were to be applied to these phenomena, Eghigian

agreed, "If the question is whether or not there is some ontolog-
ical reality behind witnesses' experiences—one that might well
be extraterrestrial in origin—then this is something where I
personally place most value on forensic, physical evidence."

But how could this be done? How could ufology become a
serious debate in both the eyes of academia and science? "Academics need to recognize that most UFO researchers are not
antagonistic toward science, but are people who share their love
of knowledge," Eghigian continued. "In an environment today
where there are many nefarious forces attacking science, acade-
micians would do well to see in ufologists a natural ally." But it
didn't end there. Those who researched UFOs also had to accept
a part of the blame for this war, having done the same to academics and even to one another. "Ufologists need to develop a
professional ethos, one in which they respectfully disagree with
one another and remain skeptical and open to changing their
viewpoints based on evidence."

Eghigian's work clearly showed, without a doubt, that a
divide existed and that it had only grown with time. The war
had manifested through the unconventional activity of the
phenomena. To the credit of the scientific communities,
however, it wasn't so much a lack of trying to study the topic;
instead, the lack of empirical evidence stymied a hard scientific
approach to much of the phenomena. But Eghigian's sobering
research would not overshadow his optimism that progress
could be made in both the physical and human sciences. And
that optimism would hit me tenfold when I came across what
was known as "The Warriors' Code."

According to many military scholars, there is an unwritten
rule during times of war. This rule, or code, is basically an act of
mercy where the victorious will allow their enemies a chance of
escape or even spare their lives. It is a code embedded in the
rules of engagement, allowing both sides of the battle to retain
their humanity in severely inhumane situations. It has even
been reported that enemies in war, through this act, have

become lifelong friends because of the bond the code had created between them. This code both surprised and invigorated me. Could this universal and deeply impactful code, in even some small way, be implemented into the study of UFOs? Surely there had to be scientists out there willing to speak out on the topic of UFOs. I'd soon learn that not only was this the case, but the code was more relevant than I had originally presumed.

A Scorched Ring in the Ground

He graduated with a PhD in synthetic organic chemistry from Queen Mary College, London University, undertaking postdoctoral research at Oxford and Nottingham. This led him to his position as a developmental chemist for what is now GlaxoSmithKline, a major pharmaceutical company known for manufacturing the antidepressant drug Seroxat. He wrote peer-reviewed papers for journals such as *Helvetica Chimica Acta* and *The Journal of Antibiotics*, all while holding several patents. It was quite clear that Dr. Erol Faruk's contributions in the fields of pharmaceuticals and medicine were highly respected, but it was his research into a completely different field that caught my personal attention: ufology.

During his time at Nottingham University, he'd come across a 1971 UFO case from the small town of Delphos, Kansas. The case involved a young man named Ron Johnson, who, while tending sheep on his family farm, witnessed a mushroom-shaped object hovering about seventy feet above. The object began to descend until it was only a few feet off the ground. Johnson moved toward it, but was soon blinded by the object's multicolored lights. Johnson called for his parents, Erma and Durel, who witnessed the object as it shot upward and disappeared. All three of the Johnsons then noticed a glowing, scorched ring in the ground below where the object had been hovering. The incident was later corroborated by another

witness who reported to local law enforcement that he'd seen an
object descending on the Johnsons' property.

Dr. Faruk, intrigued by the physical trace evidence left
behind in the case, requested samples of the soil within and
around the scorched ring in the ground. He was granted
samples from the area and used his own equipment and skills to
run a chemical analysis on several grams of soil. What he
discovered was quite intriguing. The compounds of the soil,
when put in water, could be dissolved, yet also acted as a repel-
lent against the water. Even more intriguing, however, was that
whatever caused the ring in the soil appeared to have contained
an aqueous solution that caused light emissions. Dr. Faruk
published his findings in the 1989 edition of the *Journal of UFO
Studies*, and subsequently published a book on in the same vein,
titled *The Compelling Scientific Evidence for UFOs*. The book elaborated even more on his findings, explaining how the data could
be used to move forward in examining the UFO phenomenon
from a scientific perspective.

While the inception of Dr. Faruk's interest in UFOs stemmed
mostly from this single case, I wanted to narrow in on this
chemist's ideas on what could compel scientists to look further
into these phenomena. "Since the main obstacle to scientific
acceptance of UFOs is in demonstrating that an actual physical
phenomenon is involved, then I fervently believe that the
Delphos case analysis establishes that reality, in the sense that it
strongly implicates a non-earthly luminescence technology
having left its mark in the soil." The Delphos case remains one
of many where trace evidence was found at the site of a UFO
event and analysis took place.

Dr. Faruk, focusing on chemical analysis, was quick to add,
"Mainstream science must first abandon the notion of 'impossi-
bility' denoted to UFOs. Earthly science is approximately four
hundred years old. While interstellar travel is certainly impossible for us now, who is to say that this will still be the case in
another one thousand years' time? We cannot possibly predict

our own scientific advances after such a lengthy period, so how can we be so arrogant to dismiss what alien civilizations currently 'out there' might already be capable of?"

So given the possibility that an extraterrestrial intelligence was responsible for some UFO sightings, what did Dr. Faruk honestly believe we were dealing with? "I believe the UFO phenomenon points to the probability that we are currently being visited by aliens using advanced technologies. Like many other scientists, I believe that the chances for life evolving elsewhere in the universe are very high, provided that the chemical makeup of a planet allows for such an occurrence. In our solar system, the Earth appears to be the only planet where life has developed because it is situated in the so-called 'goldilocks' orbital region of the sun, where it's not too hot or cold, thereby allowing water to be present as a liquid—considered vital for life."

Dr. Faruk's findings in terms of the Delphos case were indeed fascinating and only strengthened my hopes that such cases like this would invite scientists to look into this and so many other cases. But the issue always remained that even if they did so, would they ever consider speaking in public about it? Dr. Faruk would propel me to move from his insight as a chemist to the insight of someone in a completely different line of study: biophysics and the probability of extraterrestrial life throughout the universe.

If They Want Us to Know They're Here, They'll Tell Us

Dr. Jeffrey Bennett holds a BA in biophysics from the University of California at San Diego and both an MS and PhD in astrophysics from the University of Colorado at Boulder. So it was safe to say that his opinions and insight would be highly beneficial to my search for scientific answers. I'd attended a lecture by Dr. Bennett in early 2014, where he spoke in depth about the search for both microbial and intelligent life elsewhere in the universe. We spoke briefly after the lecture, his enthusiasm and intelligence shining through with each passing question I asked. Little did I know that the conversation would lead to his involvement in this chapter.

Dr. Bennett spent most of his time teaching mathematics and science around the country, also writing countless textbooks for college courses in astronomy, mathematics, statistics, and astrobiology. But it was his work as a visiting senior scientist at NASA Headquarters that caught my attention most. He was the first scientist hired within a science division specifically to leverage science missions for education. Working with NASA's Education Division, he helped bridge the cultural divide between education and science. He created the Initiative to Develop Education through Astronomy (IDEA) and also the Perspectives From Space concept that was ultimately adopted as the global theme for International Space Year. It was safe to say that Dr. Bennett knew a little something about space and the vast distances an intelligence would have to travel to visit Earth. He would speak prominently about this in his book *Beyond UFOs: The Search for Extraterrestrial Life and its Astonishing Implications for our Future.*

In relation to the UFOs reported here on Earth to the possibility of aliens being in control of said UFOs, Dr. Bennett stated: "Alien visitors of the type that people claim to see in UFO sightings are able to travel quite easily among the stars. They appear often, and in substantial numbers, and apparently don't mind visiting for just a few minutes or hours at a time even after the long journeys from the stars. It would seem that, for them, a journey to Earth is little more troubling than an intercontinental flight is for us, and certainly no more difficult than it is for us to reach the Moon." He also added, "I have no idea what kind of technology they might have that would enable them to do that. What I do know is that this technology is far beyond what we have, and very likely beyond what we can even yet conceive of" (Bennett 67).

He also deduced that if another civilization were out there somewhere amongst the stars, due to distance and time and the relativity of both, the youngest (besides us) would be at least fifty thousand years ahead of us technologically. He theorized, "With extremely high confidence, we can conclude that any aliens who are visiting Earth are so far beyond us that there's virtually no chance of them leaving evidence behind by accident. If they want us to know they're here, they'll tell us. And if they don't want us to know, it's highly unlikely that we could discover them, no matter how hard we might try" (Bennett 61).

What about cases similar to those that Dr. Faruk studied, and so many other reports of trace evidence or crashed UFOs? If what Dr. Bennett says is true, were these all hoaxes, misidentifi-cations, or in some cases, top-secret man-made aircraft? He was quick to add in his book: "I still won't tell anyone who claims to have seen a UFO that they're wrong. Because with all this considered, there are still laws of nature that must be obeyed. I suspect that aliens will have discovered laws of which we are unaware, perhaps allowing them to do things like 'cloaking' their spacecraft to prevent us from seeing them. But if that kind of hiding isn't possible, and if they really are visiting, then no matter how good their technology, we might catch an occasional glimpse of one of their spacecraft as it darts by. I highly doubt that such craft would look at all like flying saucers or anything else that is commonly reported. But if you see a strange light in the sky, indistinct but unmistakable and moving in a way that defies ordinary explanation, then maybe, just maybe, you've seen them."

So let's say we have seen them, as every individual in this book has reported. And let's say that some of them are perhaps extraterrestrial in origin. What, in his opinion, did he believe most valuable about having the scientific community study these reports or phenomena? "Science depends on having phys-ical evidence that can be objectively studied by many people; eyewitness testimony is never considered sufficient by itself in either court or in science. Then, if the physical evidence is to be taken to indicate something as extraordinary as alien life, it needs to be clear enough and compelling enough that most scientists would draw the same conclusions about its nature."

This answer was responsible and this answer was expected. But what I didn't expect was to hear a scientist speak so freely and so optimistically about the potential for life outside our planet not only existing, but possibly having already visited. This, of course, is if extraterrestrials are responsible for UFOs at all, given the possibility that they are controlled by an intelligence of some kind. In his book, he elaborates through the lens of the most publicly known organization that hunts for alien messages: the SETI Institute. Dr. Bennett adds, "For most people, SETI is the public face of astrobiology, holding out the potential promise of introducing us to advanced new friends in the cosmos. So most people are usually surprised when I explain that, while SETI is an important part of the search for life in the universe, it is not by any means the only focus of scientific research. It isn't even the sole focus of research at the SETI Institute..." He continues, "As the SETI scientists well know, there'd be little point in searching for intelligence if we weren't at least moderately confident that there are many worlds with microbial life" (Bennett 107).

In reading Dr. Bennet's ideas on what is being done in the fields of astrobiology and astrophysics, I still came away feeling that a gap existed between the study of UFOs and science. And that feeling was only strengthened by Dr. Bennet's following words: "Science has very specific standards of evidence, and nothing so far presented about UFOs has ever been clear enough or compelling enough to convince scientists that there's something that will meet those standards of evidence."

While it is close to impossible that life doesn't exist elsewhere in the cosmos, the question always remains whether it has ever visited Earth. "I hold out the possibility that some UFO reports might actually be due to aliens, but I think it highly unlikely that we could ever discover proof of their existence through such reports." Dr. Bennet was also quick to point out to me that if an alien intelligence was responsible for UFO reports, "… they would need incredibly advanced technology to be visiting us. In that case, if they don't want us to know they are here, they should have no difficulty making sure we can't get hard evidence. And if they do want us to know they are here, they'd make sure there was no doubt about it."

Although Dr. Bennett's remarks both from his book and in personal correspondence brought me no closer to a resolution in terms of UFO studies, it certainly left me hopeful. We were inching closer to finding alien life, whether microbial or intelligent. And perhaps there was something more important than solving the UFO mystery. As Dr. Bennett explained, "The most important thing is that if others have survived long enough to become spacefaring civilizations, it will mean that we can hope to survive our current difficulties as well. This would be a fantastically hopeful thing to learn."

While we still have so much to learn about astrobiology and astrophysics, we also have much to learn about ourselves back here on Earth. Through the work of Dr. Bennett and others like him, we have a responsible and, perhaps more importantly, objective approach to the many questions regarding the possibility of intelligent alien life. And although very exciting to think about, I had to pull myself back to the ground and use that same objectivity to remain focused on the UFO issue. That focus led me to another scientist who did acknowledge the lack of UFO studies in the scientific community. Perhaps he could help shed some more light on the issue and help bring this phantom war to a resolution.

The Who, What, and Why

Dr. Robert Davis studied audiology at the City University of New York, where he received both a BA and MA. He then went on to receive his doctorate in hearing science and audiology from Ohio State University. He is an internationally recognized scientist in his field, having served as a professor at the State University of New York for over thirty years and received numerous grants to fund research in auditory neuroscience and hearing sciences. His collegiate career and accomplishments are highly impressive, but what did it have to do with UFOs? The answer would come in the form of a book he authored: *The UFO Phenomenon: Should I Believe?*

Davis would attribute his interest in the topic to the impact of the flying saucer craze that exploded into the mainstream in the 1960s, which included the ground-breaking television show *Star Trek*. But it was a personal sighting of orange orbs in the skies of Sedona, Arizona, in 2012 that mystified him, compelling him to eventually review, analyze, and interpret existing evidence in the literature of UFO studies to better understand the nature of the phenomenon.

So in reviewing and interpreting that evidence, why does Davis believe that the scientific community chooses not to study the phenomenon in an official capacity, if such evidence truly exists? He answered: "Ufology has garnered an apathetic attitude from the scientific community toward conducting UFO research. This perspective evolved, in part, from the many extraordinary UFO-based claims by leading research ufologists, unsubstantiated by compelling factual evidence. Such unconfirmed conclusions are counterproductive. They create disillusion in the minds of scientists, which impedes efforts to help promote and enhance the quality of UFO based research initiatives."

But what about the ridicule factor? Could this stigma impede the act of even looking into the subject by many scientists? Davis answered: "They consider it an area of study filled with hoaxers, new agers, and as a popular cultural movement and/or hobby. Thus scientists feel it may compromise their career if they suddenly change course from their area of expertise to an area of study that lacks acceptance as a reputable research topic." So, in Davis' opinion, was the UFO phenomenon, in all its elusive glory, worth a reputable research initiative? "Yes indeed," he answered without hesitation. "If one conducts a thorough and objective review and analysis of the existing UFO evidence, it should be obvious that people have observed something very unusual in our skies. And given our limited understanding of this phenomenon, even just a small hint of what is going on would suffice for now. We must attempt to better understand the inherent who, what, and why's associated with the phenomenon and its associated transformative, enduring impact on those who experience the phenomenon."

And while the transformative and lasting impact has been this book's primary focus, I wondered how an initiative to study these phenomena could be scientifically undertaken. "Critical to this research is to stop studying the phenomenon as a separate science and, instead, to apply a multidisciplinary research-based approach. This is necessary since the UFO phenomenon represents many different scientific disciplines such as psychology, astronomy, astrophysics, physics, chemistry, biology, and optical physics, among others. That is, to better understand the UFO phenomenon and its impact on human behavior, society, technology, and possibly even our understanding of physical laws governing nature."

It was one thing to suggest critical research and a multidisciplinary organization. It was another to actually follow through with it. Davis was indeed involved in such an organization. It was known as the Dr. Edgar Mitchell Foundation for Research into Extraterrestrial Encounters (FREE). The organization was co-founded by Rey Hernandez, an attorney with the US Department of Treasury, and therapist and researcher Mary Rodwell. The executive director is Dr. Rudy Schild, an emeritus professor at the Smithsonian Center for Astrophysics at Harvard University. Schild worked closely with the late Dr. Edgar Mitchell, naming him a primary board member of the organization before his untimely passing in 2016.

So with such prestigious members, what exactly did this organization set out to accomplish? Davis explained to me that FREE was currently "conducting the first comprehensive multinational academic research study on individuals that have had UFO-related contact experiences. Scientists across many disciplines, including myself, are conducting research of witness reports. No one has ever attempted this type of academic research study. Our study is comprised of a quantitative survey totaling six hundred questions, written responses to over seventy open-ended questions, and a structured comprehensive interview. As of December 1, 2015, we have received over twenty-five hundred responses to our surveys." What exactly did the organization hope to discover through this research study? Davis replied: "This type of research will attempt to explore the meaning of what and how the phenomenon was experienced through the examination of specific statements and themes, and a search for all possible significant meanings. Consequently, our research is correlating reported consciously recalled UFO encounters and the person's personality and beliefs, and psychological and physiological effects, among other reported events associated with the experience."

Davis and the FREE organization were working tirelessly to synthesize data into cohesive insights. Their collective hope was that those both in the scientific community and academia could not only peer review the information, but could then accept that a true phenomenon existed. They could then contribute their own knowledge and resources toward furthering its study. This was quite invigorating. I not only respected Davis for his contributions to UFO studies, but for working with an organization that mirrored my own sentiments that the experiencers should be the focus. With their continued efforts, FREE and Davis gave me hope that there were not only scientists pursuing the topic, but that organizations and projects were being developed specifically to uncover ufology's roots and impact.

As of 2019, FREE has published the first book on their findings. *Beyond UFOs: The Science of Consciousness and Contact with Non Human Intelligence* is a detailed analysis of the FREE Experiencer Research Study—the world's first comprehensive and international academic research study of over 4,200 individuals from over 100 countries who have had UFO-related contact with nonhuman intelligence (NHI). The book provided data from thousands of experiencers in over a hundred different countries. According to the findings by the organization, the quantitative and qualitative data contradicts much of the information that is circulating about these phenomena. The group also believed that their findings would dramatically change both the paradigms of consciousness studies and ufology.

According to Davis, "In early 2020, FREE evolved into the Contact and Consciousness Research Institute (CCRI). This organization plans to undertake both a comprehensive short-term and long-term worldwide academic research study on the commonalities of the experiencers. The CCRI intends to establish a research methodology that will address both a short-term and long-term academic research study on this important question: *What is the Relationship between Consciousness, our Cosmology, and Contact with Non-Human Intelligence?*"

Davis decided to move on from the newly reworked version of FREE and focus on his own research. This came in the form of a book he published, *Unseen Forces: The Integration of Science, Reality and You*. In the book, Davis "addresses aspects of multiple phenomena like UFOs, but also near-death experiences and out-of-body experiences, which include the perceived experience of one interacting with nonhuman intelligences in this and/or an alternate reality. This served as a foundation to explain the possible nature of reality, the mind-brain distinction, and associated outcomes of such phenomena on individual lives."

The "outcome" had always been my personal focus in writing both editions of this book. I was happy to discover that this is where Davis' work was heading as well. "In general, these experiences have been reported to often facilitate dramatic and positive changes in one's personal and philosophical viewpoints on life, love, death, and spirituality. That is, we are just now realizing that the phenomenology of UFOs may be similar to and interrelated with other phenomena, and that the unifying feature of this connection may be an aspect of mind or consciousness. This represents a shift in research focus from the traditional physical 'nuts and bolts' approach to the 'nonphysical' or subjective and behavioral outcomes facilitated by contact experiences with varying phenomena."

It seemed that the data being produced was leading down a completely different path than many within FREE, and many in the field of UFO studies, had expected. It wasn't so much about the phenomena in our skies, but the phenomena in our minds and hearts. That invisible mechanism turning the gears of our subjective realities. Davis emphasized this point by adding, "The evolution of mind is simply impeded by too many closed-minded, inside-the-box egotistical thinkers. Thus, science, and the world at large, is in dire need of scholars bold enough to buck the conventional trend of academia and established concrete scientific principles and study UFOs. Nonetheless, the staggering degree of testimonial evidence alone, with thousands of incredible reports generated by seemingly credible observers, from all over the globe, has kept this long-enduring controversy from dying out. But focus needs to be shifted. In other words, one's subjective interpretation and essence of their interaction with the phenomena must be considered an imperative research initiative going forward."

So it seemed that while some scientists were perfectly fine studying the UFO phenomenon from a methodical and physical level, the real work, according to Davis, is happening somewhere in between multidisciplinary studies that have been done and need to continue being done, in order to find a convergence point of understanding. "The UAP research paradox exists because it is both a physical and nonphysical phenomenon inconsistent with traditional scientific principles. And for this reason, a new paradigm with agreed-upon laws and principles that incorporate the nonphysical aspects of reality must be developed. And it is not only essential for traditional materialist science to evolve into a new paradigm. It is mandatory."

With each scientist I spoke to, I realized that the warrior's code was stronger than ever, and the gap between science and UFOs wasn't narrowing: it was instead opening wide into new paths, new methods, and an entirely new world of possibilities. Could this manifest into the new paradigm Davis spoke of? Many of the scientists I would speak to seemed to believe so. But where exactly were these scientists and researchers putting these multidisciplinary methods into motion?

Turning Science Fiction Into Science Fact

Marc D'Antonio graduated from Wesleyan University with a degree in astronomy. He specialized in the study of exoplanets, particularly the search for planets that could harbor life much like Earth's. This led to his role as chief astronomer for a science center in Connecticut. He'd co-written a program to analyze photos before there was really any such software available, eventually discovering that the Hubble Institute was in fact using it. He also created his own special effects company that specialized in models, which is still in business today. But it was in 1971 when D'Antonio's interest in UFOs surfaced. At the mere age of eleven, he'd joined MUFON, having had unexplained experiences of his own that prompted him to look further into UFOs. As the years went on and D'Antonio's interest mounted, he became the chief photo and video analyst for the organization. "My job is to examine photos from a broad knowledge of the natural sciences, human evolution, and camera technology, determining if there is merit to photo or video evidence. Much like a forensic scientist, I have to consider how human evolution provided us with advantages and most importantly saddled us with some disadvantages when viewing an event in the sky. To that end, I have to understand the evolution and disadvantages of binocular vision with the human eye and how one can be fooled by something in the sky and think it's closer/bigger/fast/slower than it really is. I consult studies at Stanford University and the Eye Institute for metrics on tests performed on night vision of humans to understand and incorporate this into my work."

His work made him many enemies in the field of UFO studies, as some hardcore believers refused to accept many of his answers as to what was actually captured in particular photos or videos. But this wasn't something that concerned D'Antonio. He was tasked with a very critical position, and he took it on with the utmost respect for the phenomenon and for the organization. It was clear that D'Antonio's work was desperately needed by both MUFON and the study of UFOs in general to keep the analysis grounded and evolving with the times. And while he may have made some enemies, he also made some prominent friends.

One of those friends was Douglas Trumbull. Trumbull was responsible for a large portion of the special photographic effects for some of the most iconic science fiction films, including *2001: A Space Odyssey*, *Close Encounters of the Third Kind*, *Star Trek: The Motion Picture*, and *Blade Runner*. Trumbull had become acquainted with D'Antonio's special effects work and interest in UFOs; the two soon discovered they had much in common. This eventually led them to working together on several projects in the film and television industry. Trumbull was an avid UFO hunter, creating an interesting project from scratch to target UFO activity. "He showed me UFOTOG," D'Antonio explained. "It was basically a Humvee vehicle outfitted with hydraulic lifts. This would raise a telescope platform with an array of instruments out of the top for surveying the sky." D'Antonio was impressed, but suggested that he could assist in making it smaller and more efficient. Trumbull gave him the green light, and soon UFOTOG II was born.

So what exactly was the purpose of UFOTOG II, and how was it benefiting the advancement of scientific UFO studies? D'Antonio explained: "UFOTOG II was created to capture evidence of advanced civilizations' visiting the Earth. We are doing visual camera capture, yes, but we are adding detectors for various forms of radiation that would be emitted from a vehicle utilizing advanced propulsion. We are looking for what we have coined 'skid marks' of an advanced race using advanced propulsion in our four-dimensional space. If such a civilization exists, then in our regular four dimensions, we will see these bursts of other radiative energy as an advanced ship is translating from interdimensional space to our space."

This ambitious tracking system of sorts could explain, in some ways, the theories brought forth by Dr. Bennett earlier. If these advanced civilizations do in fact exist and are somehow traveling to Earth through wormholes or interstellar travel, then perhaps UFOTOG II could in fact begin to capture this technology, or the aftermath of it. "The UFOTOG II system will have multiple instruments to capture data on each event it sees. Then, if it sees something that is not a plane (it can tell) and not an expected satellite (it can also tell), then it will send an alert to us from even the most remote locations using GPS satellite bounce."

So while this project could bring us one step closer to finding answers to what may or may not be in the skies, what would be done with the data collected? "Our data will belong to humanity," D'Antonio explained. "If we find a promising result (and we think we will), then first it goes to our science team, and then an independent science team after that. Once we confirm the sighting, the data will be released to humanity via MUFON, who will be our data storage organization and boots-on-the-ground personnel who will maintain and deploy our units."

While the efforts of D'Antonio may seem like science fiction, the technology they've created and cultivated is not only possible, but is in its infancy stage of development as we speak. It's only a matter of time before it's perfected and used on a large scale. Thus, something that once seemed like science fiction has transitioned into the realm of science fact. And as D'Antonio and Trumbull move forward with their work, it only aids in translating UFOs into a scientific language. One that the mainstream may be willing to listen to much more closely. And as my excitement grew for the potential of UFOTOG II, it grew exponentially when I learned that projects to collect data on UFOs were also being created for in-air surveillance as well. And these projects were being shaped by a team of highly intelligent civilians and realized solely by crowdfunding.

Crowdfunding UFO Exploration

He graduated from Simon Fraser University with degrees in computer science and psychology, after which he worked for several prominent companies, including Google. He also created software applications for Mac and Windows. But it was a pair of personal sightings that prompted Dave Cote's interest in the topic of UFOs. In 2008, he witnessed erratic lights performing unconventional circular maneuvers in the skies of Vancouver, British Columbia. "It was exhilarating and a little unsettling. I have since racked my brain to come up with an explanation." In 2009, he witnessed a cigar-shaped craft in broad daylight while vacationing in Bangkok, Thailand. "My skeptic's mind was swayed into the wacky world of UFOs."

This wacky world soon collided with Dave's computer engineering interests. "I was reading up on tech articles, as I do in my field of computer research, and came across an article from Interorbital Systems saying that they could send a tiny cube satellite into orbit for anyone. This got me asking around if friends wanted to launch a satellite with me." With those friends also came new colleagues who were eager to see Dave's vision to completion. They included Matt Lippert, an employee at the Wright Patterson Air Force Base Institute of Technology, and Dave Shock, who'd previously launched endeavors to get a UFO satellite in the sky. Soon, they began developing what they called the CubeSat for Disclosure, a low-Earth-orbit satellite.

With many other team members from different fields, they soon had a clear vision of what they wanted. "Ultimately, we hope to identify extraterrestrial craft and visitation. Secondarily, we hope to make some interesting scientific discoveries related to low-Earth orbit, including interesting facts about meteors, solar flares, and things of that sort. Finally, we hope to inspire others to continue our work, maybe sending up a cube satellite for the UFO purpose once every year."

So what exactly would the CubeSat consist of to make these endeavors possible? "Our CubeSat will have electromagnetic and high energy ion detectors, two cameras, and the various boards to run everything. Image recognition will assist in determining anomalies, sending anything unusual back down to Earth through our duplex modem. We can then correlate the visual data with electromagnetic radiation and high energy ions. This, coupled with sightings reported to agencies like MUFON, should give us verifiable evidence of whatever we may detect."

With any new development comes many challenges. And Dave was quick to point out to me that this wasn't going to be a walk in the park. "A major challenge is how to handle data. Interorbital, our launch partner, informed me that they recommend ham radio, but we'd get a very small data speed, and we'd need ground stations all around the globe, which simply isn't feasible for us. But we've found that we can rent data services from existing satellite networks such as Globalstar. This is the route we are going." But how did Dave plan on effectively reading the many anomalies he was sure to run into? "I'm developing software that will determine differences in images, like a more advanced motion/light detector. I also have a software program that extracts thumbnails of images, so we can send those down and save the full high-definition images for only when a true anomaly is detected."

Another component to consider is how transparent the data will be. Dave explained, "We have ordered a duplex modem from NearSpace Launch, who is partnered with Globalstar network. Our data will go through their massive network of satellites. That data will come with a checksum so that everything can be verified genuine. With thousands of people independently able to log in to get the data firsthand, we will have peer review guaranteed." But if perhaps some of this data did point to UFOs that could potentially be extraterrestrial in origin, how did Dave personally feel this information would be handled by those in the scientific community? "My original CubeSat technician dropped out because of the obvious UFO stigma. However, I've noticed that the media has embraced our project, which tells me that the stigma is fading. And with such a science-based endeavor, I think our experiment, and other empirical-based experiments, will bridge the gap between science and the extraterrestrial topic."

So while Dave and the CubeSat team were willing to entertain the possibility that some of what they may find could be extraterrestrial, what exactly about those findings did he feel was most important? "It's important to investigate the phenomenon, just as any scientific endeavor is important. If the oceans are becoming acidic, it's important to study; if global warming is occurring, it's important to study; if beings from another world are visiting Earth, it's most definitely important to study. So let's build more evidence."

It seemed that Dave and his team were ready to face the UFO phenomenon head-on. As of 2016, they have successfully gathered complete funding for their launch and data retrieval. Having been a crowd-sourced mission, the public would be the first to receive the data collected. It was transparency at its most democratic. "Let's find out what is causing UFO phenomena," Dave proclaimed. "If aliens are visiting Earth, they likely have very advanced technology, perhaps technology that could help solve some of Earth's most pressing issues, such as pollution, global warming, and clean energy." If this were the benefit of the CubeSat's findings, then the sky was literally the limit of possibility.

As of 2020, the wait is finally over. After reaching out to Dave, he expressed how time-consuming it actually is to get independent satellites into space. "It has been a waiting game. Apparently, it takes an actual act of Congress to launch from United States soil to space. We have been awaiting also for the approval and license for our interorbital rocket that will launch the satellite." Dave also stressed the reality of how much time these ambitious projects truly take. "In the time that has passed, my satellite technician, Matt Lippert, has since moved on from his teaching position, and I have relocated to New Brunswick to raise a family. In the amount of time this has taken... I've had two kids now!"

Dave also wished to comment on how the recent revelations from the Pentagon, and in particular the Department of Defense statements on the Navy UFO videos, had fueled his passion to find answers among the stars. "Our mission with CubeSat remains the same: to capture several data points simultaneously on UAP. And since the Department of Defense has recently released much info on this, we hope to contribute supporting civilian evidence to the possibility of extraterrestrial life and visitation. After launch, we will collect images and electromagnetic data and see what turns up." And the most exciting thing Dave had to share: "Pending any issues with the rocket licensing, the launch is set to happen in January of 2021."

Studying UFO Phenomena As They Occur

He'd made his way through the French education system, earning degrees in business administration and commercial management. A strong interest in the cosmos eventually led Philippe Ailleris to a position at the Space Research and Technology Centre of the European Space Agency (ESA), located in the Netherlands. For two years, he functioned as project controller for Sentinel 2, an Earth Observation Satellite project. It is the first optical imaging satellite in the European Union's Copernicus program. From there, he also worked on Sentinel 1, which consisted of radar missions.

While Ailleris' interest in space was apparent, it was a 1981 newspaper article detailing the French Space Agency's involvement in UFO studies that piqued his interest in what may lie beyond the stars. He began to look into reports of UFOs himself, and in 2009 launched his own organization called the UAP (Unidentified Aerial Phenomena) Observation Reporting Scheme. Using contacts from the European Space Agency, volunteers from various disciplines helped analyze UFO reports that Ailleris would receive. The members would then check their sightings against the most common nocturnal and diurnal misidentifications. They also are in close contact with amateur astronomers, societies, and astronomical magazines that also receive their share of UFO reports, allowing for sharing of reports and investigations with Ailleris and the organization. "Reactions have generally been positive within the European Space Agency," he told me. "As long as any subject is approached in a professional, rational, and structured manner, scientists are ready to listen. UAP study seems barely exotic when compared to black holes, dark matter and energy, or brain-machine interfaces studied by many scientists."

The Observation Reporting Scheme soon caught the attention of Dr. Mark Rodeghier, director and president of the J. Allen Hynek Center for UFO Studies. And in 2012, he asked

Ailleris to be a board member for a project known as UFODATA, which would be comprised of highly accomplished scientists and researchers. "I immediately accepted because I strongly believe that this subject should be approached from a professional, rational, and scientific perspective. Researchers should try to maximize the chances of acquiring reliable and valid data. Accordingly, instrument observations are essential."

While UFOTOG II would be deployed from vehicles on the ground, UFODATA took a different approach. Ailleris explained that it would be a "network of automated surveillance stations that will include sophisticated instrumentation to monitor the skies twenty-four seven, looking for aerial anomalies. To move forward, as in other areas of science, UFO studies require the collection of reliable physical data, and we believe the best method to do so is to go into the field and capture such data in 'real time' while a UFO event is occurring."

So how exactly did Ailleris and the group intend to capture this data? "The final version of the stations will have a core optical unit, with both an all-sky camera to detect lights or objects to trigger recording, along with a suite of cameras with higher resolution capable of detecting and recording both an image/video and spectrum of the phenomenon. Stations will also include a magnetometer, instrumentation to detect microwave and radio frequency radiation, an electrostatic field detector, a gravimeter to record the local gravitational field, and a weather station to record standard atmospheric data."

So once detected, what exactly did they plan on doing with the data? Ailleris explained, "It will be stored and then trans-mitted to a central location. We have a science team, led by Dr. Massimo Teodorani, that will analyze any data collected. We plan to publish results in the scientific literature and, of course, share them on our website." I found it promising, just as I had with the UFOTOG II project, that any data collected would be shared. The transparency of these findings was integral for both public awareness and interest. But what if the data did indeed point toward the possibility of an extraterrestrial presence of some sort? "Firstly, the origin of unexplained aerial phenomena is unknown. So studying them is a 'natural' activity of science. Scientists study all aspects of the world, and UAP are a part of the world, whatever their cause. It is entirely possible that all UAP have conventional explanations, but given the highly unusual characteristics of UFO reports, there is a chance that some are caused by non-terrestrial intelligence. If that turned out to be the case, then it would be one of the most important events in human history, and as such even if the odds of detecting extraterrestrial intelligences are low, it seems extremely important to learn as much as possible about these phenomena."

Whether extraterrestrial or something completely different, the stark realization that these phenomena could once and for all be tracked and analyzed was surely a step in the right direc-tion. And whatever they may or may not be, Ailleris was quick to point out that "the continuous analysis of anomalous events may provide us with new insights into the nature of physics. Whenever there are unexplained observations, there is the possibility for scientists to learn something new by studying these observations." I felt reassured that no matter the findings of Ailleris and the rest of the UFODATA team, the most impor-tant thing was that a completely independent organization had taken a huge step in moving past the question of whether or not there was a phenomenon, but what that phenomenon was. The most important thing Ailleris stated, however, was this: "Whether or not the UFODATA recorded data suggests an extraterrestrial presence or not, collecting such data would show that UFO phenomena can be studied in a rigorous and system-atic fashion, and thereby hopefully break down the 'taboo' that has long stymied basic scientific research in this area."

In June 2020, I was able to catch up with Ailleris on the progress of UFODATA, and discovered that the project was not only well on track, but various side projects were also in the works with several other organizations to pursue UFO phenomena from every angle. In September of 2019, Ailleris had traveled to Norway to meet with Erling Strand, an Assistant Professor at the School of Computer Sciences at Østfold University College. Strand was a founder and continued project manager of Project Hessdalen. Hessdalen is a small valley in the central part of Norway. From 1981 through 1984, residents reported hundreds of highly anomalous lights that appeared throughout the valley. At peak activity, there were about twenty reports a week. Strand took it upon himself to set up a dedicated station in the area to monitor, capture, and analyze the lights. Known as Project Hessdalen, constant surveillance of the sporadic activity continues up until today. Since 2002, there have even been science camps in the Hessdalen Valley for young students to spend one week in the valley searching for unidentified aerial phenomena. While the stations have been operating with highly sophisticated equipment for years, they always wanted to continue working closely with other UFO projects to compare notes and tackle the phenomena from every angle.

This is where UFODATA came in. Ailleris told me, "We have asked Erling Strand to be part of our project, to learn from it, and eventually to deploy one of our stations over there in the near future. I went to Norway to assess the feasibility of this, and of course hopefully observe mysterious aerial phenomena." Upon setting up a cooperation with Strand and the Hessdalen Project, Ailleris shared Strand's exciting new endeavors. "Strand and his colleagues have recently opened a new research station called the Hessdalen Observatory at the top of Mount Skarvan, where it was transported by helicopter. The station benefits from a 360-degree panoramic view over the Hessdalen valley, is self-supplied with electricity, and provides sufficient working space for scientists for doing field research. The other well-known station in Hessdalen, called the 'Blue Box,' is being maintained by Strand and continues to record the anomalous light phenomena."

But the work didn't end there. Ailleris also explained: "In terms of supplementary instrumentation, Hakan Kayal, another UFODATA consulting engineer from the University of Wurzburg in Germany, has installed on top of the Blue Box a new all-sky camera. This project is called 'ASMET' and can be seen as a technology demonstration and test platform. The main objective is to detect meteors, and secondly to detect unknown aerospace phenomena. It has been operating well within its planned limits. This is an excellent test case for the planned UFODATA station, which will allow us to learn from it and to design a much better system."

Another exciting development is the current work being done by UFODATA board member Christopher Mellon. Mellon is a former Pentagon intelligence official and ex-staffer on the Senate Intelligence Committee. Most recently, he has signed onto the advisory board for To the Stars Academy. According to Ailleris and the UFODATA website, Mellon has been active during the last few years in highlighting the UFO topic within the US military and government, trying to break down the bureaucratic walls that are preventing serious UFO-related information from reaching Congress and the American people. In line with UFODATA goals, Mellon is also pushing the message to the US government to use the capabilities it already has to understand the UFO phenomenon, as it is critical to obtain a range of data from multiwavelength and multimode sensors to allow a proper analysis of the phenomenon observed.

In relation to obtaining a range of data, as Mellon suggests doing, Ailleris is doing the same in his personal work outside of UFODATA as well. "I'm also pursuing a new axis of research related to my employment in the space sector, which is to attempt using civilian satellite imagery to detect and study anomalous aerial anomalies, with the development of Artificial Intelligence methods/algorithms and the increased launch of Earth Observation satellites. The time is right to work on this, as it's very different from the task of creating and sending small satellites in orbit, as these satellites in Europe are very expensive. The instrumentations present many advantages, including the fact that the access to data from some satellites are free."

So while Ailleris continues his own work, he also confirmed the most recent partnership UFODATA has undertaken with the UFO Data Acquisition Project (UFODAP). Using cutting-edge technology, this project has many of the same goals in mind and uses similar methods. It only made sense to form such an alliance. And as we'll see, UFODAP was just as ambitious and excited to continue implementing some of the most innovative equipment to track and try to decipher the anomalies in our skies. And it all began with a single location with an intensity of unexplained phenomena unrivaled by anywhere else in the United States.

Letting the Data Overwhelm the Mystery

Christopher O'Brien became interested in UFOs at a very early age. Just short of age seven, he had a life-changing experience while living in Bellevue, Washington, in 1963. "Strange, nonhuman entities," as he described them, began following O'Brien. This would be one of four incidents with these beings that very year. Even more curious is that during this period, John Keel, noted journalist, author, and UFO researcher, was investigating several other unexplainable incidents in the very city of Bellevue. Ever since these brushes with the unknown, O'Brien has been fascinated by the subject of UFOs and the possible occupants or intelligence behind them.

As time progressed, O'Brien would never fully understand what those beings were that seemed to have entered his life, and left without a trace or explanation. But he'd now become increasingly interested in UFOs and consumed every book he could on the topic. All throughout college in New York, and living in Manhattan, he continued to keep his interests to himself. But after having a multi-witnessed UFO sighting in 1979 in New Paltz, New York, where strange lights in the sky seemed to be interacting with O'Brien and the other witnesses, he began to gradually embrace the mystery and face it head-on. He would eventually find himself out West in the San Luis Valley of Colorado, where he soon learned he was stepping in to the most mysterious place he could ever have imagined. The phenomena he'd been chasing his whole life had now fallen in to his lap.

In the early '90s, O'Brien decided to become a full-time investigator, taking after such dedicated researchers such as Keel, who had visited his hometown so many years prior. But while Keel scattered himself across the United States searching for the weird and strange, O'Brien needed not look any further than his new backyard.

The San Luis Valley is located in South Central Colorado, with a small portion overlapping into New Mexico. It measures about 140 miles long and around 60 miles wide. Legends and stories have been passed down for centuries of strange occurrences in the valley. And O'Brien soon learned it wasn't letting up any time soon. "From 1992 to 2002, I investigated over a thousand claims of unusual events and stories handed down throughout the generations." O'Brien decided to create a database to log each and every story and case he came across. "Out of the thousand or so, about 650 made my database. I worked extensively with law enforcement officials, ex-military, ranchers, and an extensive network of skywatchers, documenting what may have been the most intense wave of unexplained activity ever in the United States."

But just exactly what type of phenomena was occurring? According to O'Brien, it really ran a spectrum of the strange. "Everything from crypto-creatures to UFOs. It's the birthplace of the cattle-mutilation phenomenon. I've investigated over two hundred cases of cattle mutilations in the area. I've had sightings of fae folk and even leprechauns from highly credible witnesses. At the height of my investigative period in 1996, I got seventeen calls in one day from witnesses in five separate events." O'Brien chased each case with tenacity, unlike most armchair researchers, who never left their homes to gather data or interview witnesses. Every time he thought he'd seen it all, the valley would continue its relentless pursuit to keep the answers just out of reach. "I was run ragged. I put three hundred thousand miles on my truck in the span of my investigations.

The work showed. His ten-year investigation resulted in a trilogy of books, *The Mysterious Valley*, *Enter the Valley*, and *Secrets of the Mysterious Valley*. When it came to cattle mutilations, O'Brien became one of the most prominent investigators on this dark and disturbing phenomenon. His book *Stalking the Herd* has been called the most important book ever written on our relationship with cattle and how this has manifested into the modern cattle-mutilation mystery. But there had to be a way to continue the work in the San Luis Valley not after it occurred, but to capture it while it was happening. What if these phenomena could be tracked, captured, and investigated in real time? This is when the idea for UFODAP came about, and then soon became a reality.

Over a thirteen-year period, UFODAP was in careful development. Originally called the San Luis Valley Camera Project, it gradually took shape. But it wouldn't be until 2015 that O'Brien would bring on Ron Olch, a systems engineer in research and development, and the project became what would eventually be known as the UFO Data Acquisition Project. Olch had opened the first microcomputer store and system consultancy in West Los Angeles. He graduated from UCLA with a BS in engineering and computer science and an MS in computer science. Subsequently employed by Teledyne Controls, Walt Disney Imagineering, and AeroVironment, he retired with more than thirty years of engineering experience in 2013. He was an A inventor in eight patents and has a lifetime interest in designing, building, and programming embedded electronic systems. But he was also very interested in UFOs and was a founding member of the Los Angeles UFO Research Group from 1973 to 2015. Together, Olch and O'Brien created the UFODAP system.

According to O'Brien and the official UFODAP website, "The system involves the deployment of pan/tilt/zoom video cameras and multi-sensor data-acquisition sensors to properly record real-time UFO events. These instruments document anomalous aerial objects in a three-camera system with data sensors. Multiple cameras and sensors allow for all-important 'triangulation.' The triangulation feature will permit an evaluation and determination of object size, distance, altitude, speed and acceleration. The system's cameras are controlled by customized motion-tracking software and triangulation software. When anomalous movement is detected by the automatic motion-detection software, the system will go into record mode as the cameras coordinate their function and follow the moving objects, zooming in for better identification. With multiple cameras, the triangulated position of the object will also be located on Google Maps for precise GPS location and tracking. This position will be recorded along with coordinated video and data from the cameras and the other sensors. UFODAP is also slated to include recording sensors to determine changes in the Earth's magnetic and gravitational fields. Electromagnetic detectors and other measuring equipment will be encased in environmental enclosures—all operated over the internet under automatic control of our unique customized software."

While the Hessdalen Project uses large systems set in one area to study a certain condensed type of phenomenon, O'Brien stresses that miniaturization is key with what UFODAP is attempting to achieve. These systems are portable and can be used anywhere. And with most of the work being done remotely over the internet, a certain location can be monitored and recorded from literally anywhere in the world. "This is a historic project," O'Brien stresses. "We are currently working with several different companies and organizations across four different countries on supplying them custom UFODAP systems." (UFODATA being one of them.) O'Brien also explained, "There's no substitute for gathering hard data. Ufology is like driving a car forward but using the rearview mirror to see where you've been even though you're heading forward. We're taking away the rearview mirror and allowing ourselves to look straight forward with the acquisition of hard data. People's stories can only take you so far with under-standing what the phenomena is all about. We need hard data to take the next step. UFODAP is that next step."

So the technology and instrumentation of UFODAP is one thing. But what, in O'Brien's opinion, was the overall benefit and contribution of UFODAP to the study of UFOs? He told me, "With the holy grail of scientific inquiry being repeatability, imagine if we can show that a UFO event can be captured with a variety of instrumentation, including optical, magnetic, and gravitational, and if we can replicate that sighting event with a second data set, this will truly be unprecedented. It would allow us to approach mainstream academia and science with the proper protocol, get peer-reviewed papers, and then doors are flung wide open. Between UFODAP, things like To the Stars Academy, and mainstream UFO information being spread, this opens the doors of credibility and acceptance of the UFO topic as something that is real and something that is not to be ignored. I think we have a real good chance of letting the data overwhelm the mystery."

It only made sense that UFODATA would team up with UFODAP to implement one another's goals, technology, and strategies to furthering the scientific exploration and investiga-tion of UFO phenomena. And as UFODAP's systems begin to spread across the world, only time will tell how influential the data recorded globally will contribute to the overall UFO conversation and possibly finding answers. So in a world moving toward a wider acceptance of the UFO phenomenon, the real questions always remain. Who or what is the true archi-tect and source of the phenomena? Will we ever truly know? "I do think we are getting closer to finding answers," O'Brien commented. "The interest we are seeing in the relationship with human consciousness and the intrinsic presence of the phenomenon, there's an interrelationship between the observer and what they're observing. We're also seeing a move towards trying to understand why particular people have these experiences. The experiencer is probably more important than a UFO experience. And because we're now starting to think more outside the box, and we have applications like UFODAP, we're getting tantalizingly closer to finding an answer... or at least showing what our options are for those answers a bit more clearly."

The Not So "Invisible College"

Since 2016, many other organizations and projects have come to life through the efforts of many individuals. But perhaps one of the most respected by the scientific community has been the work done by Robert Powell. With a degree in chemistry, Powell racked up over twenty-eight years of experience in engineering management in the semiconductor industry. While working at Advanced Micro Devices, he helped develop its first flash memory technology that is used in today's flash cards for cameras, PCs, video cameras, and other products. He is also experienced in managing a state-of-the-art chemistry laboratory and managing a research and development group that worked on nanotechnology using atomic force microscopes, near-field optical microscopy, and other techniques. And as if this weren't exceptional enough, he also had a keen interest in the UFO phenomenon as well.

"I first became interested in the UFO topic in high school during the mid-1970s when I read Dr. Allen Hynek's book *The UFO Experience*. I put my interest aside for about thirty years as I went to college to get my degree in chemistry, got married, worked in the semiconductor industry, and raised a family."

Powell was able to retire early in 2006, and that's when the UFO bug returned in full force. "I reignited my interest in UFOs and began studying the phenomenon in earnest. I must give a lot of credit to my tutelage on the subject to Dr. Michael Swords, who I met in 2007. Thanks to his academic background and years of studying the topic, he and I, along with several others, were able to produce a tome of a book in *UFOs and Government: A Historical Inquiry.* My interest has never waned since."

This interest would ultimately lead Powell to volunteer his expertise and time to working with MUFON for over ten years. "I became the director of Research at MUFON in May of 2007. I viewed the main role of my position as adding science to the way that MUFON approached the UFO subject. It was a difficult task, and often I felt that I was beating my head against the wall. One finds that some individuals without science backgrounds actually *fear* science. It was a situation that I had never experienced before, and I would continue to argue for more science."

In 2012, Powell would create the MUFON Science Review Board. "I envisioned a group of individuals with science backgrounds that could be used to identify the ten strongest cases reported to MUFON each year and that could also analyze reports or claims that came out of the UFO community." According to Powell, this group consisted of individuals with a PhD in chemistry, a master's in geology, a master's in science technology, a master's in physics, an electrical engineer, and Powell himself, with a degree in chemistry. "The board would spend countless hours every month reviewing cases, and we also would provide technical expertise to field investigators that were open to receiving help."

Although the structure was in place for a complete scientific analysis of reported UFO cases to MUFON, there seemed to be a pushback within the organization in favor of more sensational or unsubstantiated claims. It seemed that this time, more than any other, scientists were willing to work hand in hand with one of the most visible and well-respected UFO research organizations in the entire world. But according to Powell, it wasn't push-back from the scientists, but from the fractured state chapters of the organization and the hierarchy at MUFON. Clearly, not everyone was on the same page, and that became very clear to Powell in 2017, when he voiced concerns of the speaker lineup at the International MUFON Symposium. "It featured speakers who made atrocious claims. One claimed to have fought on alien ships against other aliens, another claimed to be able to time travel and that he would be a future US president, and another who claimed that Mars used to be inhabited before an alien race devastated it with a nuclear attack." When Powell brought this up to the director and board members, fearing that this type of material could tarnish MUFON's reputation and image, the board overwhelmingly voted to continue with the symposium. "I felt that science had left the building," Powell admitted. "I tenured my resignation after ten years as their director of Research."

But this didn't mean Powell was done exploring the UFO phenomenon from the most scientific approach he possibly could. "I knew that there were plenty of people that had a scientific background and that had interest in the phenomenon." And that's when, in 2017, Powell and several colleagues created the Scientific Coalition for UAP Studies (SCU).

The term "Invisible College" is defined as a small interactive community of scholars who meet face-to-face, exchange ideas, and encourage one another in their respective fields of study. In respect to the UFO field, a book was written in 1975 by noted computer scientist, astronomer, and UFO researcher Jacques Vallee. It was titled *The Invisible College*, in which he details the work of a group of scientists studying the UFO phenomenon and its influence on the human race. Yet their findings and discoveries stayed secret from the outside world. With Powell's group, they took the idea but agreed to not only be visible to the world about who they were and what they were studying, but promised transparency in their findings through peer-reviewed papers, publications, and conferences.

According to the official SCU website, the mission of the organization is as follows:

To conduct, promote and encourage rigorous scientific examination of UFOs. To fully utilize scientific principles, methodologies and practices in the study of unidentified aerial phenomenon observed and reported around the globe. We provide scientific case analysis support to witness cases, other scientific organizations, and government entities who are looking for the certitude of facts to this phenomenon. We seek to share credible data with the public, the media, the government, and scientific institutions, so we can further our understanding of this enigmatic phenomenon.

SCU started out with six core members, but has rapidly grown to almost ninety. "Today SCU consists of scientists with degrees in astrophysics, chemistry, astronomy, physics, oceanography, geology, computer science, and electrical engineering," Powell explained. "It includes scientists who have worked for NASA and the defense industry as well as college professors. Most of SCU's members have science backgrounds, and its demographics are impressive: 94% have college degrees, 28% have PhDs, 27% with military experience, and 16% represent other nations. SCU is a testament to the fact that there are many scientists with an interest in the UFO phenomenon."

As we enter a new decade of uncertainty, the topic of UFOs remains just as uncertain and mysterious as it ever has. The more we discover, the more questions seem to arise. And while this may be frustrating, Powell focuses on what we *have* learned. "Our knowledge of UFO characteristics has improved marginally over the last seventy years or so. We do know that they physically exist and as far as we can determine are not a national security threat. We know that their outside shape is not consistent, but their shapes are dominated by the appearance of disks, cylinders, and triangles. They emit EM waves, sometimes in the radio and microwave range. We know that they are capable of extreme accelerations and speeds with no indication of any interaction with the atmosphere and often completely silent. But that's not much knowledge considering that seventy years have gone by."

So maybe it's not where many UFO enthusiasts, researchers, or even those in the scientific fields that study UFOs want to be. But at the end of the day, Powell stresses, "This lack of knowledge ultimately falls on the scientific community, which has avoided all approaches to this enigma. But the scientific community's perspective on the UFO phenomenon has begun to change. Whatever the cause of the UFO phenomenon—it will not be solved without the scientific community's full participation." So as the dreamers and realists, or the UFO research community and the scientific communities, may be narrowing the gap between one another and working more closely together to find answers, there is another obstacle in the way of advancing the scientific research in to the UFO phenomenon: government. "The only way the UFO phenomenon will ultimately be resolved is through data and the openness of government to share that data with the scientific community. It cannot be done only with witness reports. We have radar data that covers everything in Earth's atmosphere as well as anything in near Earth space. That data is classified because of its military implications. Additionally, the amount of data possessed is so enormous that computer algorithms must be utilized to screen out data that does not represent radar targets with national security implications, such as satellites, ICBMs, or near Earth debris in orbit. A way must be found to allow the scientific community to have access to this information."

While SCU continues to fight for more transparency and cooperation with the government, they continue to provide scientific analysis of UFOs. Powell adds, "SCU members have published two academic papers on the subject of UAP ('Estimating Flight Characteristics of Anomalous Unidentified Aerial Vehicles in the 2004 Nimitz Encounter' in the journal *Proceed-*

ings, and 'Estimating Flight Characteristics of Anomalous Unidentified Aerial Vehicles' in the journal *Entropy.* SCU also has project teams that are examining data on unidentified submerged objects (USOs) and UAP characteristics, and statistical analysis of historical UFO reports."

Along with Powell, the entire team at SCU is very optimistic about the future of both UFO studies and their role in what Powell summarizes as "... engaging the broader scientific community in the analysis of the UFO phenomenon. In order to do this, we must have data. The best source of data is from our military organizations. We plan to take steps to try to make this type of data available." SCU has and continues to do what so many have tried before but eventually found a lost cause. But as their work continues, it's quite clear that their cause was anything but lost, and the work in analyzing and exploring the UFO phenomenon has only begun.

Whether it is through high-powered satellite imagery or cutting-edge photographic technology and analysis, there is still much work to be done on capturing data of UFOs. But that isn't necessarily a bad thing. If anything, it is progress in a field of study that rarely ever has any. The testimonies I've heard so far were proof that whatever these objects were in our skies, they could be seen, felt, and heard. And with the work being done by the scientists and academics above, I have absolutely no doubt that their dedication and openness to finding unconventional answers could possibly solve some of these mysteries. But not all of them. And as I moved forward with my own research, I realized that things were about to not only become more mysterious, but downright terrifying.

8

IN A CORNFIELD

Unlike many first-time witnesses or experiencers, Chase Kloetzke was no stranger to UFOs. In fact, she'd spent over twenty years of her life investigating them. This would eventually lead to her becoming an active field investigator for MUFON. Chase, being recognized for her passion and objectivity, rose through the ranks of MUFON to become deputy director of Investigations. She also served as Star Team manager, supervising the rapid response team that handled the more complex cases brought to the organization. One of these cases in particular would impact Chase prominently and would cause her to become a primary witness in her own case.

"On April 20, 2010, I was assigned a case out of Tennessee by my chief investigator, Max Mitchell," Chase told me. "In reviewing the report, I began highlighting key elements and making notes. I saw a commonly reported claim of red and white lights in the sky in the small town where this had taken place. These lights would cluster with up to twenty-seven, at one count, maneuvering and hovering as multiple witnesses looked on." Chase explained that various reports of fireballs were being reported in the area. With all this excitement, she began her rigorous investigation into this specific location itself, checking weather patterns, phoning local authorities, and checking off each and every possibility for the aerial phenomena plaguing the skies.

As the local reports flooded in, the investigation led them to one witness, who seemed to be experiencing the peak of activity over his home. Eventually, Chase was put into contact with the man. "He was getting increasingly anxious. He stated that he and his cousin were outside every night looking for these lights. I talked him into trying to take pictures of what he was seeing." Chase wanted hard evidence. Something she could analyze. But she warned him not to be too aggressive in his pursuit. "I was more worried about his safety on the country roads in the extremely rural area."

A few days passed. Without warning, the witness phoned Chase, very excited. "Last night, I saw three distinct points of light that formed a triangle," he told her. "There are helicopters buzzing around this morning. In all my years living here, I have never seen helicopters in this area. It's like they're searching for something!"

Chase had heard enough. Whatever was happening far surpassed simple misidentification. This led Chase to vigorously dig deeper into the investigation. "The witness was a high-profile businessman in the community," Chase explained. "He had absolutely nothing to gain and everything to lose with this UFO stuff." Chase packed her bags, met with her investigative partner on the case, and soon they were off, boots on the ground, to investigate.

They arrived as the sun was quickly setting across the endless fields that surrounded the witness' property. Introductions were cordial and brief, and just as Chase was ready to ask her initial questions, the witness pointed to an area in the night sky. "Well, there's one now," he said. Chase looked up and saw a small light in the distance. The witness suggested they head out into a nearby cornfield to get a better look. They hopped into the witness' truck and soon found themselves barreling through acres upon acres of six-inch-tall cornstalks. They stopped where the witness believed they would have a solid view of the entire area. After walking a few yards out, they set up their equipment and started to scan the skies for the previous lights.

"I started to set up my equipment. Cameras, tri-field meter, magnetometer, flashlight, binoculars, my triple threat digital recorder, laser dot thermometer and several other pieces of equipment. Almost immediately, we started to witness these lights. No matter where we turned, they were there, surrounding us." As Chase focused on a set of lights, it appeared to be coming closer. Chase signaled for her partner to grab the cameras. The two of them fumbled with each camera, four in total, and found none of them were working. The batteries, though fully charged before arrival, were now completely drained. Chase moved to the other equipment, all of which also failed. Soon, a trio of white lights framing a red light in the center moved closer. Overwhelmed and stunned, Chase came to the sudden realization that these lights were not self-contained, but attached to something. The stars behind disappeared, and a massive craft now floated silently above her. Within moments, it shot off, disappearing out of sight.

"There was no hiding the excitement. I quickly turned my attention back to the equipment. It seemed to be working now. That's when I started to feel this very uneasy feeling. It was quickly growing uncomfortable." Chase peered out into the vast cornfield. "Does anyone else feel like they are being watched?" she asked. "And I don't mean from above."

The witness nodded. A complete rush of fear flooded over the three. Quietly, they gathered the equipment and began a steady jog from the area. The jog soon picked up pace, and before they knew it, they were running at full speed through the cornfield from an unknown threat that seemed to follow. The witness, flashlight in hand, hurriedly guided them. As they continued through the rows of corn, the witness came to an abrupt halt, Chase running directly into him.

"What the fuck is that!?" the witness managed to ask. He turned the flashlight back to the location where they had all just made their escape. As Chase recovered from the collision, she looked over his shoulder. For a fraction of a moment, there amongst the darkness and corn, a figure stood facing them. The figure boasted a mere three-foot height. It lingered silently, staring back at Chase and the others. Full panic set in, and they ran toward the truck. They hopped in, the witness started the ignition, and they shot out of the cornfield. The truck picked up speed, catching air several times as they made their way down the bumpy dirt road. In complete silence, they tried to process what had just occurred.

As the witness pulled into the driveway of his home, the three got out of the truck, unsure of how to proceed. Chase and her partner, having trained extensively in matters of sightings and encounters, stood dumbfounded. This was clearly not what they had expected, and as they tried to shake the initial shock, the witness found himself breaking the silence.

"What was that?" he asked.

Chase couldn't reply. The witness stood dumbfounded, out of breath, bent over with his hands on his knees. He looked up at her, desperation evident in his trembling voice.

"I'm not crazy, right? You saw it too, didn't you?"

"Yeah. Yeah, I saw it," Chase replied.

"What does it want?" he asked.

Chase looked at him, searching for words to ease the confusion. But no words came. She stared at the ground, shaking her head. This was beyond anything she had ever experienced before. That night, she and her partner left the cornfield unsure of how to proceed with the case. Although the initial event had passed, the case itself was far from over.

Within the next few weeks, many investigators visited the site to speak with the witness. It was beginning to resemble a "circus atmosphere," as the witness described it. Investigators began flooding in, no equipment in hand, hoping to merely experience something themselves rather than to conduct actual investigations. As attention zeroed in on the witness, he began to worry that his name would get out to the public. The last thing he wanted was to be the town's "UFO guy." His wife carried the biggest worry that her professional career would be in jeopardy if word got out. Promising anonymity, Chase felt a responsibility to personally return to the property to ease their worries. She was, after all, the main contact and first responder. Upon her return, Chase approached the witness' wife, assuring her that confidentiality was MUFON's priority. Immediately, the wife, distraught, pleaded with Chase.

"Do you have any children?" she asked.

"Yes. Two boys," Chase responded.

"I cannot tell you how much it has meant to me and my husband that you answered our call for help," the wife continued. "But this whole thing is causing everyone in our family so much stress."

Chase completely understood what that feeling was like. She'd seen it many times before in witnesses. Every question invariably led to countless more. This was also stressful for the investigator, especially when answers could not be given to a witness.

"What does it mean? What does this all mean?" the wife asked.

"I don't know what it all means," Chase admitted. "But I can assure you that we are trying to figure this all out." There just wasn't enough trace evidence to make anything of the instantaneous event. As much as Chase wished she could give a solid answer, it just wasn't possible. They were no longer dealing with simple lights in the sky. Something very real and mysterious had plagued the cornfields that night. And it was anyone's bet as to whether it would continue.

"I need it to stop," the wife told Chase. "These sightings have ripped my family into all directions and has distracted us from our normal lives," she explained. "My husband is obsessed with it. He just stares up at the sky all night, hoping for more activity."

Chase knew this feeling all too well. Many who have sightings and encounters are left searching for answers in the dark, hoping for some sort of reassurance that what they saw was real and had actually happened to them. They are left guarded or even secluded. It was a natural reaction, but one Chase hoped wouldn't happen to the witness, especially if it was affecting the entire family as much as the wife had said it was. The wife, desperate for some sort of closure, asked Chase a question that would bring tears to her eyes.

"Can you stop it?"

This was a plea that left both women standing there at a loss. Chase gathered the strength to answer her.

"No. I can't stop it."

Whether the wife meant the activity and events themselves, or the bombardment of attention that the case was now receiving, Chase could do nothing but promise that their anonymity would remain intact. She left that day knowing that this case was special. It was corroborated by other witnesses, and all were willing to go on the record to relate what had occurred. It has remained the most incredible experience she has had, and it was quite clear, as she related the experience to me, that its effects have been lasting. Of the events, she told me, "It was not only surreal, but quite frankly unbelievable. What do you do with that? You tell the truth of what was seen and admit that even as a witness, you yourself were having a very hard time processing it all."

When dealing with witnesses of UFO phenomena, it is often thought that if the witness has had any previous interest or knowledge of the phenomena or its history, they must be directly influenced by that biased perception. This is an argument that cannot be dismissed easily. However, one must also entertain the possibility that just by investigating, the witness is more likely to have some sort of genuine experience at some point. In my personal experience, most UFO investigators are very skeptical individuals. They are not only skeptical, but responsible to a fault. They know that in order to find answers, every conventional theory and scientific approach must be applied. But how do you explain a small grey being, presumably nonhuman in appearance, standing in the middle of a cornfield?

"It is the one second that completely changed so much for me. One second of time that, to this day, still haunts me." I wanted to know exactly what it was about the experience that haunted her. What would stick with her so strongly as to impact her life the way it did? She answered, "My mind always traces back to the two immediate thoughts: the eyes of this being. They were not the large black almond eyes that are usually reported. I was also shocked at the size of the legs. They were very thin and twiglike. I honestly remember thinking a very conscious question to myself, 'They're so thin! How do they hold the body?'"

As a thorough investigator, Chase was never too quick to assert that this experience involved aliens, but something deep within her couldn't seem to shake the possibility. I asked her what she felt was behind this dramatic event. She had the following to say: "I still ponder a manipulated event versus a truly extraterrestrial contact and sighting. Again, I know what I saw, but who was behind it? My head and heart says it was exactly as we witnessed. Another-world technology and a being that was not human. My gut screams: something was off. No witness, no investigator ever gets all of this in one night." I found this last part of Chase's answer very interesting. It seemed as though a multilevel experience was dropped directly into her, Alyson's, and the witness' laps. Almost as if planned. Were they meant to see all of this? Or was it purely by chance that not only were they seeing the massive amounts of lights in the sky, but for a fraction of a moment, they even peered into the eyes of the possible perpetrator?

So it would appear that this encounter primarily induced fear in its trio of witnesses. But even through that deeply vulnerable and desperate feeling, could she find something constructive to take from the experience? "I have become more sensitive to others with contact experiences, but especially those who report terrifying reactions." As an investigator, Chase also found herself focusing more on other theories and a consciousness side of the phenomena. "Coming from a purely 'nuts and bolts' agenda, this experience has made me look past the obvious standards."

So, did she see this experience as a positive or negative influence on her own life? Her answer affirmed many of my own reasons for writing this book. "No one single person has the answers about what is going on out there. If they try to convince you of one way or another, walk away. They're all good aliens here to help us, or they're all evil and working off bad intentions for humanity. To adopt one of these mindsets is to completely ignore the tens of thousands of reports from credible witnesses on both fronts. The initial research indicates an eclectic agenda and one that cannot be grouped into just a positive or negative box."

Although frustrating in its relentless complexity and mystery, the UFO phenomenon has become a pivotal part of Chase's life. She took the leap of accepting that some things simply couldn't be explained and would continue to defy logic. But it would drive her to continue searching for answers. "I truly won't stop until I find answers," she told me. I certainly hoped she wouldn't.

I wanted to know, just as Chase did, what truly was out there. But there was an entirely different level of bizarre and terrifying experiences happening back on the ground as well, leading me to the most controversial cases I'd come across in all my research. Cases where experiences didn't happen in cornfields with multiple witnesses, but happened in the dead of night in the homes of individuals whose privacy and sense of security were being intruded upon at an alarming rate.

9

WAKE ME UP WHEN IT'S OVER

Abductions. This was a part of the research that pushed all boundaries of belief to the most challenging corners. It took me years to actually sift through the many cases that so many books, documentaries, and even the Hollywood machine shoved down my throat. Not only were the stories disturbing, but the notion that they were actually happening was downright terrifying. I would begin to see patterns in the accounts as I drafted up a prototypical abduction experience. They are often described as vivid memories of being taken against one's will by an unknown force and being subjected to intense physical and psychological procedures.

These experiences were almost always dreamlike in nature. The experiencer is never quite sure whether they are awake or sleeping. This isn't always the case, however. Many also have these experiences fully awake and fully aware of what is happening. So here we have a dilemma: we are not only faced with the frightening possibility that some sort of alien presence may be abducting humans, but we may also be dealing with the harsh reality that all of this may be happening in the rocky terrain of the subconscious. My research into abductions began

face-to-face with Claudette Huber, a bright and sincere individual dealing with extremely dark memories.

I sat across from her and her husband at a small restaurant
in Fountain Hills, Arizona. We had introduced ourselves only a
few days prior and communicated several times over email. But
now here we were, face-to-face, the beginning of what would
ultimately become years of correspondence. Our food was cold,
but none of us cared. The conversation was more than enough
to sustain us for now. Something had drawn me to Claudette: a
sincerity unlike any I'd ever seen in an experiencer, and I knew
that her story was one absolutely worth telling.

She is a mother of three, happily married, and spends her
days gardening and tending to her acreage. After spending years
in the real estate business, she gave up her job to be a dedicated
homemaker. She would spend her days playing piano, camping
with her family, and reading an array of books spanning the
literary spectrum.

Claudette had been described to me by her husband as a
person who would give you an immediate rush of calm just by
her demeanor. But that wasn't what I observed as she attempted
to tell me her story. She struggled at first to describe the experience, pausing between each fragmented image. It became clear
to me that this was not a story she'd told often. And as I watched
her hands tremble and could hear her knee lightly hit the table
from underneath in a rhythm, I knew this wasn't going to be
easy for her. Her husband locked fingers with her, trying to calm
her nerves. I asked if she would prefer a more private
atmosphere to talk. She nodded, her eyes welling up. The
following evening, we sat down in my hotel room to conduct the
interview. I asked if she wished that her husband be present. She
took a deep breath and shook her head no. "I want to do this on
my own." And she did.

She was four years old when it happened. It was 1977. In the
small farming community called Bay Tree in Alberta, Canada, a
young Claudette was getting ready for bed. Being one of five

Somewhere in the Skies   135

children, sharing not only a bedroom but a bed was usual for her and her siblings. Claudette and her sister said their nightly prayers and slowly drifted off to sleep.

Claudette awoke, roused by an awareness that her body was no longer resting snugly in her soft sheets. Whatever surface she now lay on was unyielding, cold, and hard. Her shoulder blades pressed against the coolness of what almost felt like metal. In every sense of the word, she was fully aware that she was no longer in her bedroom. Her eyes shot open, an anxious energy filling her body. Her eyes bounced from left to right, looking for her sister. She wasn't there. Claudette desperately searched for something familiar. Again, nothing.

"There was a horrifying moment when I realized that my eyes were literally the only part of my body that I had control over," Claudette told me. She lay frozen, trying to make any sense of her surroundings. A bright white light beat down on her from above. She tried with all her might to move again. Still nothing. Her sight darted to the right, where a sterile, dimly lit area caught her attention. Suddenly, something within her sensed a presence. "I looked in the opposite direction and was startled when out of nowhere, I locked onto a pair of large orbital eyes staring back at me."

Immediately induced with fear, she forced her sights off these mysterious eyes only to discover another two pairs staring back at her from the opposite direction. "I assumed they were about three or four feet tall for the fact that I felt I was raised on some sort of table, and they were eye level with me."

Covering their slender bodies were flowing black robes. Large hoods, almost monk-like in appearance, covered their heads. Claudette went on to describe the clothing the beings wore: "Their robes seemed harsh, almost like that of a burlap sack. Their skin was black. It was wrinkled and flapped over, almost like a dog." Perhaps the most vivid observation Claudette had during the experience was that wherever she was, the area held some sort of moisture in the air. She was able to deduce this for the fact that she could see tiny beads of perspiration dripping off their skin.

"At this point, there were about six of them surrounding me." Claudette screamed in terror. Unfazed, these beings looked on with curious eyes as her screams continued. The beings drew closer. "I noticed a thick, stubby finger of one of the beings inching its way closer and closer. I could feel a faint pressure. My eyes shot downward towards my arm. I could see the fingers tightly wrapping around my arm. Then everything went black."

Claudette awoke the next morning to find that her sister wasn't there. As Claudette crawled out of the sheets and heard the scattered noises of her siblings throughout the house, she realized that their day had already begun. She hazily made her way down the stairs, trying to make sense of what had happened the night before. The smell of breakfast caught her attention as she turned to the kitchen and saw her mother at the stove. Claudette furiously tugged at her mother's apron.

"I was taken away in the night," Claudette told her. Her mother, in turn, hushed her young daughter, dismissing her admission as a nightmare. Claudette challenged her, explaining how real the experience had felt. But her mother wouldn't budge. This was nothing but a horrible dream. And it would pass.

But it didn't. And it never would.

The vivid memory of the visitors haunted Claudette for years. Growing up in a devout Catholic family, she kept silent, warned that her experience was not just a dream, but an evil one at that. Although those she told within her family didn't ridicule her, they did believe that whatever possessed her dreams that night was of demonic origin. Her mother told her to forget about what had happened. To deny it. And it was in that moment that Claudette's sense of innocence shattered. To acknowledge the presence of these small, dark beings would, in essence, be succumbing to their power. Claudette remained silent for many years, fearing a return of the beings. She found herself drawing the blinds shut in her bedroom to block out any light. "I wanted to be left in the dark so that if these beings returned, I wouldn't be able to see them," she told me. It was around this time that she also became fond of her bedside radio. She would spend hours spinning the dial, searching for any radio program to battle the silence in the room. This seemingly dreamlike experience had poured over into real life more than Claudette had ever expected it would. It was affecting every aspect of her life. She knew, deep down, that whatever this was, it wasn't going to simply fade away into obscurity. She would need to face it head-on. And then, and perhaps only then, would she have some sort of lasting resolution.

Claudette eventually sought the assistance of a licensed therapist. After many in-depth conversations about how the experience was affecting her, the therapist offered to put Claudette under hypnotic regression to see what they could coax from her subconscious. Unsure about the reliability of regression hypnosis, Claudette also struggled with the question of what may happen if it yielded answers: would she be ready to accept the revelations? "In the daytime, it is easy to be strong and courageous, but in the darkness of night, it is another beast completely." Under the careful guidance of her therapist, they tried many times, but the regression technique simply didn't bring anything new or revelatory to the surface. But she refused to give up, continuing on a journey to find answers.

She attended many support groups for those who claimed similar experiences. She would listen with an empathetic ear to the startling and completely heartbreaking stories of others whose lives were turned upside down.

Why, I asked, would these beings abduct and terrify an innocent child? She responded: "All I can estimate is that they had an interest in my anatomy, and something had to be done. But they never intended to hurt me. Whatever it was, they felt it completely necessary." If necessary, amid the fear and uncertainty that plagued her, I wanted to know why Claudette felt she was chosen against her will for this abduction and possible experimentation. Was this something that was meant to happen specifically to her? Or was it completely random? "As much as other experiencers or abductees may resent this answer, I truly feel that there is something uniquely special about each and every abductee and experiencer that these beings are aware of, and something that not everyone on this planet necessarily has. I believe it is a calculated exercise when a human being is abducted. This is not just a fishing effort."

Whether calculated or random in nature, there is no doubt that the experience itself has shattering implications. Even if there was something truly special about Claudette, I wanted to know if she felt that the aftermath of her experience was worth the pain and suffering she would consequently carry with her for years to come. "I struggle every day with whether or not it is a positive or negative 'thing' that people all over the world at any given time of the day or night are experiencing. I choose not to pick a side on this debate, except to say that the concept that there could be ill-motivated beings and well-meaning beings living and interacting with the occupants of this planet sounds about right for me... at this time, that is."

At this time, that is. I found it interesting that Claudette included that last statement in her response. Although the experience had come and gone, the acceptance of the experience is an entirely different struggle. One not taken lightly and one that would continue now and possibly for the rest of her life. Even if the slightest hint of an answer were finally bestowed upon Claudette, a thousand other questions would follow. But as she continues to search, she finds comfort and solace knowing that she is not alone in her journey. With each passing day, the courage of coming forward with her experience is what drives her to confront both the demons of her past and the possible saviors of her future.

As we parted ways that evening, I could see a brightness in Claudette that I hadn't noticed before. The proverbial weight seemed to have been lifted off her shoulders. She may not have been any closer to an answer, but she had opened up to me in ways she admitted to never having done before. Holding back tears, she hugged me, whispering in my ear, "I trust you with this. Nobody else."

As she walked away, her husband wrapping his arm around her waist, I knew that Claudette was on her way to new discoveries. With the confidence to share her story through the words you're reading now, she'd taken a huge step forward. And each footstep behind her seemed to now be propelling her on the journey ahead.

In late 2015, Claudette, along with her husband, established their own metaphysical center in British Columbia. And in 2018, they found a permanent home for the center in the heart of the city of Dawson Creek. Curious if this had anything to do with her experience, Claudette updated me by saying, "I opened up my shop to help legitimize experiencers. We are from all walks of life, and we lead very similar lives to everyone else. The key difference is that we have had incredible experiences. It's time we make the effort to reach all of the people who have been marginalized and deemed crazy because of something society cannot explain."

While Claudette hadn't endured anything as profound as her initial experience, she admitted to frequently encountering moments of high strangeness throughout the years, never being able to explain these moments, but embracing them as part of her journey, both physical and spiritual. "I continue to search for answers and weigh every bit of information I glean for how it relates to my experience."

Taking into consideration the recent acknowledgment of UFOs by the US government, I wondered if this at all solidified anything for Claudette, in terms of credibility and legitimacy she was striving for on a micro-level in British Columbia. "I do believe there will be disclosure. But not on the terms and conditions that the truth keepers have tried so very hard to maintain. I

believe a global event will upturn the world and cause instability, opening up the opportunity for a big revelation." Could this
instability lay in the middle of a global pandemic and societal
and racial unrest in the United States and abroad? Only time
will tell and history will tell. But it wasn't necessarily a revelation
by the hands, minds, and hearts of us here on Earth, but
perhaps by the visitors Claudette claimed encountering. "The
revelation will come from the beings themselves. I believe we
are living in a time where anything is possible. The world as we
know and understand it is about to make a huge shift into a new
paradigm. I do not know what role the beings I encountered will
play in all this."

With time often comes growth. And it was clear that
Claudette's experience had influenced her life in different ways,
many of which were yet to be uncovered. "I am no closer to
finding the answers that I seek than where I was when our
initial interview took place. I continue to debate within myself
each idea that is put forth by researchers. I know what I saw. I
know what I experienced. Others have seen the very same creatures and I have. I just hope I am brave enough to face whatever
the truth is about our place in this vast universe and how we
relate to these others who continue to interfere with us. They
have moved their attention to the next phase of their involvement with us. I feel things are about to change."

10

CAN WE COME VISIT?

In an old farmhouse on the outskirts of southern Illinois, Bret, a mere five years old, was getting ready for bed. It was a cold autumn night as he drew the covers close, trying to stay warm. The calm, serene darkness began to take hold of his heavy eyelids, and soon he drifted off to sleep.

The brightness was what awakened him. So unbelievably bright that it pierced through his eyelids, sending him straight up to his feet. It seemed to be pouring in from the living room window. The house, surrounded by fields of corn and soybeans, boasted no streetlights for countless miles. Whatever the light was, it was coming from a source that clearly hadn't been there before. Suddenly, a voice called out to him.

Bret, it whispered.

Was it his stepfather? Bret frantically looked around but saw no one. The voice coaxed him even further. *Don't be afraid, don't be afraid. I have something special to show you.* Bret told me, "For some reason, I felt that the corner window was where I was being guided toward. Whatever this voice was, it was pulling me there."

As he approached the window, he grasped the thin white curtain and pulled it back. "It was in that moment that I knew my life had changed forever." There, staring straight back at him beyond the glass, was a pair of black, curious eyes. They tilted slightly as they met Bret's gaze. He stood in awe before a small androgynous being with a pale grey complexion. Bret could sense something out beyond this being. There, about twenty feet away, stood two more identical beings by the tree line in the front yard. Whatever this being was, it was not alone. Bret's curiosity was shattered by visceral fear. "Before I could muster a scream, I completely blacked out."

Darkness. Not a sound. His senses kicked back in, waking him to yet another bright light. He could feel a solid structure below him. A platform of some kind. His eyes scanned his surroundings. He could make out a blurred suggestion of figures in front of him. As the figures came into focus, Bret couldn't help but scream. They surrounded him, slowly closing in. Suddenly, Bret noticed a complete shift in their appearance. They now looked almost human. In fact, he could see surgical masks covering their mouths. Were these doctors? Had he been unaware that he'd be undergoing an operation? Why would his parents subject him to such a horrible thing without his knowledge or consent? He began to scream for his mother. But his mother never came. As his screams became louder and louder, the doctor facade soon faded, and the beings before him returned to their alien form.

"I was then taken to a room where there was a half-moon-like seating area that was sunken down and seemed to be built into the craft itself. Several of the greys were sitting in this area, although one of them was dramatically taller than the rest. They sat me down with them and just stared at me." This is when Bret remembers that the tall grey began to communicate with him. "I didn't understand how he was speaking, though. I could hear his words, yet I didn't see his mouth move. His words, or perhaps his touch, had a very calming effect on me."

The voice spoke in a soft monotone: *We're not going to hurt you. We are your friends. Do you understand?*

Bret nodded.

We want to learn about you. Can we come and visit you from time to time?

Bret was scared, yet a calming sensation seemed to steadily brush over him. He went on to tell me, "I didn't understand what was happening or why it was happening, but a bond was being formed. I had nothing in this strange place they had taken me to. I had no one. I saw nothing that looked even vaguely familiar. So I grasped onto the only thing that offered me any degree of comfort and friendship, even if it was this tall being. It was all I had. The effect that being had on me has lasted my entire life up until this very moment."

Can we come visit you from time to time? Bret heard it once more. It was then that he reluctantly replied, "Okay." And with that, he blacked out once more.

Bret awoke the next morning excited, yet also very uneasy. This had indeed been the most vivid dream he could possibly remember in his short life. But something wasn't right. Whatever had happened, Bret knew deep down that it wasn't just a dream. It couldn't be. He would eventually tell his mother about the "little men" who came and took him in the night. His mother, in turn, explained to young Bret that these were nothing but imaginary friends.

But the friends would continue to visit Bret time and again. And as he grew older, it became very apparent that this wasn't a childhood fantasy to be pushed aside. Strange, unexplainable marks began to appear on his body, which he believed came from the deeply violating examinations he endured during the frightening abductions. The unsympathetic intrusions by the beings continued. Bret began to feel a perverse connection to them, a feeling that this was supposed to be happening. Although a small sense of ease floated on the surface with this growing connection, a strong disconnect ate away at him. The trauma of both the childhood visit and subsequent experiences would prove too heavy for Bret to ignore. Anxiety began to fester.

"Since I have had multiple experiences, I can tell you that it usually evokes a myriad of emotions depending on what was done to me. The physical stuff I could heal from, but the emotional things caused real damage. Many symptoms can be compared to that of post-traumatic stress disorder. Your self-worth is compromised. You feel like a lab rat. You have no say or control over anything that is done to you. When you are returned, the next day you feel as if every ounce of energy in your body is depleted. Yet you have to get up and pretend to function in a normal fashion as if nothing ever happened."

To play the role of "down-to-earth" Bret, he continued to live his life as if nothing had happened. The vivid memories of each experience would race through his mind even while he tried with all his might to blend into the routine of everyday life. But the greys seemed to have different plans, continuing their mysterious intrusions. And the more he tried denying them, the stronger his anxiety became. Nightmares plagued his sleep as the thin line between dream and reality became increasingly blurred. Anxiety turned to depression. "I had fought bouts of depression throughout my life, which I'm sure is in direct correlation to the experiments and procedures that I've endured at the hands of these beings. And what angers me most is that they appear to be completely devoid of empathy toward their unfortunate subjects."

I wanted to know if, as in Claudette's case, Bret held deep religious beliefs. Besides therapy to deal with such mentally and sometimes physically exhausting experiences, one's faith can often be a driving force in dealing with such traumatic experiences. "My family was very religious," he told me. "They were Southern Missionary Baptists and I was raised and taught the Christian faith. These experiences did indeed change my religious beliefs. I am not religious at all anymore, but I am a deeply spiritual person. I have a deep love and regard for our planet and especially the creatures that inhabit it. This was all set in motion by my experiences. They caused me to seek out other paths to the truth. I realized the strong inaccuracies of religious dogma, and how fear is used to control in most religions."

Bret had been acutely made aware of the world around him. Religion aside, faith had become a much more integral part of his life. A higher level of belief was tearing down any walls raised by normality. "It's caused me to view the world on a much broader scale. It's caused me to be more loving and accepting. I used to be jealous of people who didn't have to deal with what I have to, but since then I've learned to let that go, and I live my live completely free of jealousy. It's made me a much stronger person than I ever would have been had I not had these experiences. It's given me a deep appreciation of my life and those in it, and an ongoing sense of gratitude."

It is clear that these beings have had a lasting impact on Bret. So what, in his opinion, was their purpose in abducting him and so many others who claimed similar experiences? "I don't believe that anyone truly knows the agenda of these beings. I can only express my views and opinions on what they may be doing. After having endured countless procedures and experiments, I can only deduce that it seems that they are extremely interested in human emotions, of which they themselves lack and don't understand."

These experiences often make those who endured them feel either completely alienated from their surroundings, or perhaps even special. I wanted to know if Bret felt any sense of having been specifically chosen for these experiences, or, as Claudette put it, could this all be a "fishing effort"? Bret had the following to add: "I don't believe that I am special and that's why I was taken. This is a generational phenomenon. It seems to run in families, even though most don't remember it, or if they do, they never talk about it. As far as the beings I have come into contact with, once they find a certain genetic makeup that they for some

unknown reason favor, they stay with it. I believe that I simply
have the DNA they favor."

With a lifetime of experiences, both incredible and intrusive,
the question that I inevitably circle back to with the experiencers is whether or not they view this entire phenomenon as a
positive or negative. Brent went on to tell me that he saw it as
both. "I believe that we, as a planet, have been given certain
technologies from these beings. But at what price? I don't think
that after thousands of years of existence, we suddenly became
vastly more intelligent as a species, and yet when you look at the
scientific and technological progress we have made in the last
sixty to seventy years compared to the rest of the timeline of our
existence, the answer is rather obvious." If proven, this could be
an intervention of epic proportions. And while technology can
be seen as a positive, I sensed that there was more to Bret's
opinion on this than met the eye. He added the following:
"Other than that, I see it as a negative. I know that there are
others who believe that these beings are our 'galactic space
brothers' and are here to help us. But I've seen no evidence of
that except the sharing of technology. Thousands and thousands
of abductees have paid the price in terms of these deeply
violating and confusing experiences at their hands."

As Bret's experiences continue, he takes solace in knowing
that his closest friends and family support him throughout these
deeply complex interactions with a possible alien presence. And
as the contact between him and the beings became more
intense, he found it easier to accept it. To open up further to
whatever it may be that they wanted from him. The last thing I
asked Bret was just exactly what he believed he'd taken from all
of this. What did he hold most vital about the experiences. He
answered: "Knowledge." Whatever that meant to Bret was yet to
be fully encapsulated, but his confidence in just exactly what
had happened, and what was yet to happen, was a journey he
was more than willing to continue taking.

It was now 2020. And Bret's story was far from over. Though

the experiences had lessened with time, they *did* continue. Bret told me, "It's something I have come to accept over the years. There came a point in my life when I realized that *they* were not going to stop taking me. Even though the abduction events happened less frequently, they are still profound." While profound, the experiences seemed to take on a much darker and mysterious nature. "Over the last couple of years, there has been an appearance of large bloody, what appears to be, handprints on my sheets. This has happened three separate times now. I have tested the substance with luminol, and it is indeed blood. Every single time I have found the bloody prints, I have tried to find a rational cause for them. I have not been able to find any source."

This was admittedly quite an unexpected update from Bret, and I was curious to learn more. Could this blood have been from either him or his wife? "Neither my wife or I have had any blood on us or any cuts or injuries. Given the amount of blood, it would have had to have been a rather large cut anyway. I could find no source for the bloody prints." So naturally, my next question was what he believed the handprint to be. Bret told me, "One of the handprints clearly is a four-digit hand with long fingers, just like the greys I had come into contact with. I believe the handprints were left there on purpose as a sign or message." What the message may have been, Bret was uncertain.

Given the bloody and cryptic nature of these occurrences, had Bret's thoughts or feelings changed on the overall motives or purpose of the beings that seemed to be taking him throughout his life? "Over the years I have lost count of the number of people who have had abductions or contact that I have personally counseled. Two common denominators among them are fear and anger, stemming from what happened to them. I used to feel the exact same way. That has all changed now. It was a long healing process, but I reached a point where I was able to forgive these beings for what they have done to me."

Given the deeply intrusive actions taken by these beings, it would presumably be hard to allow it and even accept it. But Bret now thought differently. "One must come to the realization that the beings are not human and thus not wired like we are. Regarding the greys, of whom I have had the most experiences with, they do not exhibit the emotions and feelings that we do. They lack human empathy as we know it. When you accept that, you come to an understanding that they don't fully comprehend the psychological damage they cause by taking us against our will and using us for procedures and experiments."

Bret seemed to be taking control of the situation, moving from fear and anxiety to an unspoken agreement that whatever *they* were doing, it was much bigger and vital than curious experiments on human beings. "To some degree, I actually feel sorry for them now," he admitted. "There is a strong sense of desperation and urgency in what they are doing."

As mentioned, it's one thing to accept it, but another to embrace it and integrate it into one's life. Bret explained, "I learned to focus on the positives of my alien abduction experiences. I've been extremely healthy my entire life. Every doctor who has ever seen a blood test of mine has commented how remarkable it is. Not just for my age but for any age. I attribute that to the greys. I think they have kept me healthy all these years. Not from the kindness of their heart but because I have been valuable to them. Most likely because I have the genetics they favor for their hybrid program. So it is, and has been, in their best interest to keep me healthy."

While the US government has publicly acknowledged the existence of legitimate unidentifiable aerial phenomena in our skies, we have individuals like Bret claiming contact with nonhuman intelligences. There seems to be a large disconnect in terms of where we are in the overall UFO conversation as a society. "I believe that there is a slow drip of disclosure happening. Even people like me and my case is disclosure, but no one really pays attention to it. Sometimes I wish disclosure would happen. It might be just what this world needs at this point in our history, but are we, as a society, really prepared for that kind of acceptance? Has humanity advanced to that level yet? Humans can't even accept each other's skin color or religious differences. Are they ready to accept an alien species who not only look different from them but who are far superior intellectually and technologically? I hope we get there someday. I really do."

A large stigma still surrounds the entire abduction phenomenon. It always has, and it most likely always will. Though many may find Bret's lifelong contact with beings from another world impossible, implausible, or simply just a story, Bret steadfastly stresses that he lived it. He continues to live it. And it's quite obvious that whatever he has learned and taken from his experiences, it has made him the person he is today. It is *his* truth. And Bret also admits that he doesn't necessarily care what the public thinks. He has laid out the story, provided evidence, and it's up to the individual to decide what to do with it. "I have given more proof than any case I know of. I have provided physical evidence. I have been examined by doctors who can't explain the mysterious scars on my body. I have taken polygraphs administered by top examiners. I have taken and passed a brain scan, which showed that while recalling the events of my story, they came from the part of my brain associated with memory and not the creative part which they would have if I were making them up."

Even when experiencers try with all their might to provide evidence, still there will always be those who refuse to believe. Was it not enough evidence? Or was it merely a refusal to accept any of these stories because they could in fact be real? Bret believed, "It is scary enough for them to fathom the idea that we might and continue to be visited by an extraterrestrial species, but way too much for them to handle to think that one or more of those extraterrestrial species are taking us by the thousands on a regular basis. So, for these reasons and for my safety, these days... I remain quiet."

Though Bret has decided to now keep his experiences private, he continues to reflect on them introspectively, trying to unravel the memories from the past and the cryptic and visceral events taking place most recently, and quite possibly in the years to come.

11

MY CHALK-COLORED FRIENDS

A week in Mexico would have sufficed. But ten days seemed like a rare opportunity that Michael Carter and his girlfriend just couldn't pass up. As he dug his feet into the warm Cancun sand, he knew this was exactly what he needed. A few days of relaxation turned into a small expedition to many sites that Michael had always wanted to visit. The Mayan step pyramids were first. Then came Tulum, and Chichen Itza on the Yucatan Peninsula. It was ten whole days of exploration and escape from his bustling life waiting impatiently back in New York City.

It was 1989. Michael and his girlfriend boarded their plane in eighty-degree weather and returned to an uninviting winter in New York. It was one night later when Michael, having shared his vacation experiences with friends at a dinner party, said goodnight early, still feeling the pangs of jet lag. He took the subway home, his exhaustion growing stronger. He stumbled into the apartment, kicked off his shoes, and fell face-first into bed. His girlfriend pulled the covers over him, and they both drifted off to sleep.

His eyes shot open. Something inside him was urging him awake. "I distinctly remember not wanting to get up because I was warm and comfortable under the blankets." He looked over at his girlfriend, who remained fast asleep. He wanted the same. "There was this persistent feeling that I must be awake at this moment, however." And just as he was about to remove the blankets to get up, he noticed a bluish-white light enveloping the entire bedroom as if it were daytime, although the bedside clock argued that it was still the middle of the night. Something caught his eye at the end of the bed. What Michael saw next would leave him petrified.

"Standing at the end of the bed was this being," Michael explained. "It had an egg-shaped head and wraparound eyes. Deep. Black. It was very short, its head just peeking over the end of the bed. It was dressed in a silver tight-fitting suit with a tunic collar." Michael went on to describe the being as similar to what he would later learn was called a grey. However, this being wasn't grey, but what Michael described as a "chalk-white color. It glowed brightly, light just emanating from it. It stared straight at me for what seemed like an eternity."

Frightened by the sheer presence of this intruder, Michael pulled the covers over his head, trying to assess the situation. "I thought and felt that my heart was going to come out of my chest," he recalled. "I looked over at my girlfriend, who didn't even stir, still in a deep sleep."

Michael stayed under the covers, hoping the being would just go away. Perhaps this was all just a figment of his imagination. Suddenly, the temperature in the room dropped drastically. He began to shiver as a loud whooshing sound consumed the room like a violent windstorm. "For a moment, I felt as though I had somehow been transported outside," he told me. With all the courage he could muster, Michael slowly removed the covers from over his head and took stock of his surroundings. He was thankfully still in his bedroom. But the being was nowhere to be seen. "The room was dark and all was eerily quiet," he remembered. "I tried to shake my girlfriend awake, but she was so deeply asleep and unresponsive that I actually had to check if she was breathing." Michael tried to gather himself, the nerves throughout his body slowly waning. He forced his eyes shut and eventually fell back asleep. The morning would promise relief. This was all just a terrible dream, he kept convincing himself. It would all be forgotten when he awoke. But to his dismay, he remembered it all the following morning.

He awoke to find an empty spot next to him in bed. Michael thought to himself how rare it was that he had slept in this late. He debated whether or not to tell his girlfriend what had apparently happened to him in the night. But she had always been very open-minded and spiritual. He took the chance and told her everything, anxious about her reaction. She listened with a compassionate ear and slowly but surely took it all in stride. This would all pass. Life was sure to return to normal. It had to. For his well-being.

Nights were spent with the lights on for a very long time after that. "I was a wreck," Michael admitted to me. "I was afraid of what would happen if it came back again." His girlfriend would wait until he fell asleep, and then—and only then— would she turn off the lights. "When she was home, I felt a bit more at ease, because I was not alone." But this wouldn't calm his nerves when she wasn't around. He only grew more anxious. Was he going crazy? Was a part of him hoping that this being would return? Its tangible existence would ascertain that he wasn't slipping into a dangerous realm of delusion. But at the same time, it would also change his entire perception of reality. What if it returned? This thought stuck with him as days and months passed. And just as he had feared, it did return.

"The visits continued for about six months or so." Michael also acknowledged that the visits always happened "on a night with a full or new moon. Each visit was frightening, but they never harmed me." As these visits continued, it grew apparent that Michael was no longer dealing with one chalk-colored friend, but many. He went on to explain to me how most of the visits played out. "I'd be lying in bed attempting to sleep. The room would be eerily quiet. The air would become still. I would hear a faint humming sound in my ears seconds before their arrival. Suddenly, without warning, I would be paralyzed. I couldn't even open my eyes. They would show me images of what was happening, almost as if I were outside my own body, watching this all happen. One being would extend its hand towards me and a bright ray of light would appear from it, touching me. It felt like electricity was surging through my whole body. As I watched all of this from above, I tried with all my might to open my eyes. When I did, the beings would disappear. I would then awake in my bedroom, as if nothing had happened." Michael acknowledged that this pattern continued for some time, and the fear he'd initially felt began to dissipate. "I was now getting somewhat used to the visits." But just as he was getting used to it, it started to diminish. This is when the fear morphed into something completely different. "I now found myself almost longing for their return." These profound experiences were becoming more attractive to Michael. He wanted to talk to someone outside the comfort and care of his girlfriend about it. Someone who could take an unbiased approach to examining his case. And the opportunity presented itself one late afternoon in a bookstore in downtown Manhattan.

"I was browsing in a bookstore down in SoHo. I found a book by Dr. Edith Fiore, *Encounters*. While glancing through the book, I noticed, in the back, she had a list of symptoms an individual may display if they were having encounters with an extraterrestrial intelligence. It also had a list of professional therapists who specialized in dealing with those who claimed contact. I felt like I had hit the jackpot!"

As Michael timidly made his way to the counter to purchase the book, he had already begun imagining the ridicule he would endure upon checkout. "I felt like a teenager buying condoms. I couldn't even look the cashier in the eye. I just wanted to buy the book and get out of there," Michael told me. "The cashier asked me if this was just a hobby of mine or if I truly thought it was for real. I wanted to lie. Say it was for a weird friend of mine. But I didn't. I looked straight at him and told him that it was in fact for real." What the cashier said next was an answer to Michael's prayers. "The cashier told me that he knew a place where I could go and be with others like me. A support group. He told me that if I was interested, he had a number I could call, and that he himself used to attend the group." Michael had found another experiencer right in front of him. And he was about to meet many more when he attended the first meeting.

"In the group, there were not only those who had similar experiences, but something that really stood out to me was that there were others of color, like me. This was significant for me because most UFO or abduction literature often paints this as a Eurocentric phenomenon. Naturally, the media perpetuates this image, rarely if ever interviewing anyone of color." It was almost as if Michael had found a new community. Something extremely disquieting had now connected him with others who had very similar outlooks on the experiences they were all having, and how it affected them as a human race. "I noticed that although there was varied interest amongst the individuals in the group concerning the phenomenon itself, most view their encounters as spiritually transformative. Barriers such as nationality, religion, ethnicity or race... these played second fiddle to the identity of being one with all creation."

Creation caught my attention most. Between that and his remark of spiritual transformation, I sensed that religion had somehow been a part of his life in some sort of capacity. I had been looking for experiencers who perhaps viewed their experiences through a religious or spiritual lens. While many admitted spiritual awakening, I wondered if entire beliefs were ever changed or altered. As I would soon find out, my curiosity would be sated in the course of my and Michael's correspondence. "I was wrestling with how Christianity and my experiences would fit into my worldview. I have always been into comparative religious study, and these experiences only enhanced my interest. During one of my experiences, I was shown a picture of a pair of hands in the prayer position with a lightning bolt going through it. I took this as encouragement to pursue energy healing and prayer."

Michael had always had respiratory problems, suffering from severe asthma all his life. Nothing seemed to help. But after visiting a physician who dealt in Eastern medicine, it was recommended that he perhaps try the Japanese technique known as Reiki. This is basically a healing technique where energy is transferred through the palms into an ailing part of the body, promoting a state of equilibrium. This type of practice is still considered pseudoscience, and Michael wasn't quite ready to accept it. But after his first experience, his inhibitions faded and he opened himself up to different possibilities. After about six weeks, he noticed a dramatic change to the point of almost being cured of this lifelong struggle to breathe normally. "I attribute my acceptance of this practice entirely to my experiences. They opened something up inside me, and I wanted to share that with others."

Michael's path took a dramatic turn when he decided to join the seminary. "I had made a conscious decision to dedicate a large portion of my life to spreading the message of God," he told me. "I wanted to continue searching for meaning in this other realm of what I considered extraterrestrial intervention in tandem with my own spiritual journey. This led me to write my Master of Divinity thesis on the connection between UFOs and the Bible, something I know sounds controversial, but with an open mind, it is quite apparent and can be interpreted many different ways."

After realizing that his spirituality and techniques had worked for him personally, he took to learning how to spread the healing to others who he felt needed it. He became a chaplain at a New York City hospital in an oncology unit. He worked there for the next ten years, healing patients left and right. "Let me be clear. There is a big difference between being healed and being cured. I have witnessed some miraculous events by using this energy, but I do not diagnose and I am not a doctor."

After many years of spiritual evolution and continued experiences, Michael eventually moved to North Carolina to become the minister of a Unitarian Universalist congregation. He now lives a happy life with his wife and nine-year-old daughter, continuing to spread his positive experiences to any who will listen. And while he still hopes to find answers for his deeply complex experiences with the beings, he knows one thing for certain: "These are my experiences. They are powerful and empowering. My prayer is that my story will help those on their trail in this life. I hope I have been of service. I take life one day at a time and that's all I can do. I am grateful for my family, my friends, and the gift of life." I could sense that although the experience would always be there, it never defined Michael as the person he once was or the person he would become. He was a man of faith, spirituality, and acceptance. But most importantly, he was gracious. "My needs are always met, and I choose to continue to grow spiritually and to continue to love myself as well as others. Because when it truly comes down to it... what else is there?"

Michael, for me, was the prime example of how these experiences can completely alter the path of a person's life. And after even more time had passed since last speaking with him, I was eager to see where that path had led him. Had he had any follow-up experiences with the beings? He told me, "To date I have not had any follow-up experiences, at least not consciously. I find that this happens at times, with years going by between visits. Especially if my life is busy and I am pretty much on my path, which I feel I am at this point in my life."

Spirituality had been a huge focus of Michael's life during and after his experiences, so much to have compelled him to become a minister. Where had his faith and practices led him? "I am very much influenced by Eastern thought and philosophy, particularly Buddhism and Taoism. I try to live my life by 'going with the flow' and non-attachment. By this, I mean I try not to worry about things I cannot control. If something can be changed, why worry, and if it cannot be changed, why worry? It has brought me an inner peace that I would not exchange for anything in the world. I meditate daily. The Serenity Prayer is one that resonates with me on many levels as well as the Rumi quote, *'When I was young and clever I wanted to change the world. Now I am older and I just want to change myself.'* I bring this attitude to my ministry and to my everyday life."

As for the experiences themselves, I would learn that many interpret their experiences differently as time goes on. Had Michael's thoughts changed at all in terms of the beings, their motives, and the messages they were trying to convey to him? "My thoughts on them haven't changed. But *I* have changed because of the experiences. At the outset, when I was a younger man, my experiences with nonhuman intelligences was all consuming. It's all that I lived and breathed. But as time went on, I realized that there was so much more to my life that I was ignoring. I was living in a bubble. I find that when I am speaking at conferences, the audiences were very much into my stories about my experiences and the religious aspects I bring to the table, but you could hear a pin drop when I spoke about my spirituality after the experiences."

While the acknowledgment of unidentified aerial phenomena has grown in the past few years, bringing more people to accept the fact that alien life must exist somewhere in the universe, still a large portion of society isn't willing to marry these two topics together to explain the hundreds, if not thousands, of abduction and experiencer accounts. But Michael thinks differently, optimistically reminding us: "There are so many people nowadays who are open about their contacts, so it's not so novel anymore. Yet people still are questioning, and they want to know how do I live with wisdom and integrity in these trying times as a new paradigm emerges on the planet? How do I coexist with people who are different from me on so many levels? Where can I find wisdom instead of just information? I try to provide those answers as best I can."

In a world that is rapidly changing before our very eyes, I couldn't help but wonder how Michael felt about where we are as a society and as a planet. Were we going to experience any type of contact with these beings he had? Would we ever learn the message Michael continued to learn from them? In terms of any grand disclosure, he confessed, "I'm still not sure when that will happen, but as Dr. King and Victor Hugo remind us, no lie lives forever. I'm not sure someone from another planet or galaxy is coming to save us. After all, it's our mess and we made it. I do believe that we have a choice and we are reaching a tipping point. Anything can happen."

So while the true message of these beings has yet to be spoken, Michael continues to listen. But he's also not holding his breath. "There's too much here on Earth to learn and to grow from. I can see a new world being born, but the choice is ours and the hour is getting late. I am encouraged with the changes that have come along globally after the murder of Brother George Floyd. We *need* a revolution and it will be a revolution of consciousness. Changes must be made and a new consciousness must come to us and our leaders if we are to survive as a species. We must learn to live together as brothers and sisters, or we will certainly perish together as fools."

So while Michael continues his spiritual journey, he takes comfort in knowing that *he* holds the map, no matter what or who the beings were who might have and may continue to visit him again. "Rest assured that I will see them again. When the time is right."

12

UNKNOWN CHILDREN

Shane Kurz Sia is a history buff. Active in her local historical society as a secretary, she is also a member of the Medina Tourism Committee in her hometown of Medina, New York. In her spare time, she also teaches Tai Chi classes and exhibits her artwork at sidewalk art shows across town. In the past, she co-owned a commercial cleaning business with her husband. A life full of prosperity on many levels. You'd never expect that this seemingly normal woman would have a story hidden deep down like the one she told me. And as Shane opened up to me about her experiences, it became clear that her life was anything but normal.

It all began in April of 1968. Winter was turning to a mild spring in Westmoreland, a small town on the outskirts of Syracuse, New York. Shane was nineteen at the time, the oldest of four siblings. On the brink of entering her twenties, Shane had interests that differed greatly from those around her. While most were focusing on small-town aspirations, Shane was searching the skies above. Her fascination with astronomy was quite apparent and had even led her boyfriend to buy her a telescope for Christmas the year prior. On an unusually warm night that April, Shane invited her boyfriend and mother to join her outside their home to gaze at the stars. Lawn chairs in hand, the three planted themselves on the damp grass and talked the night away, staring up at the small white lights that littered the black beyond.

As Shane's eyes bounced from left to right, she noticed a single bright light that stood out amongst the others. It was very high up, traveling at great speed from west to east in an elliptical fashion. As she pointed it out to her mother and boyfriend, it completely disappeared from sight. Had it been a figment of her imagination? Just as she was ready to brush it off, the light reappeared directly above her, legitimizing its presence to the entire trio. It descended slowly. Shane could faintly make out an oval shape to the light, giving a sense that there was in fact a structure emanating the light. All three could feel a prickly sensation throughout their bodies, as the hair on both their necks and heads shot straight up. Just as quickly as the object appeared, it shot upward and disappeared from sight. The three stood dumbfounded.

Days passed before Shane made the return to the same location. This time, she and her mother witnessed an almost identical object making similar maneuvers. After about ten minutes, they watched as the object disappeared from sight yet again. It was obvious that whatever this was, it wasn't just a onetime event. This object's sudden appearances were swiftly becoming a pattern in Shane's eyes. Her mother, accepting that this was indeed out of the ordinary, phoned nearby Griffiss Air Force Base. Having been a civilian employee for the local base for some time, she inched her way through the red tape to finally speak to someone on the base. She asked if this object had either been tracked or if the base claimed responsibility for it. They denied both, leaving Shane and her mother at a complete loss as to what they had seen twice in one week. She and her mother went to bed that night just as perplexed as ever. Hopefully a good night's rest would calm the nerves in both of them.

As Shane dozed off into a heavy sleep that night, she was

awakened by her mother in a complete panic. "There was this incredibly bright light shining in our upstairs bedroom windows. My mother shared the bedroom with me, and the light was so intense it illuminated the whole front of the house." Shane's mother pulled her to the front window to look out, and there, in a field across the street from their house, was the oval-shaped object hovering about thirty feet off the ground. "It appeared to be yellow with orange lights surrounding the middle rim, which was rotating around the middle of the craft," Shane described. "We could not make much else out, except the light emanating from the craft seemed very contained around it —not shining in a big area around it. I don't recall hearing any sound, only possibly a very low hum."

It was at this time that Shane and her younger sister, Pam, ran outside to the front porch to watch. They yelled for their mother to once again contact Griffiss Air Force Base. Again, she was told that they had nothing to do with this object. Shane's mother even went as far as to contact Hancock Air Base in Syracuse, which, in turn, also denied any involvement with this object. Outside, Shane watched as the object abruptly shot up and vanished yet again. *How could this be happening again?* Shane thought to herself. She went to bed that night, more tired than ever. Perhaps this would all pass with a good night's sleep. Perhaps when she drifted off, this would all fade away, and life could return to some semblance of normality.

It was approximately 8 a.m. Shane's mother shook her awake yet again. Had the object returned in the morning sun? Was this all happening again? Her eyes focused on her mother, who asked what had happened to Shane. Confused, her mother pointed at her daughter's robe. Shane looked down to see herself lying on top of her bedsheets and covers. "I had my robe on, buttoned all the way to top," Shane told me. "My slippers were on, and the front of me was covered in mud, as were the sides of my slippers and soles. There was mud splattered on my hands and on my lower legs."

Shane and her mother sat at the edge of the bed, trying to make sense of the situation. Her mother had noticed that Shane had not been in her bed around 4 a.m., and assumed that she had gotten up to use the bathroom. She thought nothing of it, going back to sleep. But Shane had clearly made her way outside without remembering. Had she been sleepwalking? She had never shown any signs of such a condition before. If this were the first time, it had been a rather dramatic one at that. The two of them made their way out of the room, following a trail of muddy footsteps from her bedroom and down the stairs to the back door of the kitchen. There, they found the door unlocked and wide open. Scared and confused, Shane became distraught. Her mother helped her get in the shower to wash off the mud and hopefully calm her nerves. But as Shane began to disrobe, they both noticed on her lower abdomen was a small triangular burn mark. Accompanying it was a thin red line that started at her navel, trailing downward. Lastly, a gel-like substance could faintly be seen running from her abdomen upward toward her breasts. Her nerves were turning to anxiety at a rapid rate.

Shane's mother feared the worst. Had Shane been taken in the night by a predator and assaulted? Was this all somehow connected to the events that seemed to be escalating above their home? Memories of the night prior remained hidden somewhere deep, and as the mysterious marks on Shane's body slowly began to fade, so did any hope that she would find answers to whatever happened to her that night. Strange symptoms arose, as Shane told me: "My eyes began to feel as if I had been staring at the sun. They felt burned and puffy. And I had a terrible headache that lasted for days." As the physical symptoms began to take hold, it left Shane rather cold and numb. "I felt very tired and depressed, and I didn't sleep well at all. I felt like this had something to do with whatever happened between sleeping and waking that night, but I just couldn't find a memory of any of it. It was as if I were suffering from total amnesia."

The physical ailments only escalated from there. "My hearing seemed to be heightened, almost to a point where it was painful," she told me. "I would be lying in bed at night, and I could hear someone talking as if right next to me. But as I'd follow the voice, it would lead me blocks away from my house. There, I would find the conversation, and it would be almost deafening."

If this weren't curious enough, what happened next only intensified and left her even more confused. After months of gradual weight loss and many visits to physicians, Shane found herself in the care of a medical specialist. Upon close examination, he diagnosed her with severe amenorrhea. The doctor determined that there were no signs of sexual assault and asked Shane what, if anything, could have caused this to happen to her. Shane was up front, explaining that she and her family were experiencing unexplained sightings of some sort of craft above their home. The doctor was completely at a loss. "He gave me some pills to try to start things normally again with my cycle," Shane told me. "He assured me that it wouldn't affect my ability to get pregnant, which had been a concern of mine. It wouldn't be until five years later that I finally had normal menses again."

The mental toll of these experiences on Shane was becoming increasingly unbearable. She knew this was somehow all connected to the craft in the sky that had entered her family's lives, and that in the span of that singular night, something insidious had occurred that she just couldn't remember. As time progressed, she began to have nightmares of an ominous face with huge black eyes. She found herself catching glimpses of it repeatedly. And although the marks on her body faded and her hearing soon returned to normal, she was living in a constant state of anxiety at this point.

She sought the help of several hypnotherapists to see if any regressed memories could be salvaged from that night. While some progress seemed to be made, no compelling impressions surfaced that could fully account for what had happened. As the years passed, Shane found herself weaving in and out of several local UFO support groups, trying to find a connection to someone or something. Eventually, through one of these groups, she met noted psychiatrist and author Dr. Berthold Schwarz. He had been working on a book about the psychiatric and possible psychic aspects to the UFO phenomenon and those who have experienced it. After many failed attempts at hypnosis, Dr. Schwarz advised Shane to move away from using hypnosis to recover the memories. "Instead, he suggested that I let it happen organically. Eventually, my mind would remember what it was ready to remember if and when it was ready to do so." Apparently, this tactic proved successful: a flurry of memories rushed in.

The first memory emerged in the form of a dream. "I awoke to a low humming noise outside of my upstairs window that was facing a large field across the street. I checked the time on my side table and it read 1:15 a.m. I saw a light hovering in the field. I put on my robe and slippers and walked downstairs and outside to get a better view of this very bright hovering object." Something seemed to then compel Shane to move directly underneath the object. "I felt like I was suddenly going into an altered state, as if I couldn't move on my own. I found myself trying to run away. But I couldn't. The object opened up, and I felt myself go weightless and lift up into the object." Shane found herself ascending through a glass-like elevator further upward. Once she reached a certain level, she stepped out into a large room, where there seemed to be some sort of diamond revolving in the center. "Around the diamond were these small figures looking at what appeared to be computer screens of some sort." It was at this moment that Shane blacked out.

She awoke again to find herself in a completely different room. It was very dark. The only light seemed to be from a large viewing screen of some sort. Shane could see herself in the screen, almost as if she were being monitored. She couldn't move. From the darkness, a face appeared to her. It was the same face that had haunted her dreams in the past. Shane told me about the face this figure had: "White skin, a large forehead, a small jaw, thin lips, and large dark eyes. It was looking straight at me. And it spoke, but I never saw its lips move. It was communicating through my mind somehow. I could hear it say nothing but, 'You are alright. You are alright.'" All around her, small robot-like creatures scampered about, each seeming to have a certain job in Shane's examination. A large light from above began to scan her from head to toe. As the light passed her vision one last time, she blacked out yet again.

Shane awoke in the field. It was cold and damp. She could feel the morning sun just beginning to rise as she stumbled back into the house, her feet completely covered in mud from the ground outside. She made her way back up to her bedroom, fell onto the mattress, and passed out, exhausted beyond comprehension. It wouldn't be until her mother shook her awake in a panic to find her muddied. The missing time and experiences had finally made themselves somewhat apparent. Shane had some recollection at this point, but her entire world was now changing before her very eyes. If the dreamlike revelations were true, she now had to accept that something completely unknown—perhaps alien—had taken her in the night and performed intrusive examinations on her.

Years passed. Small snippets of memory would come and go. It was now 1974. Shane had moved to a new house with her mother in upstate New York. Shane awoke in the middle of the night, tears streaming down her cheeks. It was another dream. Whatever had happened in the dream sparked immense emotions within Shane. "In the dream, I was holding a baby," Shane recalled. "I was sitting on a couch and crying over this baby because I thought the baby was deformed in some way. It also seemed physically unusual. It had a very large head and big eyes. It was very thin as well. Sickly looking." It was at this point in the dream that Shane remembers her mother coming over to comfort her. In the dream, Shane feared this baby was dying.

But her mother reassured Shane that the baby would live. A voice in her head reassured her, just like the being in her past memory had: It's alright. You're alright.

"After that dream, and ever since, I have always had this feeling that there is another part of me out there somewhere. I can't fully explain it, but it's just this sense," Shane continued, "a sense similar to that of a mother who has given up a child for adoption. A feeling that I had an unknown family member that I was unaware of, but was somehow deeply connected to." It would be almost a decade later that another visit to the doctor would make this feeling even more apparent to Shane.

She was now married. She was also now the mother of a healthy baby boy. Soon after, she needed to have a tubal ligation. After the surgery, her doctor approached her and explained that during the operation, he had found something rather odd. "He said that he went in to do the operation, he noticed that I had neither a right ovary or fallopian tube. He had also found a tiny 'nub' on that side. He then asked me if I had ever had laser surgery, to which I told him I never had." At this point the doctor looked at her quizzically, telling her that it looked as though it was a piece left over from a laser incision of the fallopian tube. He also stated that this was the first time he'd seen something like it in his twenty-five years of medical practice. Coincidentally, this was all in the same area, albeit internally, where Shane had found the burn mark the morning after her missing time experience.

Shane left the doctor's office with more questions than answers, and the small pieces of the puzzle once thought in place were now pulling apart with each passing day. What exactly had these ominous creatures done to her? Was this some sort of breeding program? A hybridization of sorts? Abduction cases throughout the world have included reports of male and female abductees having sperm and eggs extracted from their bodies. There have even been extreme cases where female abductees have reported having been pregnant before an experience and finding themselves no longer with child afterward. Could Shane have been a part of such a program? And what exactly would be the purpose?

I wanted to know how this all affected Shane. What about this experience spoke to her the most? What drove her to dig deeper into its complexity rather than shrugging it off, or even denying its occurrence? She told me, "At first, I didn't feel that this experience had any positivity in my life. It took me many years to even admit that it had happened, much less talk about it. I wanted to believe that it could be easily explained and that I would someday find a logical, down-to-earth explanation. But I simply couldn't. So, in realizing that there are many, many others out there like me who have had similar experiences, I've found solace and comfort that I am not alone."

Comfort. Many abductees have stated similar feelings after finding others who have been subjected to the abduction phenomenon. But why had it happened? "Because of what I've been through, I find myself having far more awareness of humanity. I am also more aware of what we are doing on this planet and to our planet," Shane said. "I try to do my part in preserving and protecting our environment. Also, I find myself far more broad-minded in both my views and others' as well. I am far more open to other ways of living and opinions."

Again, I found myself also asking Shane: *Why you?* Whatever was behind the experience itself, why had it chosen you? Was it, as Claudette and Bret both believed of themselves, something within her that these beings found integral to their examinations? Was this part of their agenda? Her answer struck me: "I believe I fit what they wanted at that time. Partly, to try to conduct a kind of scientific approach on their part of us human beings here, in how we develop, grow, mate, give birth, and survive." These were all very interesting theories as to what they want. But why did they need to know these things? Why were they taking humans, against their conscious will, to conduct these extremely personal experiments? Shane responded: "Perhaps we are of help to them in some way. Maybe they are looking for potential evidence of who we are and that either they evolved from us or us from them. Or perhaps they are on some sort of 'humanitarian' mission to save us and our planet from destruction, and in essence, saving themselves as well."

No matter the case, Shane had endured lasting effects, both mentally and physically. Could the more physical symptoms of the experience have been purely coincidental, a product of nothing but Mother Nature herself? Perhaps. But as the chains of logic break link after link, one is left wondering if the coincidences of the experience, with corroboration by family, friends, and doctors, are more than pure chance.

I was both touched and shocked by Shane's story. Her detailed memories and sincerity had built a solid foundation for her to continue searching for answers to the unknown child she'd encountered. And while that path may lead to more questions, Shane took comfort and solace in that mysterious path. "I feel that I, along with the countless others who have had similar encounters and abduction experiences, were part of an extraordinary experience at the hands of another life form, whose purpose we will someday truly know. Perhaps now is not that time. But someday."

13

A MOTHER'S PRAYER

Patty Blackburn had always been an avid stargazer. She lived a normal life in the Michigan countryside, surrounded by miles of forest, Lake Michigan's shores only a mile or so from her front door. The secluded surroundings kept the night sky full of bright stars, an occasional view of the Northern Lights, and hundreds of satellites sprinkled just beyond the atmosphere. It made for some amazing sky watches in the quiet night.

Working in quality control for a multinational corporation, the stress of Patty's long, rigorous days gave way to relaxing nights at home with her family. There was nothing more calming than the vastness of the pitch-black heavens above her. But it was on the night of March 12, 2005, that Patty and her daughters would gaze at something far more extraordinary than any star or satellite. And it would set into motion a string of events so bizarre, it would shake the family to the core.

It was approximately 7:30 p.m. Patty was heading out for an evening walk to watch the stars strewn about the sky. Accompanying her were Zoe and Bonnie, her two dogs. But as she tried to lead them down to the front yard, she noticed that both dogs were acting rather unusual. Instead of following behind her, they sat on the porch, pressed up against one another as if they were scared of something. This usually only happened if a coyote was in the area. Patty scanned the surrounding woods, but saw nothing. She noticed Zoe staring at the northern sky. Patty's eyes shot upward. In the distance, she saw a huge beam of burning bright light. The beam followed the curvature of the Earth, its edges perfectly straight and defined. "It was as though someone took a curved ruler and drew two lines from the west horizon to the east horizon and filled it in with this brilliant white light," Patty told me. "I watched it for about five minutes or so, trying to figure out if it was some sort of weather anomaly or possibly a different beginning to the Northern Lights." Whatever it was, it just didn't seem to match anything she'd ever seen before. Her curiosity led her further into the yard.

The light grew brighter. So did Patty's excitement. What exactly was she looking at? Perhaps another witness could explain away what was happening. Patty retrieved her cell phone from her pocket and dialed her husband, who was inside. No answer. He'd most likely fallen asleep. She then called her son, Jeremy, who was staying at a friend's house in the city. Jeremy told her he didn't see anything, most likely due to the amount of city light pollution. Patty went so far as to call her parents, who lived about ten miles away. They told her that they too could see nothing, the trees in their location much too tall and thick to see over or through for any type of light. All this time, she kept her eyes on the light, not wanting to move, for fear that she would miss it if it disappeared. The phone calls ended with one last attempt to contact her older daughter, Jenifer, who was having a sleepover with family friends. Jenifer rushed outside, looked in the direction her mother told her to, but saw nothing. Her hope for another witness proved futile. Was Patty going crazy? Was this all in her imagination?

"What is that?" asked a voice from behind her. It was Jessica, her youngest daughter. Her husband stood directly behind Jessica. They both stared upward, just as mesmerized as Patty.

"Whatever it is, it's not from this world," her husband

responded. Patty looked at him, stunned. It was very unlike him to say something like that.

They continued staring up at the light as Jenifer and the family friends pulled up to the driveway, getting out of the car and joining. Soon, the entire group stood mesmerized. Patty recalled the following: "The beam suddenly starts getting wider and wider. We then notice the beam start moving ever so slowly southward in our direction. It was reminiscent of a scanner's light as it slowly moves across the scanner bed." Soon, the light began to get closer to the group, eventually shining directly overhead. "You could now see through it. Surprisingly you could see so much more definition and depth of everything in the sky within it than you could outside of it, almost like you were seeing everything through a gigantic massive horizontal tele-scope that scanned the sky." Trying to rationalize it, Patty attributed this to the transparent light within the beam, illumi-nating the stars. "I'm puzzled by this, though, as normally light, especially of this magnitude, should make it much harder to see anything. Let alone thousands more stars."

As many in the group retired inside to escape the chill outside, Patty and her friend stood planted, refusing to give up on finding the source of this strange anomaly. They watched as a few scattered clouds drifted in front of the beam. It suddenly disappeared.

"Look at all the lights!" her friend shouted, pointing to the southwest. Patty turned to see a flock of small red lights heading in the direction that the beam had disappeared in. "It's almost like they're following it!" the friend shouted. What were these strange red lights? Patty wondered if they could possibly be from the National Guard station. But that was more than seven miles away, and these lights were constant and didn't seem to be from any type of conventional aircraft. The two watched as the red lights faded into the clouds. And with that, the event was over. Patty went to bed that night, excited but scared. Exhaustion set in, and she finally fell asleep.

The next morning brought about an anxiousness to find answers to what had happened the night prior. Patty reached out to local airports, meteorologists, and even the sheriff's office to see if they had any sort of explanation or similar reports. She found nothing. As the rest of her family seemed to move on from the event, Patty wasn't so quick to put it to rest. Little did she know, things were about to get much more interesting.

Almost a year had passed when Patty found herself back to her calming ritual of going into the yard and looking out at the sky. Cautious now of anything out of the ordinary, she slung a camera around her neck every time she went out. Maybe another beam of light would appear and she would be able to snap a photo or two. Dogs in tow, she headed down through the front yard. Located just across the road from her front yard were acres of a farmer's field. As she looked over the field to snap some photos of the moon, something in the distance caught her attention. "What I saw was a brilliant white light in the shape of a rectangle. Its edges were rounded and smooth. At first, it appeared to be stationary. But as I watched closer, I could see that it was ever so slowly moving in my direction."

The rectangular light crept forward. Just like the beam of light she had seen prior, this one seemed to be self-illuminating, absolutely nothing around it catching any of its residual brightness. It floated closer and closer toward her. Patty's heart began to beat furiously. "It was now over a wooded area across from my home, and I could not figure out why it didn't crash or fall out of the sky. It seemed to float just above the snow-filled treetops. Soon, it was right over the field in front of me." The closer it got, the more formation the light began to take. That was when Patty realized this wasn't just a light, but a solid object. And it wasn't rectangular but triangular, three distinct points visible now. It was completely silent. Entranced by the experience, a voice inside her head knocked her out of her daze. "I said to myself... I need a witness."

Not wanting to lose sight of the triangle, Patty made a

beeline to the front door to find Jenifer passing by inside the house. Patty slowly opened the storm door to get her daughter's attention.

"Jenifer, will you please come out here?"

"What is it, Mama?" Jenifer responded.

"Fast. Come out here, would you?"

Patty ran back down into the yard, feeling the pull of curiosity inching her closer to the edge of the road. The triangle was almost directly overhead.

"A triangle! A triangle, Mom!" Jenifer yelled.

Patty turned to see her daughter standing directly behind her, staring up at the object, a look of sheer terror on her face. The triangle fixed itself directly over the family's property. Though assuming the triangle was silent at first, she could now hear a faint whooshing sound, like that of a hot air balloon when the gas lever is pulled. The low frequency remained constant.

"Can you hear that low whooshing sound?" Patty asked Jenifer. Jenifer didn't answer. Patty turned to see her covering her ears, her eyes tightly closed.

"It's so loud!" Jenifer finally responded.

Patty looked at her, confused. It was barely audible, yet her daughter could hardly bear the noise. As Patty's eyes returned to the triangle, which was now only a hundred feet or so from the ground, she began to take in every small detail: "It was an equilateral, rounded-cornered triangle. It appeared to be no more than eight feet in height. No visible engine. No wings. No appendages. No seams or bolts. Nothing. Just very smooth. There was a white glow around the triangle and what appeared to be three round white lights under each corner. Yet there was no actual light fixture or source. There was another large circular light at the base of it."

"It's so dark. So black," Jenifer said.

Patty once again looked at her, confused. "It's white," she told her daughter. "Do you see that huge bright light in the middle?"

"It's a portal," Jenifer replied.

"How do you know what it is?" Patty inquired.

"I just know," Jenifer shot back, a quiver in her voice.

Patty continued staring up. Jenifer began to back away, scared.

"I don't like this. I don't like this, Mama."

"Just keep watching," Patty told her, a rush of calmness consuming her.

With her daughter scared, Patty couldn't help but stand still, fixated on the triangle. "I suddenly felt this overwhelming euphoria, peace, calm, and love come over me. It was unlike anything I had ever felt before. I can't explain it. It was like something else was producing these feelings in me."

As Patty embraced the event, Jenifer's fear continued to escalate. The triangle began to ascend and float away from the yard. Patty's fixation broke momentarily as she registered a weight pulling on the back of her neck. "It was in that moment that I remembered, duh... I have a camera with me!" She fumbled to take the lens cap off, turned the camera on, and was able to take one quick photo of the triangle above them as it continued to move away. Although the camera's battery was full, it went black after she took the single photo. She flipped the switch on the digital camera to a video setting and continued filming the triangle until it disappeared.

"I'm going inside. Are you coming?" Jenifer asked to prompt her mother.

Patty remained stationary. She told her daughter to head inside while she stayed out another ten minutes or so. What if it returned? She had to be sure. As time passed, Patty could feel the cold, thick air piercing her skin. Disappointment crept in as she finally accepted that the event had ended. She headed into the house, exhausted.

She went to bed that night feeling completely at odds with what had happened. She knew deep down that the event was terrifying and possibly dangerous. The look on Jenifer's face alone was all the proof she needed. But for some reason, somewhere deep within herself, she wanted nothing more than to experience that sensation of euphoria that overtook her. But the next morning brought about different feelings. "The next day, I became very cold to the touch," Patty told me. "Ice cold. It lasted for a few weeks. On the flip side of this uncomfortable feeling, I also had energy like never before. I didn't need much sleep. And I didn't need to eat or drink much. I ended up losing almost fifteen pounds in the next two weeks or so." Fearing too much of a loss of appetite would drastically affect her well-being, Patty conditioned herself to eat a little bit more each day until her eating schedule returned to normal. She hoped that life would also return to some sense of normality. But after I personally spoke with her daughter Jessica, it was apparent that the strange events had only begun.

Jessica prepared for bed late one night. As she turned down the narrow hallway toward her bedroom, something caught her eye. Emerging from the open door of her sister's room was a small dark shadow. Assuming it was her sister, she moved closer. That was when she stopped cold in her tracks. "I saw this little being," she told me. "It was about three feet tall. It had a slightly disproportionately sized head to its body. There were no distinct facial features except for large black eyes, two small slits for a nose, and a single line for a mouth. Over its head was a hood connected to a robe that covered its whole body."

Their gazes met, the being staring at her with curious black eyes. "They were shining," she told me of the being's eyes. "Almost like an animal's at night when light hits them. But this being's eyes remained black, almost as if it were producing its own light." After a moment, the being quickly moved into her parents' bedroom. Still in shock, and somewhat paralyzed with fear, Jessica finally was able to react, sprinting into her bedroom and jumping into her bed. "I had cocooned myself under the covers, completely at odds with what to do. I just lay in bed, hoping it was all in my imagination." A voice suddenly called out her name.

"Jessica, just saying goodnight, honey." It was her mother. A flood of comfort rushed over her. She quickly took the covers down from her eyes to see Patty in the doorway. After having just witnessed the robed being entering her mother's room, Jessica was relieved to find that Patty hadn't seen anything. It all must have been some sort of hallucination, her mind playing tricks on her tired eyes. But it wasn't. As her mother entered the room to kiss her goodnight, something followed a few steps behind, slowly and silently. It was another strange being, unrobed and much taller than the last. Jessica shot up in the bed, unable to take her eyes off it. "The skin was grey," Jessica remembered. "Its eyes were pitch black, just like the other."

Jessica, fearing that this was all in her imagination, tried to remain calm, still questioning if this was all in her head. Her attention remained on the being, who moved throughout the room, curiously taking stock of everything. "It didn't know I was watching it. It was looking at my furniture, almost studying it. It moved toward my mother and tried to touch her back." Jessica gasped for air, not wanting it to come into contact with her mother. The being reacted, quickly taking cover behind Jessica's dresser as Patty turned and left the room. Jessica also took cover under her blankets. She could hear the faint sound of footsteps moving toward her. She closed her eyes tight, awaiting the touch of the being's hand.

"Nothing happened. I gathered the courage to peek above the covers. I looked just in time to see the being leaving the room." Jessica sat in bed, not sure what to do. Though she wanted to scream and run to her mother's room, something kept her frozen in bed. "And then that was it. I fell asleep moments later."

The next morning, Jessica told her mother about what she had seen in great detail. Completely in shock and disbelief, Patty questioned her daughter, asking why she hadn't said something while it was happening. In reference to her mother's question, Jessica admitted to me that she was completely terrified. "But I think the main reason I didn't say anything, despite my fear, was that I didn't feel that the beings were there to hurt us or anything. They were just curious. The experience itself was unexpected and most definitely different."

So what was it that Jessica believed she encountered in the hallway and bedroom that night? "I don't know what they are. Some would call them aliens, but they are simply 'beings' to me. That's how they feel to me personally." And why exactly did Jessica believe they had visited the house that night? "I do wonder why they were here, and exactly what it was they were looking for. But other than that, I prefer not to talk about it much. I'm the type of person that likes answers, so the fact that I don't have any makes me uncomfortable. So I just chose to move on with my life."

While Jessica chose to put the dramatic experience behind her, Patty just couldn't let go of the ongoing high strangeness that followed her after the initial experiences with the beam of light and the triangular craft. And as many who have had similar experiences can attest, that interest and intrigue can often lead to borderline obsession. "I'm okay with discussing other experiences that I wasn't a part of. But not my experience directly. My mom became obsessed with the experiences and would talk about them nonstop."

Whatever was happening to Patty, it seemed like these strange events had hit somewhere deep inside her. Jessica had stated that she had become obsessed. So I wanted to go back to the event that had presumably started it all, which was the triangle. As I had originally heard the story from Patty's perspective, perhaps speaking with Jenifer, who had also been present during the sighting, would shed some light on the inarguably lasting impact on all three.

Jenifer recalled a very similar timeline and narrative for what she had seen in the sky that night. But her emotional state during the event was far different. "I felt more uneasiness than anything. While watching it, I remember telling my mom I wanted to go back inside, but I did not want to leave her alone. I wanted it to be over with. I don't think it was evil, but it had an energy about it that I was nervous about."

The talk of energy intrigued me. Even Patty noted the clear distinction between her and her daughter's reactions to the craft looming overhead. It was as if the fear Jenifer was experiencing was manipulated into an almost spiritual awakening of some sort for Patty. Jenifer added, "I feel as if she was open to seeing the triangle, and because she was open to seeing it, she was open to viewing it the way they wanted her to see it. I also believe that people who are open to these experiences can be manipulated by that energy because it then calls to all energy, not just the happy, positive kinds."

That energy would follow Jenifer as she recounted several follow-up experiences that eerily connected to her younger sister's encounter. She explained to me: "The most pivotal moment for me was when I would begin having dreams about beings. I had dreams of myself and this small grey being walking down the road in front of my house. I had another dream where I saw two large oval eyes looking down at me. I'd turn to the side on my pillow, and the body of the being seemed to bend impossibly so that the eyes were staring directly into mine. One of the most dramatic dreams consisted of Jessica and I alone at a local playground. I noticed, in the distance, a tall, robed figure walking toward us. It had a hood that covered its eyes, and it carried a long stick. It finally confronted us, touched the stick against my sister's forehead, and somehow immediately put Jessica to sleep. I couldn't wake her up. This is when I was emotionally shaken out of the dream."

Dreams like these would leave Jenifer suffering many sleepless nights and trickle into many incidents of high strangeness in the home. "I began seeing shadows run around our house in the hallway by my room. There were knocks on our walls and windows. All of us experienced this. Not just me. Sometimes, when I'd lay my head down on the pillow to sleep at night, I would hear voices talking and whispering. It always sounded like a radio or television left on downstairs in the basement. We'd go down to look, but nothing would be on."

So Jenifer, albeit in a dream-state, had also encountered both these small and tall beings. Were these the same beings that Jessica claimed to have witnessed in her bedroom? Had Jessica's encounter influenced Jenifer's dreams of these curious little creatures? The fact that all three would hear strange sounds throughout the house was definitely a safety concern, and Jenifer explained how seriously her mother took this. "She wanted to see and know more about what was going on so that she could keep us safe. Never once had she ever talked about UFOs or aliens before all this. But once it started surrounding our family, she started researching everything she could. She was finding more people with things happening to them, and she'd go out of her way to talk to these people and see how they dealt with it."

As Patty opened up further to the unexplainable experiences, her daughters chose to distance themselves. Jenifer, being the older sibling, also chose not to divulge much about her dreams to her younger sister, not wanting to scare her any more than she already was. But remaining silent would only create more tension. It would eventually reach a fever pitch, and all three could no longer ignore the fact that confronting the energy was the only way they'd be able to accept it. They would finally sit down with one another and have an open discussion about all of it. "It made our family even stronger," Jenifer told me. "We were finally able to tell each other everything. At the end, when our house felt like there was just evil around it, we became more religious. We began praying to ourselves every night and realized only positive light and energy would make us feel better about what we were experiencing." Patty elaborated on this religious approach. "For me it had a definite spiritual and religious undertone to it. I have no doubt our eyes were opened to a new level. What or who 'they' are, I can't say with certainty, but I have no doubt that we are not alone."

With a flurry of both positive and negative, alien and spiritual, I wanted to know where each stood now that the events seemed to have subsided. Jessica told me she was heading off to college, ready to move on with her life and focus on her studies. But she left me with the following: "I don't know what's happening. All I know is that it's not just me, and I don't think I'll ever know until they want me to. Don't think that you know everything there is to know in this world. It's naive to believe that out of all the innumerable stars and planets in our galaxy alone, that Earth is the only one with life on it. Especially any form of intelligent life. Just accept it."

As for Jenifer, she was also moving on to a new chapter of her life. "I have since started a family and have mostly cut these experiences out of my life. I do not want to invite anything into my life, nor my son's, and have him too afraid to sleep at night like I was for a long time. I believe things are meant to be shown to people if and when they are ready. It's out of our control."

Though the events seemed to slow down, they never truly ended for Patty. Today, she continues to experience the occasional bout of strange occurrences around her. A few mystery objects also continue to plague the skies over her Michigan home. But she has slowly accepted that some things just aren't meant to be explained. "Our eyes, minds, and souls are being opened," Patty told me. "There is just so much more out there, and no matter how hard we try, I don't believe we'll ever truly be able to comprehend the complexity and depth of it all." Her final words would mirror so many others' that I've come across when explaining the impact of their experience. "These events have had an extremely profound effect on me and how I look at the world. You can't ever go back to the way things were before. It most definitely changed me."

In September 2019, I was speaking at an event in Houghton

Lake, Michigan. And while I was eager to present my research, I was more eager to meet yet another witness I'd interviewed for the book, and that was Patty. Interviewing witnesses remotely is one thing. Meeting them in person elevates the story and brings so much more nuance and humanity than mere words on a page. I remember Patty approaching me with one of the brightest smiles I'd ever encountered. We hugged without a moment's hesitation and immediately began to catch up on everything that had happened since the release of the 2016 book.

With the passage of time, thoughts and feelings morph and change. So naturally, I was curious if the same could be said for Patty. "As far as if my feelings have changed about what I and my family experienced, no. And neither have my daughters'," she told me. "We have never said that we knew with certainty what/who it is we were dealing with. We experienced so much so fast that just when we thought we could catch our breath, something else would take place, and all these events appeared to run the entire supernatural spectrum."

The spectrum of events had certainly affected Patty's entire family, especially her daughters. Was she able to discuss these experiences openly with her daughters many years later? "We experienced so much more than what was able to be told about in your book that our experiences would take a book of its own," Patty admitted. "Just when we thought, *okay, we got this*, something totally different would happen, and many times some of our events were very unnerving. We learned real quick that the more attention that was given to the phenomena, the more that would happen. Because of this, it would be hard at times for my daughters to want to talk about specific experiences and events. I knew in the back of their minds (myself included), they were wondering if talking about it might trigger something more. My daughters are adults now and have lives of their own, but the more time that has passed, they have been much more open to discussion. We've discussed our experiences sometimes, but it really depends on their mood when it arises."

The Navy UFO videos and Pentagon UFO program were popular topics of discussion at the Michigan conference where Patty and I sat and talked. And she agreed that a shift seemed to be occurring in the overall UFO conversation. How did this affect Patty, someone who'd been thrown in the middle of an unexplained hurricane of phenomena? Patty told me: "The past few years of announcements and revelations have brought the topic forward, and though it's had its pros and cons, at least it's moving the topic into the mainstream, which has definitely opened up the conversation." However, Patty explained that "... there is so much more work to be done in that area. Who knows what tomorrow will bring? But I would like to think that an official announcement of historic significance and worldwide status would be forthcoming. For that to happen, it is going to take many at the very top level that are in the know who just finally say *enough is enough*. They will need to be honest and forthcoming with undeniable proof and just say either it's ours, another country's, nothing man-made/terrestrial from Earth, or all of those. They need to just do it. The world deserves to know the truth... good or bad."

So with her collective experiences behind her, and undoubtably more to come, I wanted to know what was most important to Patty when it came to telling her story then and reflecting on it now. "There is so much more in the world than we can ever even begin to remotely imagine. No one knows for certain who/what all is among us. I, as a person, have changed as a result of all that has taken place. I can never go back to the person I was before, nor can I ever look at the world the same as I did before. I'm not supposed to. None of us are. Nor would I want to."

One of the biggest questions I always have for witnesses and experiencers is if they felt they were chosen to experience these events or if it was completely random. And every individual has a unique and personal answer. Or they had *no* answer. And while many struggle to find meaning in their experiences, Patty's conviction was palpable: "Our experiences were intended for us and any witnesses that were there were for confirmation, at the same time opening their eyes to the subject. The chain of events that took place was uncanny. It was not simply coincidence, nor was I or my family just in the right place at the right time. The events were deliberate, calculated, intentional, for us and the other witnesses. Each event was meant to play out the way it did. There are *no* coincidences. Synchronicity... yes. Coincidences? No."

Witnesses and experiencers often seek closure or vindication. Deep down, I was searching for that myself. Throughout every interview I'd conducted, I was recording the events of those who'd felt the way I did at one point or another. *We* wanted answers. And though each experience was vastly different and the subjectivity remained constant, it was comforting to find an unspoken connection between every person I'd spoken to throughout the process of my own research. And that connection was no more apparent than when I looked Patty in the eyes and thanked her for coming forward and for her unflinching vulnerability and honesty throughout it all. Patty's final words matched the sincerity she had always had, and would continue to have, moving forward in her own journey. "My family and I understand that there will always be those that may question not only our experiences but *us*, as well as the phenomena itself. But we have nothing to hide nor anything to fear. We can't deny what we have experienced. It is what it is. It happened. And all we and/or anyone can do, is to face it head-on and tell the truth, hoping that one day we will get the truth revealed to us all. It will help not only ourselves, but everyone else in understanding as well. Everything is connected. We are all one."

14

A WEEKEND IN THE WOODS

It was late March of 2015. Winter had officially turned to spring, but you wouldn't be able to tell from the frigid temperatures plaguing the east coast. Jane and I rode the train upstate from New York City to Saranac Lake, a beautiful town tucked snugly into the Adirondack mountains. We had been craving a weekend away from the city for months now, having suffered a very harsh winter that didn't seem to be letting up any time soon. As the train chugged its way out of Manhattan, the ride gradually became a sight to behold. Endless stretches of frozen lakes and snow-filled pine trees surrounded us like a Colorado winter.

We'd been invited by a close friend and colleague, Mike Clelland, to join him and a few others for a weekend of rest, relaxation, and friendly conversation. Mike had recently moved from the Rockies to New York State, taking up residence in a cozy bed-and-breakfast run by his partner, Andrea. With skiing and hiking season winding down, the town truly served up the dead silence we had yearned for. The bed-and-breakfast, appropriately named the Doctor's Inn, had once housed many physicians who treated tuberculosis patients at a nearby sanatorium. Now the sanatorium sat vacant, its iron gate rusted open and its many buildings rotting away from years of abandonment. This was going to be an interesting stay indeed.

The Doctor's Inn, experiencing its slowest time of the year, would fill its current vacancies with our company. Greeting us upon arrival was Spazzy, a creme-colored feline with stunning black eyes. She timidly welcomed us with nudges and barely audible purrs. Welcomes in the human category began with Lee, an energetic Brit who flew in from London. A bit closer to home, Rachel, a young woman from the suburbs of New Jersey, also joined us. Andrea, with a warm smile, took our coats and made us feel like we'd just walked into a family gathering.

Besides Jane and me, everyone in the house had met at an event in Portland, Maine, in September 2014. The event, called "Experiencers Speak," included about a dozen individuals from around the world speaking out about their experiences. Mike had met Andrea at this event, and a romance blossomed almost immediately. Rachel, hesitant to attend this particular event after her friend dropped out, mustered the courage to drive north by herself and attend. There, she met the other three individuals who now stood before us. Lee, claiming no direct experiences with UFOs or alien presences, had always been fascinated by the topic and had impulsively attended the Maine event.

We arrived just as dinner was being prepared. I was immediately put on preparation duty for the food. Mike wanted me to peel and mince garlic, something I had never done before. Having just bragged about making dinner for Jane a few night's prior, Mike jokingly scoffed at my ineptitude. I laughed, a sense of ease rushing over me. Knowing I was in a house of experiencers was rather intimidating, but not knowing how to mince garlic in front of a seasoned cook was definitely a modest crush to my ego. As I continued following Mike's instructions, I began to realize that I wasn't an outsider observing these individuals as subjects for a book. I was here as a friend and to eat home-cooked meals, something rare in my daily routine. Everything else would have to wait.

As I watched Mike prepare a bowl of spices, I began to remember when I had first met him a few years prior. Although we'd previously communicated online several times, we'd yet to converse face-to-face. That all changed in 2013 in Phoenix, Arizona, when we met at the International UFO Congress, the largest UFO conference in North America. We'd spend the next week running into one another and having impromptu conversations lasting late into the night. Throughout those conversations, Mike's highly viewed blog, Hidden Experience, would come up many times. I'd spent many sleepless nights pouring over this blog, and it was rewarding to finally put a face to the words.

Mike was a life-long experiencer who chronicled his events in great detail on Hidden Experience. He would introduce the blog on the homepage of his website as such: "This was a time when I was swallowed up in a sort of existential crisis. The blog originally started as a way for me to try and make sense of some weird personal experiences. I did it as a kind of sociological experiment. I wanted to wrestle with some challenging memories in a very public forum. But, as time went on, I started adding other content, things I found interesting or relevant to the core topics."

The sociological experiment was indeed working, as hundreds of new readers began visiting the blog site every week, and other experiencers came forward to tell their own stories. Mike had opened the doors for many individuals, and even found connections to others that would aid him in his personal journey to find answers.

One of the first entries I had come across was an event that happened to Mike when he was twelve years old. The year was 1974, and he was living in a quiet suburb of Detroit, Michigan. After attending a football game at the local high school, he and a friend made the leisurely half-mile trek home by foot, taking in the pleasant autumn air. "We were in front of a house where an elementary school friend lived at the time," Mike recalled.

Just as they had passed the house, a sudden flash of orange light lit up the entire sky. "It was bold and jarring," he remembered. "It felt like someone just flipped a switch, and the sky lit up and then went back to normal. As soon as it happened, it was gone. It was completely silent. We were surprised and both responded with, 'What just happened?'"

Mike and his friend parted ways, still shaken by the sudden flash of light. When he finally made it home, Mike noticed something even stranger. "I was excited to get home and watch a television show I really loved that started at 10 p.m. I remember having left the football game in order to get home in plenty of time so I could watch the show." But just as Mike entered his home, his parents were waiting for him, upset. Mike, assuming he had arrived home around 9:30 p.m., was shocked when his parents told him it was now 11 p.m. Where had the last hour and a half gone? It was as if the time had been completely stripped from his memory.

When Mike returned to school the following Monday, he sat with a group of friends in the cafeteria. They huddled around him as he began to explain the strange burst of light he had witnessed. His friend, who'd shared the experience, chimed in eagerly as he joined the group.

"It was a UFO, with lights and everything!"

Mike sat, confused. *I didn't see anything with lights*, he thought to himself. *Did he see something I hadn't?* He replayed that bright flash in his mind, the smoldering colors burned into his memory. But no UFO. Feeling almost a sense of jealousy that he hadn't witnessed a solid object, Mike remained quiet, the event simmering in his mind for many years to follow. Could a UFO, as his friend had described, have been responsible for the apparent missing time Mike had experienced as he stepped foot into his home that night? This would be one of the first major events Mike experienced. But it most certainly was not the last.

"So I thought maybe after dinner we'd all sit by the fire and share some stories," Mike said to me, placing a few items of food in the oven. My mind returned to the kitchen, the smell of fresh spices hitting me. A burst of laughter from the living room filled the cabin. Things were turning light as Lee entered the kitchen, having hit the punchline of a joke Mike and I had clearly missed out on. He prepared English tea for everyone. He handed us both a cup, heading back into the living room to entertain an attentive crowd.

I could faintly hear Jane in the other room, her warm, familiar laugh assuring me she was opening up to this new group of people just as I was. Months earlier, she had agreed to be my editor for this book. I had read several sociological papers she'd written and was impressed with her attention to detail, expansive insight, and solid grasp of grammar. This, besides her unconditional support, compelled me to invite her to this weekend getaway with Mike and the group. Being very interested in the UFO topic, Jane was also curious what the aftermath held for those who'd had experiences. So it made perfect sense to invite her along not only as my partner, but to glimpse into the everyday lives of these seemingly normal people with extraordinary experiences.

As Mike moved a heaping pile of noodles from colander to pot, I could see Spazzy creeping her head around the corner of the dining room doorway. Her nose and eyes shot up, looking at me with a sense of urgency. The activity in the house was clearly more than she was used to. She stayed in the doorway, her deep, orbital eyes bouncing my reflection back at me. I stared at her for a moment, those eyes reminding me of another experience Mike once detailed in his blog.

It was February of 1993. Mike was now thirty-one years old and living in rural Maine. As he lay in bed that winter evening, a bright light began to illuminate his bedroom window. This wasn't that uncommon, for the mere fact that a motion sensor light had been set up to catch any sudden movement approaching the house. The most common culprits were cars passing by, or the occasional deer wandering off the beaten path.

Mike, fully aware of the extreme sensitivity of the motion light, did not think much of it, but as he propped himself up and looked out the window, it was clear that this wasn't the sensor light. And it most definitely wasn't a deer.

Backlit by a small unknown light source, five small figures stood on top of the snow, walking toward the house. These figures, in Mike's own words, were "spindly entities that had very skinny bodies and big black eyes." These entities drew closer. One would assume that in this situation, he might hop out of bed, attempt to call for help, or even approach the possible threat. But his actual response surprised even him: "I nonchalantly laid my head down on the pillow and promptly fell back asleep. I felt absolutely empty of emotion," Mike explained. "It was almost as if I was somehow controlled. Like, Oh yes, they're here. Let's just shut down and black out."

While his first experiences was undoubtedly steeped in reality, Mike struggled for some time with this memory of 1993 and the entities on the lawn. According to him, it all could have just been a dream. But one that seemed all too real. "I saw something, but at the same time I truly do not think it happened in this reality," Mike explained in his blog entry. "That may sound hard to grasp, but it is the only way I can honestly depict the experience." This sense of a dreamlike state was eerily similar to that of Claudette and Shane, two of our previous experiencers. Mike would awake the next morning remembering the experience vividly, but unable to shake the feeling that whatever had happened, it was leading down a road that he couldn't seem to navigate logically.

"Maybe tomorrow, you and Jane can head down to Lake Placid. We'll give you the car." I snapped back to my current reality, a delicious aroma in the room hitting me all at once. Dinner was almost ready. I smiled and nodded, seeing Spazzy's tail sweep along the doorframe as she disappeared from sight. Mike headed into the dining room to help set the table. I trailed behind for a moment, now noticing the bright glare of the ceiling light shining down on me. I stared into it, remembering one of the most intriguing of Mike's experiences to date.

It was May of 2010. Mike was now living in Idaho. A close friend of his, Natascha, flew in from Germany to explore the beautiful canyons and sandstone of the surrounding areas in Colorado. He would meet up with her to join in on a two-week camping trip. Late into the trip, the brakes on Mike's car began to give out. Fearing danger, they found themselves in an auto repair shop in the small town of Cortez. They learned that it would be a few days before the proper parts could be shipped. This prompted Mike and Natascha to spend the night camping in the nearby town of Dolores. "We chose a secluded spot with an old fire ring and some broken beer bottles. Perfect for our camping needs," Mike recalled in his blog. They pitched their tent, crawled into their sleeping bags, and soon drifted off to sleep.

It was in the dead of night that Mike was abruptly awakened by a harsh shriek coming from Natascha. "My instantaneous response was to bolt upright and scream with an intensity that would be hard to describe," Mike explained. "I was screaming in fear, sure enough, but it was also a primal outburst of defense." He switched on the headlamp above him, immediately asking Natascha what had happened. She couldn't respond, frozen in the upright position. "Tell me the first thing that comes to your mind. Don't think, just tell me what happened," Mike said to her. She looked at him, wide-eyed, and answered with trepidation.

"I saw a face."

Panic welled in him. What Mike said next to her was completely unlike him. "Look, if we need to, we can just leave... right now. We can leave the tent set up and just drive to town and get a hotel room."

Natascha looked at Mike, desperation following her words. "Do you believe in evil ghosts?" she asked.

"No," he responded, more out of an urge to comfort than

sheer honesty. He moved a bit closer, putting an arm around her. They lay in the tent, their breathing slowly returning to normal. "I ended up chanting a repetitive mantra in my head," Mike remembered. "Love and Light, Love and Light, Love and Light." Their close proximity to one another was all they had as they both finally fell asleep, hoping that the night would soon be over. But it wasn't.

"Later that same night I had a vivid dream," Mike explained. "It took place inside the same tent with no dreamlike distortion. It was curiously void of any emotion, good or bad." What he saw in the dream would leave him completely at odds with what was real and what wasn't. "I saw a big round mandala figure up and to my left, situated in a very specific point in the tent. It was a simple circle, about the size of a large pizza, with a lone dot in its center." As Mike took stock of what he was seeing, something strange began to happen. "I was floating up off the floor of the tent. The elevator-up sensation of slowly rising. I thought to myself, 'I need to remember this... I need to remember this...'" As the sensation of floating upward continued, Mike recalled something else rather vivid about the dream. "The environment of the tent changed to a backdrop of white light. I thought, 'Am I on a table?' I didn't understand where I was. It was a mysterious realm with a uniform white glow around me."

The dream abruptly ended when Mike heard Natascha's voice. She nonchalantly remarked, "Mike, you are floating." Though the words were clear, whether she had said this in reality or merely in the dream was another point of contention in Mike's recollection. No matter the case, those words seemed to pull Mike back down to the ground both in the dream and in the tent. Upon waking the next morning, Mike and Natascha immediately began to try to make some sense of what had occurred.

"I saw a face within a circle," Natascha told Mike. The circle, she went on to explain, was strikingly similar to the mandala image Mike had seen in his dream. "This was very curious,"

Mike commented. "She didn't know about my dream yet. I asked where the face was positioned. At the time, I assumed it was directly over her, centered above her face." But Natascha broke that assumption, pointing up and off to her left in the tent. "It was exactly where I saw the glowing circle in my dream," Mike explained. The two would spend the morning discussing the entire event, trying to make sense of it all.

"What actually might have happened is very difficult to say," Mike added. "I cannot dismiss the immense fear that overcame both of us. This feeling of terror was entirely different than any emotion I have ever experienced, amplified in a way that seems extraordinary." The nature of Mike's dream, vivid in ways he couldn't fully put into words, was strikingly similar to Natascha's reaction when she'd seen the face in the tent. Pure terror.

"Dinner is ready!" Mike proclaimed to us all. We took our seats at the table. The rest of the group joined us. We opened a bottle of wine, passed around the various plates of food, and drifted in and out of one another's various conversations. I couldn't help but veer my attention toward Rachel. She had been noticeably quiet the entire night, and my curiosity got the best of me. I impulsively interrupted the conversation.

"Rachel, would you be comfortable sharing your experiences with us?"

She sighed and finally spoke. "The first experience I can remember was when I was a child."

For the next half hour, Rachel opened up to us about her startling experiences. While not being able to record or take notes in the moment, I asked her to convey these experiences through email correspondence a few weeks later. She bravely agreed.

Like many young children, Rachel found herself afraid of the dark. She would often sleep on the floor in her parents' bedroom. They didn't mind much, knowing that she would outgrow the fear. But it was in the wake of her first experience that the fear would not only remain, but intensify.

It was in the middle of the night when she awoke, her heart pounding. She sensed something in the room. She could faintly see something peeking out from the side of her father's dresser. As she lay on the floor, she could feel something lightly tugging at her legs. Frozen with terror, she soon blacked out. She awoke in the morning, assuming it was all some horrible nightmare that would fade. But whatever it was that she saw and felt was making an extremely uncomfortable home within her dreams and in the cold, hard reality of her life.

"On another occasion, while sleeping in the same room, I had an episode of paralysis where I was struggling to get a grip on it. I could sense something in the room again and tried desperately to get my parents' attention to no avail." Rachel awoke the next morning and confronted her father in a fit of anger, wondering why he hadn't done anything if he'd heard her panicking from this apparent reoccurring nightmare. He told her that he didn't do anything because he was afraid. "I was shocked," she remembered feeling after his response. "I couldn't believe he said that. And I certainly couldn't even wrap my head around my father telling me he was afraid of anything, let alone acknowledging that what was happening was real."

Whatever that reality was, it was deeply affecting Rachel in ways she was yet to fully understand. Was this merely a spell of sleep paralysis? Night terrors? She struggled with these notions. "At that point, I think I was still trying to explain it away as dreams. Really bad dreams. You try so hard to hold onto the idea of this all not being real, chalking it up to having some serious phobias. Thinking you're crazy is almost more comforting than believing there are aliens in the house at night."

The thought that an unknown and possibly nonhuman intelligence was visiting her in the night was something she wrestled with on a daily basis. Would this be the night it would happen again? Would she be helpless against its intrusion? Unfortunately for Rachel, things only seemed to escalate. "It was in my preteen years that I would wake up with twigs and leaves in my bedsheets," she explained, though she had no recollection of ever having been outside. "My father once accused me of sneaking out at night. I thought that it was completely ridiculous being that I couldn't even look out of the windows if it was dark at night." It was in these years that the visits in both her parents' room and her own seemed to be most frequent. She would wake from the paralyzing feeling time and time again. These bouts with what she believed to be sleep paralysis left her suffering extreme insomnia, afraid that there was much more to the experiences than met the eye. "I would try to stay up all night reading and usually fall asleep when the sun came up. Honestly I don't know how I functioned."

As time passed, Rachel tirelessly fought with the mysterious presence that creeped in and out of her life. She would try so hard to ignore it, but it seemed to always thrive on the periphery, almost begging to be seen. One night, she woke up to the tail end of a bright white light consuming the room. She felt like she was floating above her own body. The white light lingered for just a moment longer and then blinked out completely. Snippets of small figures would pass by her vision for years to come, which turned the fear somewhat normal but never completely manageable.

She was now thirty and living in the outskirts of New Jersey. "It was a farming community with a lot of open space. I live on the side of an interstate, which gives me a completely false sense of security. I hear the cars and trucks passing by at night and am comforted by the noise." Although the ambient noise comforted her when she slept, it didn't stop the experiences from occurring. "I have woken up to what I thought was a shoulder turning into the wall in the bedroom. It was a brownish grey."

She continued with another experience. "Another time, I woke up on the couch in a very dreamy slow-motion state with one of my cats being shoved in my face so I couldn't see around her. What I saw was the very top of a hairless head. That's it. I can't remember if I was awake from that point or if I woke up again."

Perhaps one of the most disturbing experiences that Rachel recalled was when she was lying in bed one night and could sense something underneath her bed. "I could feel a pair of hands reach out from underneath me, and then having the hands inside my body, moving my organs around." When I asked her why she felt this was occurring, she stated, "I believe they wanted to get something from me." What that was, Rachel was not entirely sure. She also felt an extreme sense of fear before each experience. "It's like a wall of force that is pushing against you as you are pushing back to remain with it when all you want to do is just fucking rail against it and lose your shit."

Whatever was happening to Rachel, it was clear that it was severely affecting her everyday life. The constant feeling of something just around the corner or in the dark, watching her, its motives ominously unclear, would make anyone feel at least a bit paranoid. Even worse was not knowing exactly what it was or what it wanted. All she knew was that it was hiding in the night, waiting for its moment to sneak into her dreams and possibly into her reality. Whatever this truly was, one thing was clear. Rachel was scared. And that fear was slowly eating away at her. And as we sat at the table that night and listened to her tell her story, tears began to run down her cheeks, a slight tremble in her hand as her fingernails tapped the tabletop. I looked at Mike, whose gaze was so intent on Rachel that it was clear he too had known these feelings of fear and helplessness before. We all sat in silence, with nods of gratitude to Rachel for sharing.

The long day of traveling and the flood of stories being shared was taking its toll on my tired mind. We moved to the living room, drinking tea around the fireplace, making lighter conversation to cap the night off. Jane and I found ourselves saying goodnight and heading to bed.

I awoke to the sound of tapping. It almost sounded identical to that of Rachel's fingernails on the dining room table. But this was behind me. Glass. On the window in our room. We were on the second floor of the house, though. What could possibly be tapping? A tree branch? A heavy snowfall? Whatever it was, it awoke me abruptly. I glanced over at Jane, who was usually a light sleeper. But in this moment of sheer panic that I couldn't fully describe, I watched her sleep deeper than I'd ever seen before. My eyes shot to the window, and as I tried to sit up, something stopped me from looking out the window. I felt paralyzed with fear. My eyes moved to the closed door of the bedroom. A shadow moved past the faint light that poured in from underneath. Something was definitely behind the door.

"Jane?" I inquired in a whimper.

No answer.

I looked under the door again. The light remained, but no bouncing shadows. The tapping creeped in again. I had listened to the stories from Mike, Rachel, and so many others, yet I'd always shied away from the possibility that anything like what they had experienced could happen to Jane and me, save my dramatic, but not traumatic, childhood sighting. But as I sat straight up in that bed, staring into the darkness, my mind began to swirl with what could be outside that window. I could feel sweat dripping from my brow. I felt alone in the universe, everything closing in on me. Whatever was outside that window, I knew that by facing it, I'd never be the same.

Finally, I gathered a shred of courage, battling with the possibility that by pulling the curtain aside and looking beyond the glass, I might stare into the eyes of something I didn't want to accept. Perhaps it would be an extension of a dome-shaped craft, or a triangular formation. Perhaps a swirling ball of energy. Or worse, it could be the fingertips of a chalk-colored being, or a pale grey figure, its black eyes staring back at me. Whatever it was, I wanted to know. I needed to know for my own sake and perhaps even my own sanity. It was in that moment that a small part of me felt a deep connection to Rachel. That fear of the unknown. Whatever lurked in the shadows didn't care what I felt or how I'd react. It would just happen and I'd have no control over it. My sweaty palm moved toward the curtain and slowly pulled it aside. I peered hesitantly through the window.

Nothing.

A sense of relief flooded over me. I let out an audible sigh, which woke Jane up. She turned toward me and whispered, "Is everything okay?"

I didn't know how to answer. I let the curtain fall and sat silent. Was I okay? Was this all a figment of my imagination? All I knew was that I'd never felt such intense fear in my life. I simply nodded to Jane, rolled on my side away from the window, and stared at her as she fell back asleep. I longed for that state and tried with all my might to fall asleep, awaiting the bright morning ahead more than ever before. It was around 3 a.m. that I finally drifted off.

We awoke the next morning to a fantastic breakfast. As I sipped my morning coffee, I saw Spazzy peeking out from beyond a potted plant. Her eyes were as deep as the night before, though she looked at me with comfort. She clearly had warmed up to us as guests, and my severe allergies to cats seemed to stay at bay for the time being. A pair of keys suddenly hit the table next to me. Mike made good on his promise, letting us borrow his car for the afternoon. He suggested we head to Lake Placid, once home to the 1980 Winter Olympics. I graciously accepted the offer, wanting to shake whatever had happened in the bedroom the night prior with some local sightseeing.

We arrived at Lake Placid to an array of local shops boasting hot chocolate, maple fudge, and cider donuts. We absorbed the beautiful landscape around us as young children skated and played hockey on the frozen water. Jane spotted a truck that held several snow dogs in its bed. I watched her beam as she tried to pet them. I felt a warmth from her excitement, but something deep down in the pit of my stomach wouldn't let the fear of the previous night fully subside. I kept getting flashes of something outside the window, and the shadows moving under the door. We headed toward the lake as I pushed the thoughts further back into my mind.

We found ourselves walking straight onto the water, a flurry of soft snow brushing past us in every direction. It brought me back to many winters growing up in Syracuse, New York, where snowfall would often reach my chest. It also brought memories of more innocent times in my life as I caught sight of the children sliding across the ice with their used and tattered hockey sticks. I felt a huge sense of gratitude and fortune for friends like Mike, Andrea, Rachel, and Lee. Not only had Mike and Andrea given us their car for the day, but they had invited us into their home to hear their stories. It was in that moment when the darkness of the night before began to dissipate once and for all. As I watched Jane climb a large mountain of snow that had collected on the ice, I felt a calming sensation rush over me. And that's when I realized that whatever was outside the window that night no longer had a hold on me.

Day slowly turned to night as we headed back to the Doctor's Inn for dinner with a special guest. Tom, a close friend of Mike and Andrea, joined our group. Tom, as we learned, was from a nearby area known as Tupper Lake. There was also something rather unique about him. He was a practicing shaman. Having never met a shaman in person, I wasn't exactly sure what to expect. But I can honestly say that Tom wasn't it. He had the grizzled, yet well-groomed, look of a professional woodsman, topped off with a healthy white beard and tattoos wrapped intricately around his forearms. He reminded me more of a biker than a spiritual practitioner who used altered states of consciousness to interact with the spirit world. But the weekend had surely opened my mind already, and I wasn't going to let it stop now.

Just as with the night prior, conversations ran the gamut. As Lee, Jane, and I listened intently to Tom explain his work as a shaman, I could see a troubled look on Rachel's face. She appeared tired. When prompted, she admitted to us that she'd had a really tough time falling asleep the past few nights, sensing that the beings were still visiting her, even on this weekend retreat. That was when she asked Tom something I'd heard many other experiencers ask: How do I stop these experiences from happening?

I felt it inappropriate to record Tom's answers that night. Rachel's emotional and vulnerable state was palpable, and it was clear that this moment was for her and her alone. But I contacted Tom several weeks later to ask him what he recalled from that night and to again relate the vital information he had imparted to us all. I first asked him about what he believed was happening to Rachel, according to her descriptions of the beings she witnessed and the fearful experiences she continued to endure. He stated the following on the beings: "In my opinion the aliens are entities from other worlds sharing the shamanic worlds with us. I think the shamanic worlds are possibly 'community property' accessed by several different physically manifested energies. It's not uncommon to encounter other life forms in the shamanic worlds. It's a richly inhabited environment. So crossing paths with 'aliens' has a high probability."

But what did Tom believe was the true nature of these specific beings that Rachel briefly encountered? What about their presence scared her so much? Tom replied:

"All of us have guides around us, working for our good and observing our lives. The guides interact with people open to seeing them, but they also interact with people only partially open to them. This makes for interesting interactions. If a guide gets insistent with guidance, if it refuses to not be seen and continues to be a presence impossible to ignore, the consciousness will frame it in something familiar when expressing it. If we are fearful at the time, then the expression will probably be fearful in its interpretation. I feel Rachel's guides are trying to get her attention over something important to her, and they keep coming back because they have failed to deliver the message."

What this message was, Rachel was not quite sure, as it never seemed to come through in a way she could comprehend or accept. Was it, as Tom had mentioned, clouded by the immense fear the experiences often harbored? Tom explained why this is so often the case with many who have had experiences like Rachel's:

"My thoughts on abductions is that some, not all, but certainly some, are people slipping into shamanic journeys without training, unaware they are journeying. They find themselves in a place unfamiliar, and the consciousness of the individual tries to frame the new experiences into familiar forms such as nightmares or abductions. Walking shamanic worlds without any training can be daunting and scary. Fear does strange things to us, and we often respond with fear when things are unknown. The entities one sees in the shamanic worlds are rarely in human form. What one runs across is often bizarre or strange looking to us. Rather than find out what the entity wants or is, we draw away and awake with a fear-filled experience of an 'alien.'"

And while Tom's observations may or may not have shed some glimmering light on what Rachel had been dealing with, it didn't fully put her at ease. It only opened the door to more questions. How does one keep a level head and begin to alleviate the constant fear? Tom's response to this question struck me most, and by the look on Rachel's face that night, it seemed like it had reached her as well:

"All experiences are different and all solutions are different. Some people come ready to let go of the event, while others have it so immersed in their being that it becomes a part of their identity, a feeling that by letting it go, they will lose themselves. Every instance will have emotions attached to it, raw and fresh, easily feeling like it will overpower the individual. We think we have a finite ability to embrace emotions, but the reality is that we have the ability to embrace emotions far deeper than we usually do. Fear holds us back. In that feeling lies our humanity and our reason to be here. These experiences are opportunities for each of us to move into a new way of being, one with little or no fear, and with a level of emotional depth few could imagine for themselves. It's a place of our true power."

There was a distinct moment when I could visibly see a rush of relief overtake Rachel as she sighed and wiped tears away. The thought that she could potentially have control over these experiences gave her hope. It would be condescending to suggest that she hadn't sought different ways to try to deal with her experiences. But Tom's words only solidified her progression in knowing that not only was she not alone, but that she could focus on the positives in her life rather than dwelling on the fear that these beings would return. "I will continue to try to focus on me and my soul's journey," she told me. "Maybe over time, I'll have more insight into this and the reason. But really, I'd be happy if they left me alone. I hope to fill my life with happiness and surround myself with positive people on a level that these fear-inducing beings can't touch."

As our final and most emotional dinner concluded that night, I found myself battling with my heavy eyelids, hesitant to go to sleep. Whatever had happened the night before had clearly affected me on a visceral level. The very thought of encountering something similar to what Rachel, Mike, or so many others had seen was almost too terrifying to consider. Reluctantly, I wished everyone a good night and headed upstairs to bed. Jane, who had retired earlier, was already fast asleep as I crawled into bed. The window suddenly caught my eye, and my heart began to pound.

As I lay there, I began to think about Tom's message. No matter what was behind the glass of the window, I had complete control over what it was and what it made me feel. If it wanted to give me a message, it was up to me to let that happen. I opened the curtain wide and stared out, the faint sound of wind and snow hitting the glass. I stared and stared and stared. Nothing seemed to be happening. I turned in bed to face Jane, watching the moonlight hit her in a most brilliant way. She slept peacefully, a faint smile on her face. An immediate rush of comfort and happiness consumed me. And no matter what was or wasn't out there in the dark, it couldn't compete with the light I felt in that moment. I had controlled the fear, and I knew that deep down, Rachel was beginning to do the same. That night, I slept more soundly than I had in a very, very long time.

We said goodbye to Lee and Rachel early the next morning as they made the long drive back to New Jersey. Lee would be spending a few days in New York City, so we knew full well it wouldn't be the last we'd see of him. As for Rachel, I didn't know when I'd ever see her again. But through her experiences, she'd taught me that no matter the level of intensity of an experience, it was possible to move on with one's life. This was something I wished for her more than anything.

We arrived to the train station just in time. Andrea and Mike hugged us goodbye. It had been a weekend of laughs, cries, and everything in between. What Mike had done by bringing us all together was something truly special. It was a weekend of sharing without any prompting, pressure, or presumptions. And it had certainly changed all of us in many ways. It was the beginning of friendships and the strengthening of others. And as we pulled out of the train station, I knew that whatever the message was that these phenomena were trying to convey, it was getting much louder the more I engaged in the lives of those having the experiences. And perhaps I was engaging more openly with the phenomena as well.

Mike's experiences were far from over, and in 2019, along with Andrea, he had a very interesting UFO sighting. At about 6:30 p.m. on April 25, they were driving toward Providence, Rhode Island, for a small weekend UFO conference. But it seemed they didn't even have to go far to get the full experience. Mike recalled that while traveling on the highway approaching

Providence, "We both saw an odd thing in the sky. My first thought was that it was a partially inflated balloon, or a thin sheet of plastic that was floating in an updraft. What I first saw seemed lumpy and irregular, like a giant potato chip. It was grey in the partially overcast sky. My first thought was that it was just a small dark cloud, but it stood out differently than a cloud would."

Deducing that it was much too dark to be a cloud, they continued driving while trying to also get a better look at what this object could be. "We were heading southeast on Highway 146, and the road twists and turns through sections of trees and buildings. We would lose sight of it, and it would reappear when our car came around a corner for a view. After a while it seemed to change shape. It now looked like a slightly curved 'credit card' and we were seeing it from a side angle, so it seemed very thin. I sensed it was slowly rotating, so when it reached its thinnest orientation, it seemed to disappear—then it would rotate just a bit more and would pop back into view. The rotation was an eerie slow motion, and didn't seem to match how something big might be effected by the wind."

Stuck now in traffic, there wasn't much they could do. Andrea attempted to snap a photo, but wasn't able to capture anything. Mike also noted a strange detail about the object. "This floating grey thing was positioned directly under a single dot in the sky. I kid you not, it looked like a credit card hanging from a pin by an invisible fishing line!" So while this odd display certainly caught their attention and they hoped to see it more clearly, they eventually turned a corner, lost sight of the object, and it never reappeared.

Knowing Mike and the intricate connections he always made with events like this, I was of course filled with excitement to hear what he had to say next: "This happened to two experiencers in a car, on the way to the home of two experiencers, and all of them would spend the next few days at a UFO conference." It most definitely was an encounter that seemed all too perfect. And while it was certainly compelling, Mike was very tempered in the power he gave each experience. "There has been a steady *hum* of synchronicity and odd life events. I've been in the eye of this hurricane for a long time, and I've gotten better at keeping my balance. I'm a lot more stable than I was a decade ago. The amount of synchronicity has been plentiful and consistent, and I trust this as a way to keep me on this path." This would be yet another piece in the large swath of unexplainable events that touched Mike's life, and paved the path ahead in many ways.

Mike had always had a deep fascination with owls. Throughout his many years as an avid outdoorsman and experiencer, he made many connections with owls either preceding or following a UFO event. This has been a major observation by many who have seen everything from simple lights in the sky to having contact with what they consider nonhuman intelligences. Mike took it upon himself to document these stories, and has become an authority on the connections between owls and UFOs. In fact, he's written three extensive books about these connections, collectively totaling over a thousand pages of material. "Real people are having real experiences with UFOs, and there are symbolic elements that show up within these stories. The owl is more than just a bird with big eyes—it is a symbol. Mankind has been having powerful experiences with owls all throughout our history; there is nothing new about the stories in my books. I'm certain our ancestors were confronting owls while we were still in caves, and this is the source of the folklore and mythology surrounding owls. Yet we are no longer in a place where we can look to these myths for the support and comfort they once provided; we dismiss them as meaningless fables. These experiences are still happening, but we are adrift— unable to find any meaning."

Meaning was something Mike had always given any experience he'd ever had. It was a trait I'd always envied, and taught me how special and powerful a subjective experience can truly be. It was comforting to know that not only did he grow from his experiences, but he continued to give meaning to something most would simply shrug off or flat-out deny in their lives. "I would argue that the modern UFO story is the same recurring narrative that has been woven into our ancient legends. We are still confronting gods and angels, but the togas have been replaced by tight, shiny space suits. I'm convinced that the source of our mythologies are still alive, and owls are still performing their vital role. They are the messenger between our world and that *other* world. The UFO is a challenge to how we think, and how we face up to ourselves. Any thoughtful person who has seen a UFO will, on some deeper level, be *transformed* by the event. The owl can be seen as the totem of the transformational experience. This haunting bird has a minor role on the grand stage of the UFO mystery, yet the unknown scriptwriter must have created its part for a reason."

So the next time you see a UFO, keep an eye out for those nocturnal creatures. Or, if you see an owl, keep an eye out for those elusive objects in our skies. Maybe, just maybe, you can add to the script being written before our very eyes, and we can finally find that reason Mike and so many others continue to search for.

15

THE OUTSIDE LOOKING IN

No matter how hard I tried to examine experiencers' lives before the event or focus on their state of being throughout it, it always came back to what happened post-experience. Having spent that weekend in the woods, I knew that even facing the fear of the unknown didn't change the fact that those who'd had experiences were staring into a mirror that reflected back nothing but confusion, contention, and sometimes obsession.

Most of these individuals did have confidants. But these familiar eyes and ears could only empathize so much. And just like any who find themselves backed into a traumatic corner, sometimes the only option is to seek professional help in the way of therapy. But it's one thing to accept therapy as an option. It's another entirely to approach a therapist with the issue. The issue of experiencing the illogical. And the fear of ridicule begins to manifest into questioning one's own sanity.

For those who have the courage to seek therapy for these experiences, a certain respect must also be given to those who provide these services. We've all seen the often dramatic and distorted images of individuals recalling, under hypnosis, terrifying experiences with evil creatures who kidnap their victims and drag them into their examination rooms, inflicting unbearable and intrusive procedures on them. And while this may be the case in some individuals' experiences, it simply isn't the case for all. So when these individuals approach a therapist or professional in the fields of psychology or psychiatry, the real question is: Where do you even begin? I wanted to seek those professionals out who were not only willing to ask this very question, but attempt to possibly answer it.

I contacted many psychologists, psychiatrists, counselors, and everything in between, always starting my inquiry with the same cautionary preface: "I'm writing about individuals who have experienced the UFO and abduction phenomenon." Some immediately stopped me mid-sentence with a blunt "no." Others politely declined to comment at all. And some went on to tell me that they had indeed worked with individuals claiming certain experiences, but they just couldn't seem to find any plausible explanation to prove the experience ever truly happened.

I was getting nowhere. Where were these supposed therapists who not only worked with those claiming abduction, but made it a priority to work with them? I decided to start with the source. With the assistance of many of the experiencers I'd interviewed, I was able to track down several individuals. I was now on a path to hear from the compassionate minds and hearts of those who were willing to listen.

The Ninety Percent

Upon graduating from Nova Southeastern University in 1996, Michael Melton began a coveted internship with the Veterans Administration Hospital in Coatesville, Pennsylvania. There, his focus was primarily on chronic mental illness, with a specialty in post-traumatic stress disorder. That internship quickly turned into an offer for employment, and Michael remained in Coatesville working with veterans for over the next two decades. Primarily focusing on hypnotic therapy and eye movement desensitization and reprocessing (EMDR), Michael saw the worst of the worst when it came to the vastly different manifestations of PTSD. "Needless to say, they were a tough crowd," Michael told me. "But working with those veterans was also very rewarding. It was really a pleasure and an honor."

His work led him to various Vietnam veterans who would sometimes bring up UFO sightings they'd had during their service. "One soldier owes his life to a sighting he had of a large glowing orb," Michael explained. "He followed it through the jungle in enemy territory to safety, rejoining with his unit after having lost them during a firefight. Divine intervention or UFO, something happened that day to save that man's life." Michael heard many other stories of UFOs, but as time progressed, he began to hear other stories that went far beyond mere sightings. He was now unraveling the memories of both veterans and others who claimed abduction experiences. Michael found himself thrust into a world he knew very little about, but that would become an integral part of his life for many years to come.

"I was awestruck when I first begin hearing about abduction experiences," Michael admitted.

"There was a quality about these people. It was very similar to the expressions and presence I saw in the combat veterans when they would describe an experience with the enemy in the jungles of Vietnam. I knew that they were trying to convey the truth as best as they could, considering what they'd been through. Many of the people I spoke to or counseled about their experiences were pillars of the community. They were parents, doctors, professional people from every level. At the same time, they were also housewives, husbands, and children. Why would anyone risk everything they worked for just to tell a story about being taken by aliens for the hell of it? You'd have to be absolutely crazy to do something like that. And please understand: most of these people were as sane as they could be." Michael gained a respect for these individuals, knowing the risk they took revealing their experiences. "They were very special people. Brave," he explained. "Exceptional, even."

Michael started including abduction experiencers in his work, finding striking similarities between the combat vets and the experiencers. Naturally, I wanted to know what those similarities were. "The symptoms were blatant. Very clear from the start. The withdrawal, the anxiety, paranoia, vigilance and scanning the environment surrounding them. Nightmares. Sleeping with the light on, or under the bed. There was great fear of it happening again, reliving the experience when confronted with anything that reminded them of their experience. These were very similar to the veterans."

Michael, working with experiencers, would go so far as to argue that PTSD could be directly connected to abduction cases, thus coining the term PASD (post-abduction stress disorder). "The only difference between the two, as far as I am concerned, is that PTSD is listed in the *Diagnostic and Statistical Manual* as an official disorder, with the designated identification number 309.86." This seemed an ambitious statement, and I wondered why he felt so strongly about it. He continued to explain, "PASD is not recognized in the official manual, and therefore, to the professional psychological community, it doesn't exist. I see PASD as a subset of PTSD. In PTSD, notice that the *T* stands for trauma, covering all types of trauma from battle to car accident and then some. PASD identifies the stressor right away: abduction. Thus, it is a part of PTSD, as a specific diagnosis. Someday, PASD will hopefully be listed right in there with PTSD."

In terms of working through these experiences with the individuals, Michael admits that most of his work is now done over the phone, as most of these patients span the globe. "With those I can't meet face-to-face, I use a type of supportive therapy. I believe psychotherapy should be done in person. There is so much more to attend to, such as body language, facial expressions, micro-expressions and the like. So, I have given support to about a hundred or so people, working regularly, face-to-face, with about a dozen."

Just like any research into a disorder, I assumed that examining trends or demographics would be a huge factor. This became my next pair of questions to Michael. What trends did he observe? Did the phenomenon, and essentially the proposed disorder itself, seem to favor a certain demographic? "People are becoming more willing to share their experiences these days. We are very close to getting an answer, and that will come by way of the abductees. My theory is that each abductee holds part of the answer, and at some point, the information they are holding in their subconscious will become conscious. It's not magic or mystical. As for demographics, I would say that there is no true trend within this. It seems to be evenly split between male and female, I have noticed more middle-aged adults report more than young adults, but most importantly, there is one demographic—if you want to call it a demographic—that needs further and more intense research: genetic profile. Comparing the genome of abductees versus non-abductees might just open up a new area of investigation. Somebody is probably working on that already. However, that's way above my pay grade!"

So if the abduction phenomenon wasn't favoring a certain gender, ethnic group, or any other demographic, then, in Michael's opinion, how great were the similarities between experiencers' claims and memories? His answer: "If you strip away all of the demographics and just look at the process and sequence of events, you will notice that there is about a 90% strong similarity to each and every one of the abductee's stories. Now one would think this would be considered irrefutable evidence that this is happening. However, mainstream science and psychology might just say it is the product of hysteria, imagination, or some other ludicrous explanation. In my opinion, this is not so. How does a person in Rwanda have the same abduction experience as another person in Greenland; or another person in the Ukraine and another in Michigan? All similar by 90%, and all verbally described with 90% similarities? Is this a worldwide hysterical folie a deux? I don't think so. Abduction by nonhuman entities seems to be a real phenomenon."

So if these cases seem to have a staggering 90% similarity rate, as Michael states, what about the variations between experiences? What might that say about the individuals? He went on to tell me: "Now we will talk about the other 10%. Just because a person's experience differs significantly from that 'norm' doesn't mean that they are lying or perpetrating a hoax. There are indeed different types of abductions. There are different species of aliens who are doing the abducting. You cannot discount their experiences just because they are different. However, and that's a big however, there is a point where an experienced researcher or interviewer might think, Okay, this is just too farfetched to be real. There are three categories of people in this 10%: People having real, very different abduction experiences. People who, for some psychological or social (psychosocial) reason, are 'wannabes.' These are individuals who somehow need to be a part of the alien abduction culture and really believe they are what they say they are, but are not at all. I guess you could say here is where the fantasy-prone personality fits in. The third category contains those who are hoaxers, fakers or pretenders. Those who do this just to stir up controversy, or who are in the process of debunking the phenomenon. To the experienced researcher or interviewer, the ability to detect the differences here is almost second nature."

So here we have Michael focusing on the individuals. But what about him? How did his peers or colleagues approach the work he had done with these individuals? Presumption would whisper to me that they probably didn't think too highly of the reality of this phenomenon in terms of its existence. "I don't really discuss this work much with others in my field," Michael explained. "When I have tried, they consider it all folly or a novelty; they might say the people who see these things are crazy, psychotic, or just making it up. This is the result of closed-mindedness and fear. Fear being the driving force behind it all. I do discuss this with others who are psychologists, doctors or scientists who are open minded and who have conquered that fear of the unknown."

It was clear from the moment I first spoke to Michael that he was a compassionate person. In dealing with something so fragile and controversial, it would be irresponsible to be anything other than empathetic yet objective when dealing with these individuals. Some felt victimized. Others welcomed it into their lives. But it was clear that most, if not all, were still suffering the initial fear of something so extraordinary happening to them.

I wanted to know, in Michael's professional opinion, what he honestly felt was happening to these people? The possibilities to rationalize the abduction phenomenon were many, but one thing seemed to be hidden under Michael's compassion. Was he a believer? "I believe they are being taken by more advanced races, and being used in many ways—more than I wish to talk about here. They are being taken by many different species, each, I assume, with their own agendas. And, as I said earlier, there is about a 90% match—thus a 10% variance. I really don't want to speculate, because your ideas are as good as mine. No one really knows for sure. And if someone calls themselves an expert, then I highly suggest one excuse themselves from their presence with grace and then run the other way. There are no experts. Only speculators."

Invigorated to help as many experiencers as he could, Michael went on to co-found a nationwide support group in 2012. His partner in the endeavor was Audrey Hewins, herself an experiencer. They named the group Starborn Support, with the mission of reaching out to as many experiencers as they could, offering counseling and demonstrating unconditional acceptance and support. Michael and Audrey included the assistance of Julia Weiss and Laura Weisser, field investigators for the

Mutual UFO Network. In 2015, the group started a radio show on the acclaimed alternative network, KGRA (Global Radio Alliance), which only strengthened their cause and garnered worldwide attention. The show was a safe place for experiencers to call in, educate themselves on therapeutic techniques, and converse with like-minded individuals. Lastly, Starborn Support began hosting their very own annual conference. This conference, aptly titled Experiencers Speak, features talks by experiences for experiencers.

It was clear that Michael, having established himself listening to combat veterans' traumatic accounts, was finding it equally as challenging to hear testimony of alien abduction. But his compassion would prove his greatest asset, and he continued to work with anyone who came to him. But even if he continued the work, would others follow in his footsteps? "It would seem that whatever these experiences are, we as humans are being assessed at every possible level of awareness, intelligence, viability, and perhaps even spiritually. We need more professionals, primarily mental health professionals, to help us handle the ever increasing number of people who are speaking out about their abduction experiences. The number of professionals who are waking up is definitely growing. Things are changing in a positive way. And that is all we can truly ask for."

As my search for professionals who involved themselves in this mysterious phenomenon continued, I was able to get into contact with Yvonne Smith, another hypnotherapist who dealt with those who claimed abduction experiences.

Abduction Experiences Continue

It was in 1991 when Yvonne received her certification as a hypnotherapist from the Hypnosis Motivation Institute in Tarzana, a small neighborhood in Los Angeles. There, she began her practice with many clients who mostly wanted help in losing weight or shaking their smoking addiction. But she also worked with many individuals who were slowly coming to terms with their cancer diagnosis. This would challenge Yvonne, seeing the impact that a life-altering diagnosis could have on an individual. But it was only months into her professional career that an entirely new form of life-altering experience would thrust her into a world she never could have imagined.

"It was in late summer of 1991 when my first 'abduction' client walked into my office," Yvonne told me. "He was an engineer in his thirties. Very conservative, and highly educated. Since childhood, he had vivid memories of little creatures in his room. These would bleed over into reoccurring dreams." Yvonne put him under regression hypnosis, and the memories began to trickle in. "He became increasingly nervous. It was a very emotional session," she recalled. "I was impressed with his sincerity."

Following this session, referrals from others who claimed abduction experiences began to flood in. Word was out that experiencers had finally found someone to talk to. Someone to listen. And as Yvonne began to unravel more and more memories from these patients, it became clear that there was something more than mere misconception or cultural impact affecting these individuals and their memories. The more individuals Yvonne treated, the more she began to see consistencies in their purported experiences. This would eventually lead her to create a questionnaire for experiencers to fill out prior to coming in for their first hypnotherapy appointment.

While there were many differences, there were also striking similarities in her patients' experiences. "Some of the similarities are described as seeing a bright white or blue-white light shining in their bedroom or other areas of the house with the feeling they are unable to move." This struck me as being very similar to many individuals I'd interviewed. "Some have described seeing a strange person(s) in the room. They also recall experiencing one or more hours of time lost with no memory of what happened, and sometimes even report scars and marks on their body that were not there the night prior."

While these observations are familiar to us as a culture through literature and movies, there are deeper connections within these experiences that Yvonne has come across with each and every individual she has worked with. These observations would open new doors of possibility as to the reasoning behind the abduction experiences. "The abduction experiences usually start in early childhood and will follow that person throughout their lives, as well as family members. It is most certainly inter-generational. Every client I have worked with, at one time or another, will describe procedures of sperm and eggs being extracted. Also during the course of their experiences, men and women are shown 'children' from babies in incubator-type enclosures to children at various stages of growth." This proto-typical experience rang familiar with that of Shane in our earlier chapter. Yvonne continued to tell me: "When I have asked the abductees to describe these children, they are clearly not completely 'human.' They are described as having larger than normal eyes, and their hair is quite wispy and their bodies appear to be very frail. They are told one or more of these chil-dren are theirs, and they are brought to their environment to bond with their offspring."

So while the information within these hypnotic regression sessions was intriguing, the process of uncovering these memo-ries was equally as compelling. "Each person is different and unique in how they will react through the process of hypnosis," Yvonne told me. "The first session is usually the most difficult since most people who come to me have never been hypnotized, in addition to the fact they are delving into the unknown. That first session may open floodgates or may yield very little infor-mation depending on the individual. The regression process is slow, but once the hidden memories do come forward, the indi-vidual experiences much relief in the long run."

I was curious, however, about what type of relief could

possibly come from digging up such traumatic and strange memories. Yvonne's answer rang true, legitimizing the therapy end of hypnotherapy. "I use several techniques to allow the abductee to 'report' what is happening without feeling pain, discomfort or fear. Even after the first session, the abductee will begin to feel relief from their symptoms of PTSD. They will begin to sleep more soundly as they incorporate this experience into their daily lives. However, progress depends on the individual."

Aside from these private hypnotherapy sessions, I learned of Yvonne's ambitious endeavor, CERO (Close Encounters Resource Organization). Founded entirely by Yvonne, it is, in her own words, "monthly support group meetings, which give experiencers the opportunity to meet other people who share these experiences. This is private and by invitation only in order to provide a safe haven for individuals to share their lifelong experiences without the fear of ridicule." The ridicule factor was something I came across with many individuals I had spoken to, and the inhibition to come forward because of it weighed heavy. But groups such as CERO are beginning to crop up across the United States and abroad, prompting experiencers to become more confident in telling their stories and finding solace in each other's accounts.

"The abduction experiences continue," Yvonne reminded me. "Because we are talking about this more openly in public forums, people who have been 'in the closet,' so to speak, feel more comfortable reaching out to find help." This made groups such as CERO integral to helping experiencers cope with the unknown. And while it was difficult to find qualified individuals such as Yvonne who would work with experiencers, she was doing all she could to make sure that this wouldn't always be the case. "This is the very reason that I will be setting up training sessions for established therapists who wish to work with abduction cases. My goal is to create a referral list of therapists across the country, as well as to educate the general public about the reality of the UFO and abduction phenomenon."

Michael and Yvonne struck me as extremely compassionate individuals. Even if one were to strip away the alien abduction topic, it would devalue nothing from their work. But what about those who didn't seek therapy or regression? Surely there were individuals out there who researched the topic but chose to keep a distance from the controversial hypnotherapy approach. This brought me to someone who did just that. She not only researched the abduction phenomenon heavily, but was a blood relative of someone who was involved in one of the most prominent accounts of alien abduction ever recorded.

Shades of Grey

She'd earned a degree in social work from the University of New Hampshire. She also participated in graduate studies in education while working as a teacher and education services coordinator. She also spent time volunteering at the New Hampshire state psychiatric hospital. Kathleen was a dedicated individual, a lifelong learner even while she passed on her knowledge to others. She would spend the next fifteen years in the education system, designing, innovating, and implementing education programs. During this time, she was also a supervisor, coordinating and training education staff members. And while her work as an educator always shone bright, there was another light flickering in the distance that just wouldn't fade away. And it all began with a phone call from her aunt Betty.

Kathleen was thirteen years old when Betty Hill phoned her childhood home on September 20, 1961. Betty reported that she and her husband, Barney, had encountered what they described as a flying saucer hovering over the White Mountains in New Hampshire. Betty then went on to report that she and Barney had been kidnapped by nonhuman entities and taken aboard their craft. There, they were examined and returned to their

vehicle some time later. Under hypnotic regression, they sepa-
rately recalled traumatic, invasive, and strikingly similar experiences. The Betty and Barney Hill case soon made national
headlines and exploded into the mainstream, spawning TV
shows, movies, and books directly inspired by the events of that
night. Perhaps most notable was a film starring James Earl Jones
and Estelle Parsons as Betty and Barney, respectively. Kathleen,
having been a witness to the aftermath of the events, stood by
her aunt's testimony. She would eventually become the foremost
investigator of the incident.

Her personal involvement never overshadowed her diligence
in remaining objective, and Kathleen continued researching the
case, eventually co-writing a book with former nuclear physicist
and UFO researcher Stanton T. Friedman, entitled *Captured!:
The Betty and Barney Hill UFO Experience*. The book gained
worldwide attention, especially from experiencers. Kathleen
was receiving letters from individuals around the world who
claimed similar experiences. "This led me to broaden my
research through the acquisition of reports and my own
personal investigations," she told me. "I recognized the need for
support services and have worked toward that end through my
association with the Mutual UFO Network." And while Kathleen didn't run any type of support group, nor had she ever
trained in hypnotherapy, she reinforced the fact that her "primary focus is and always has been upon research and investigation as opposed to support."

What intrigued me most was how Kathleen went about
interviewing the individuals involved in the abduction experiences. Was there a certain criteria or formula she used to obtain
the most credible information? She explained the following: "It
is important for experiencers to have the opportunity to explain
their event(s) without interruption during the first interview.
When I'm investigating an event, my first step is to listen to their
account carefully while I record their statements and take notes.
Then my interview will begin with questions that pertain to

their statements. I'll ask for precise dates, witnesses, memories of the presence of unconventional craft, and so on."

While many individuals claim nonphysical encounters involving vivid dreams, out-of-body experiences, or something deep in the subconscious, Kathleen made the following very clear about the focus of her work: "My primary interest lies in the collection of nuts-and-bolts evidence that the event was physical and involved nonhumans in close proximity to structured craft. The more recent focus upon nonphysical events and consciousness studies is interesting, but from a scientific perspective, I'm interested in the collection of physical evidence."

So in the case that hypnosis isn't used to recall possible regressed memories, how did Kathleen feel that these cases differed from those that were done strictly through hypnosis? "I have not found a major difference between memories that were consciously recalled and memories that were recalled for the first time through hypnosis." So hypnosis, it seemed, wasn't the be-all and end-all to recovering accurate memories. So did it hold any relevance in terms of abduction experiences? "Hypnosis has been employed to fill in information that had been forgotten and to add additional details around a certain event that was consciously recalled. I am aware of the fact that the first hypnosis session might produce distorted memories, due to fear and the emotional release that occurs. This is obvious in my uncle Barney Hill's first hypnosis session. I have discovered that when the proper techniques are employed, the memories recovered through hypnosis are often less traumatic than the experiencer suspected they would be. These are generally used by certified hypnotherapists, as opposed to licensed mental health professionals."

In conducting her research, what data did Kathleen obtain? Could it bring us any closer to discovering a pattern among experiencers? "Academic research studies in the US and Canada indicate that those who meet the criteria for having experienced a real abduction are no more psychologically aberrant than the general population. These experiences span all socioeconomic groups, ethnic groups, religious groups, intellectual levels and educational achievement levels. I have interviewed many high-achieving members of society who have one thing in common: they have troubling memories of alien abduction."

So it would appear that the only comparison to be drawn between experiencers was that they had experiences. This is sobering, to say the least. There must have been some correlating factors that tied these individuals together. Kathleen began to dig deeper in 2012, conducting a yearlong study of commonalities with a colleague, Denise Stoner. "We conducted the study for the benefit of experiencers and researchers alike. Our purpose was to identify and quantify specific traits that experiencers have in common, and to expand the UFO research community's knowledge of nonhuman contact phenomena."

So what exactly did the study consist of? How would it further insight into the abduction phenomenon? "The most efficient scientific method for obtaining this information, in our opinion, was through the use of simple straightforward questionnaires designed to identify commonalities among experiencers. Each of us brought to the table knowledge of several unique, unpublicized characteristics of the alien abduction experience. The commonalities study would ascertain how widespread these commonalities are across the abduction experiencer population. We were able to identify twenty-three traits that the experiencers shared and were not experienced by our control group of non-experiencers."

So it would appear that commonalities were indeed making their way to the surface. But what were they, and what might they mean for those who have had the experiences? "As far as gender is concerned, nearly twice as many women (32), as men (18) completed the 'Abduction Experiencer Questionnaire.' Does this indicate that abduction is far more prevalent among women? Not necessarily. While statistical evidence indicates that men are less likely than women to answer surveys of any kind, this trend was not supported when we tallied the results of the 'Commonalities among Non-Abductees Questionnaire.' The majority of respondents were men (15) as opposed to women (9). If trends in human behavior have not skewed the results, it suggests that more women than men have been abducted by aliens. This finding has been widely reported by other researchers."

Many of the experiencers I'd come across in my own research varied drastically in age. I wanted to know if this factored at all into Kathleen's study. "We were interested in identifying possible trends among age groups, partly due to the fact that a significant number of abduction experiencers in the 50+ age group had reported their experiences to us within recent months. Our suspicion was correct. 44% of the AE Group participants were born in the 1950s, although only 20% of the NAE Group was in the same age group. This figure drops dramatically for those born in the 1940s (18%) and the 1960s (26%)."

This and many other commonalities can be found in a book Kathleen published, along with Denise Stoner, entitled *The Alien Abduction Files*. And while many commonalities may shed some light on the abduction phenomenon, it doesn't change the fact that those having the experiences suffer very traumatic aftermaths. While Kathleen didn't use hypnotherapy in her work with experiencers, she worked very closely with those at MUFON, which Michael Austin Melton was directly connected to, and also with CERO, run by Yvonne Smith. These connections assured that data, with permission from the experiencers, was being shared.

So what did Kathleen believe we were truly dealing with in terms of the phenomenon? "There is evidence that leads me to believe some contact experiences are physical," she told me. "Many others are subjectively real but psychologically, psychically, or spiritually based. I have not found correlating evidence that leads me to want to place the variety of experiences under one heading, although there is a current trend in this direction. If we continue to move in this direction, we risk the possibility of removing all scientific interest in this phenomenon. In my opinion, this would be a tragedy and would negate all of the good work that has been accomplished by many researchers."

So if this is a physical phenomenon, why are those responsible for the abductions traumatizing some experiencers, enlightening others, and leaving most, if not all, completely at a loss for answers? Kathleen explained: "The current trend is for researchers to be polarized at each end of the spectrum. Some believe that alien contact is highly undesirable and we are undergoing an invasion for the aliens' purposes. At the other end of the spectrum are those who believe their experiences are highly positive and will lead to ascension." So it appeared that the intentions of what that lay at the source of these experiences was completely dependent on how each individual perceived the experience. "I am a conservative researcher who sees many shades of grey along the spectrum," Kathleen added. "Many experiencers have experienced both positive and negative contact. I believe that we must be cognizant of the fact that human emotions, both hope and fear, can color our perception in a distorted fashion."

The Measure of Meaning

While the work of those who propose and promote hypnotherapy as a way of uncovering unexplainable experiences in their lives is compelling, it certainly isn't the only approach to be taken when dealing with these unanswered questions in one's life. In fact, there are those who believe it only complicates things. And this was no more apparent than when I met Dr. Chris Cogswell, a chemical engineer who'd earned his PhD at Northeastern University.

Cogswell and I had been conversing for years as fellow podcasters, even appearing on one another's shows to discuss the various UFO cases. But it was in June 2019 when we finally got to meet in person at a conference in Los Angeles known as Alien Con. Cogswell and I were guests on one of the panels taking place at the "UFOs in Podcasting" event. We were joined by moderator David Flora of the *Blurry Photos Podcast*, Brent Hand and John Goforth of the *Hysteria 51 Podcast*, Derek Hayes of *Monsters Among Us Podcast*, and Ben Bowlin of the *Stuff They Don't Want you to Know*. It was a very enriching and insightful panel discussion with a packed audience. It was a very positive experience for everyone involved. But later that same day, an emotional whiplash would hit me unlike ever before.

For the third time at Alien Con, I was selected to moderate an event known as "Experiencer Sessions." These were put on by the conference, where anyone could convene at a set time and share their experiences. I was merely steering the ship and trying to get to as many people as we could in an allotted amount of time. This was a very challenging moderation for the mere fact that attempting to have someone summarize something as profound as a UFO event or abduction experience was almost impossible. While I enjoyed the opportunity and was appreciative of every person who came to these sessions and did share, I had to admit that these sessions were emotionally and mentally exhausting. It was clear that some of these individuals had gone through *something* either so traumatic or so puzzling that it was driving them in to a state of disoriented vulnerability. They wanted answers. And every time they looked to me for those answers, I would always have to confess that I was no expert, merely a listening ear. And it broke my heart that I couldn't do that for them. Until Cogswell stood up at the end of one of these sessions and said the most profound, yet simple thing that could have been said in the room. We'll get to that shortly.

While studying at Northeastern, Cogswell started *The Mad Scientist Podcast.* He explained that the podcast was "built off a foundational question for my philosophy and scientific research: Why do some technologies take off in the public imagination while others are left behind? Part of that question is the related question of why do people believe nonscientific things, and why do some scientific ideas never become accepted fact by the public at large?" Cogswell often covered UFOs on his podcast as well. When asked how his interest in UFOs began, he explained, "I got involved in UFOs because of a lifelong love of the subject, and really all things weird and mysterious. I always liked UFO stories, and the study of UFOs is an interesting case because it is a world where the science is pretty well accepted that aliens likely exist out there, and that we are looking for them with things like SETI. But the pseudoscience is also super popular, as in things like ancient alien theory and places like Skinwalker Ranch."

In his time, Cogswell paid close attention to how UFO researchers and self-proclaimed investigators conducted their work. And while it was interesting to Cogswell, he noted several concerns off the bat when reading the literature, listening to podcasts and watching the television shows, and observing the work being done by independent UFO investigatory organizations. "I believe the UFO world cannot structurally change without leaving a significant portion of its current proponents behind, similar to what happened in the transition from pseudo to real science in other fields (or vice versa, from real science to pseudoscience). This is what happened, say, in the study of demons and witchcraft, with witch hunters and clergy intent on the rooting out and study of demons being quickly forgotten or removed from the roles of 'serious' scientific or legal study, while simultaneously witches and other folk healers became left out of the transition of some of their practices to medicine and early pharmacology. The same thing will happen with any true science that comes from UFO studies."

In terms of the organizations studying UFO reports and investigating them, Cogswell was brutally honest about the work being done by one of the most visible of the organizations.

"What I would love to see is a serious response and alternative to MUFON being created, as well as a place for serious and rational discussion of the subject. A lot of academically serious studies are based on nothing 'real' or at least not materially real as science requires. The concepts and ideas behind UFO questions, and even the cases themselves, could be put into an interesting and useful framework for study if we just got away from the idea that these things need to be measurable events for them to be meaningful."

Now, back to what Cogswell had to say to the experiencers at Alien Con. "Go talk to a therapist. A therapist with absolutely no experience working with alien abductees." And while many in the room scoffed at his suggestion, many also agreed with him. The idea of being put under hypnotic regression by known alien abduction researchers was something Cogswell took certain points of contention with. "Experiencers are often told that they must regress their memories or undergo hypnosis, or just generally their experiences are immediately placed into a neat box that fits someone else's paradigm. The reason early cases are so interesting is because there is none of that paradigm to draw from. Experiencers should be listened to and heard, but judgments on the physical provability of their cases is sort of a secondary point for me."

So while Cogswell felt no need for hypnotic regression with those who claimed experiences, did he personally feel there was a true, physical reality to the claims made by experiencers? "I think there probably is a reality," he said. "But I'm not sure that really matters. Religious experience is often physically immaterial, and empires have risen and fallen on the whims of gods who may or may not have ever actually been there in the first place. There are enough experiencer stories I have heard, firsthand, to make me think that something worth investigating *is* happening, and there is clearly a physical component of some sort, because these people are experiencing something. But whether that physical reality means there are really aliens taking people out of bed, or there is a specific trigger in brain electrochemistry that causes disparate people to have extremely similar reactions, is impossible to say at this point."

What exactly did Cogswell think was necessary to further the scientific exploration of the abduction and experiencer phenomenon? "If we were to test experiencers scientifically, the first thing to do would be a survey of them and their experiences. See how many people actually fit that umbrella term, and see if there are commonalities to them. That is the sort of data that is not easily hoaxed as opposed to an individual case, and can be statistically relevant regardless of the reality of the phenomena itself."

Cogswell's words at Alien Con had a lasting impact on me. Ever since researching, interviewing, and writing the 2016 edition of this book, I began to feel a responsibility to explain the cases I'd presented. I felt an immense pressure to not only defend those in the book, but to even attempt to find answers to their experiences. But the hard truth of the matter was that there will always be a divergence in approaches to researching and investigating the experiencer phenomenon. While Cogswell may not agree with the work being done by abduction researchers and hypnotherapists, the fact of the matter is that nobody knows what is actually going on with these experiences, no matter what they say. "If someone tells you they have the answers, they are lying," Cogswell asserted. "Another thing I think is so important is that this really is a subject, or at least a type of subject, that has been around forever. Study how other belief systems like this have evolved and fallen away, and how some survived. You will find a lot of commonalities that allow you to begin to look at this subject from a more investigative side while still enjoying the more sensational aspects."

So while the more skeptical minds may find issue with attempting to dig up memories of alien abductions, the work of those who do take this route continues. Will they find common ground with someone like Cogswell, who strives for more scientific methodology in researching and understanding the experiencer phenomenon? I would meet someone else at Alien Con that certainly gave me hope of such. And her approach to the entire experiencer phenomenon was unlike anything I'd ever researched before.

If An Experiencer Survives It, They Get To Define It

NK Kranda is a Southern California native. She went to school for horticulture sciences and graduated with highest honors. She then continued her education in the fields of psychology, PTSD and trauma therapies, eventually landing in Texas to call home and pursue her various fields of study. Little did she know that a side interest in various esoteric topics would lead to a merging of her worlds in ways she never quite expected.

After attending a local MUFON chapter meeting in her hometown, Kranda began to hear stories from people who had claimed encounters and contact experiences with what they presumed to be nonhuman entities. Intrigued by the possibility that these stories could be true, and seeing a need for some sort of contribution to helping these deeply affected people, Kranda decided to join MUFON and become a field investigator and chapter secretary. She would work closely with other researchers and investigators to record not only UFO sightings, but the much more mysterious and controversial cases of abductions and close encounters. This is where she began to harness her skills as an interviewer, and realized, just as I had after working on this book, that a story truly meant little when compared to the person telling it.

Though Kranda found her time with MUFON rewarding and it gave her access to stories she may never have been privy to prior, she wanted to take her work in a different direction, instead of merely recording an incident and trying to solve a case. She wanted to work directly with those having the experiences on her own terms, and theirs. "I began speaking with people quietly after MUFON meetings, giving them the respect and empathy they deserved once they walked through the door. I eventually left MUFON, developed my own interview and research methods, and have been continuing to learn and evolve ever since."

Kranda's empathetic approach to working with experiencers began to set her apart from those just seeking a good story to exploit, which unfortunately was more common than I had first realized. Just like any good true crime story, sometimes it's easy to go for the most sensational or impactful story, not realizing that there is a victim always on the other side. This will often make experiencers hesitant to share their stories, knowing that it easily could fall in to the hands of a disingenuous storyteller. So what made those, who were clearly in a vulnerable state, trust Kranda in her approach? For many, it came down to how she described her work to them. Rather than considering herself an "abduction researcher" or "investigator," she simply called herself a preservationist. "I speak with people from several different countries, age groups, and demographics about their encounters with something they could not explain," Kranda explained. "I then preserve these stories for research, and to assist other experiencers in finding solace that they are not alone in having had these experiences."

What made Kranda's work different from many of the other experiencer researchers is that she didn't use any type of hypnotherapy to attempt getting to the often blocked memories of an experiencer. She simply talked to them as equals. And soon I learned that the empathy Kranda possessed came from somewhere deep inside. "I am also a longtime multi-phenomena experiencer," she admitted. "I know firsthand what it is like to be ignored, belittled, and ostracized as being 'weird and crazy' just for trying to share some of the things that have happened to me."

One of the most important things I personally came across

in all my research in the UFO world was the idea of relating to an experiencer in any way you could. It breaks down the walls of hesitancy and often leads to the most true and honest relation of a story. "I am informal, compassionate, and encourage the experiencer to set their own firm boundaries over how this experience is to be shared. We start when they want to start. We stop when they want to stop. Some interviews are never recorded and I do not even take notes. I gain an experiencer's trust not by my reputation, but by simply earning it little by little."

Something else that stood out to me about Kranda's work is that she goes into each and every preservation with no preconceived notions. There is no history of being labeled an "alien abduction researcher" or a "UFO researcher." In my own experiences, when someone comes to me to tell a story knowing I am considered a "UFO person," it's apparent that they are attempting to make their experience just a bit more *alien*. Instead of filtering an experience to seem more prosaic or "not crazy," they take the opposite approach and paint something to possibly be more than it actually was. Finding a middle ground is crucial when dealing with such anecdotal evidence and stories.

There is an immense trust between an experiencer and those they choose to confide in. It is a powerful and intimate relationship that I formed with each and every individual I interviewed for this book. And while it always remains a learning process of how to deal with each person in a unique way, there are certain approaches that remain consistent. Kranda was becoming, in my opinion, the perfect example of an experiencer-researcher. "I feel that what sets me apart from most other researchers is that there is never any attempt on my part to disassemble, investigate, or label an experiencer based on my own needs or preconceived ideas," Kranda continued. "If an experiencer survives it, they get to define it. I only give opinions or perspective about testimony if it is asked of me, and I *never* pressure an experiencer to disclose."

And while on the surface, sitting with an experiencer and just listening seems easy, the pressure, often forced upon an experiencer by themselves, can be immense. Society, as a whole, has yet to fully embrace the idea that people, from all over the world, are having experiences with something truly incredible and, often, with no evidence of the experience having occurred. Kranda explains: "One of the dark sides of working in this field is realizing just how much data and testimony we have lost over the decades. This is because the stigma is too high for people to speak about these things. The risks vary from loss of friends, loss of employment, and up to even being institutionalized, all of which have happened to experiencers I have spoken to."

Kranda also admits that it's not just people who believe they'd had an experience with a UFO or something alien that come to her. "I document the different experiences of a wide array of people. I have preserved everything from the UFO phenomena and paranormal, to religious miracles and demonic activity." So when it came down to it, it wasn't primarily about which specific or intersectional phenomena Kranda worked to preserve or research. It was about the people who had the experience, how it impacted them, and how she could help by merely listening to and talking through an experience. "I hope one day that the combination of numerical data, and the commonalities between experiencers that I have been documenting, will begin to show people just how frequently these 'strange and impossible' experiences are happening."

Finding patterns and making connections is always a primary goal of any researcher. Our entire scientific method is based on the very premise of repeatability and consistent data. But what happens when you're dealing with something that seems to push and challenge every boundary our own science has constructed around us? Kranda also admits that this is one of the biggest challenges when people come to her. They want answers. She explains, "As painful as it is at times, many experiencers come to me with questions not only about their own traumatic experiences, but also about UFO phenomena in general. I can only answer as gently as I can that sometimes there is no *why*, only *what is*."

So while some may attempt to answer the why for these people, Kranda remains steadfast in a world of uncertainties, focusing on the journeys of those experiencing the unknown and not the destination. "For me personally, it would narrow my focus too much if I concentrated on the why, and I would miss so many wonderful aspects of this beautiful, strange phenomena and all of the voices who have experienced it. There are many constellations in the sky. But if we only look at a small fraction of those stars, we would never see the beauty of how all the dots connect."

As we begin to rebuild our world after a pandemic, Kranda and so many others continue to work with experiencers—not to chart their path or course, but to be there with a helping hand and a listening ear to rebuild. Without the testimony of so many coming forward in this book, and so many more across the world, we would have no cases to investigate. No stories to hear. Nothing to build upon. We as researchers are nothing without a witness or experiencer. And while many choose to study UFOs, the paranormal, and the unexplained through the rigorous lens of science, others approach it completely differently. And while at times these different approaches may seem at odds with one another, perhaps they will someday merge into a clearer picture of understanding and acceptance. But for Kranda, and many others who bear the burden of coming forward, that burden can become strength and pride. "Whatever age you were when you had your experience, whatever happened, whatever you had to do to keep going and survive, honor yourself. If it wasn't for your past self going through all those things, you would not be here today," Kranda said. And her final comment on the importance of witnesses coming forward spoke more than any case file, any set of data, and any scientific evidence pertaining to UFOs could. "We need you. We need all of you. Honor yourself, and keep going."

Generally, the abduction or experiencer phenomenon is widely debated among believers and skeptics alike. And it most likely always will be. While physical evidence remains scarce, accounts continue to be reported all across the world. And while this may leave us at what seems like a standstill in terms of proof of a legitimate phenomenon, the cold, hard truth remains that something is definitely happening to most of these people. And with the bold and extremely controversial work being done by Michael, Yvonne, Kathleen, and many others, we may begin to narrow in on what that something is, one experience and experiencer at a time. Or it will multiply our questions tenfold. The preservation by Kranda assures that these stories will not be lost in time, or be distorted by regressed memories possibly being manipulated. That is not to say the individuals above ever attempted to lead their patients, but there's simply no way to prove the memories are entirely accurate. So the work, as always, continues for those who dedicate their time to researching, studying, and attempting to deconstruct the abduction and experiencer phenomena. Perhaps we will one day find common ground and understanding between one another. While we may not always find the answers we seek, we can learn and grow from the *new* questions we ask, together.

16

IT WAS RAINING UFOS

It was December 17, 2017. In Cave Junction, Oregon, Kevin Day was volunteering at a local golf course that was nearing bankruptcy. He'd been working there for almost four years at this point, mostly for free, watering the course at night, tending to grounds maintenance, and even bringing the golf course restaurant, the Hole in One Cafe, back to full service. He did whatever it would take to help bring in any money he could for the Illinois Valley Golf Club. This particular day, Kevin was helping wait tables in the dining area. He and several patrons were watching a golf tournament on one of the televisions in the restaurant when someone abruptly changed the channel to CNN.

"Hey, who turned the channel?" Kevin inquired. But he soon looked around the dining area to see everyone intently watching the breaking news coming across the broadcast. This was when Kevin's jaw dropped. "Oh my God…" In shock, he dropped a plate of fish and chips on the ground, shattering the plate. Several patrons jumped up to help Kevin clean up the mess as he stood there, not sure quite how to react to what he was seeing on the television screen. Down on one knee, picking up small pieces of the plate, he noticed tears dripping to the ground from his eyes. He watched through the tears as the news broadcast showed a grainy black-and-white video of some sort of object moving through the sky, cloud covering moving rapidly behind the object. It appeared to be recorded by the camera of a plane, targeting systems and numbers littered across all four sides of the camera footage. Suddenly, a familiar face popped up in the broadcast as Kevin watched intently. The man being interviewed for this segment explained what the viewer was seeing in the video. "It was a white object, oblong, pointing north, moving erratically. As I got close to it... it rapidly accelerated to the south and disappeared in less than two seconds." Kevin shook his head in disbelief, hanging on every word this man in glasses on the television was saying. "It was something I had never seen in my life..."

Kevin got up, his eyes widening. *Why now?* he asked himself. He knew the man on the television. He knew the video as well, because it wasn't the first time he'd seen it. In fact, the video never would have existed if it weren't for Kevin. A rush of excitement, fear, anticipation, and uncertainty consumed him. He turned from the television and rushed out of the restaurant. He passed the pro shop of the golf course, where his brother-in-law was currently working, and yelled to him, "Dave, I gotta go home... I'll explain later!"

As Kevin made his way home, he didn't know exactly what was going to happen when he got there. But he knew that something he'd kept silent about for so many years, something that had changed his life the day it happened, was about to change his life again. The world was about to learn about one of the most mystifying UFO events to ever become public. But how had it made its way on to the nightly news? And who was responsible for the video making its way out of the levels of classification where Kevin thought it had been so carefully hidden away? Things were not only about to change for him, but the many others who'd been quiet for so long. And soon, the entire conversation about UFOs was going to change within the US military, the US government, and perhaps the entire world.

It was November 10, 2004. Kevin Day was a US Navy senior chief operations specialist in radar systems. He was a TOPGUN air intercept controller with more than twenty years of experience in strike group air defense, including wartime operations. On this particular day, he was working the evening shift in the Combat Information Center aboard the USS *Princeton* carrier. The *Princeton* was making its way through the Pacific, accompanied by the USS *Nimitz* carrier strike group. Both vessels were preparing for a training exercise taking place in the waters and airspace of Southern California on November 14. Kevin was operating the SPY radar at the time. The SPY was brand new and, at the time, highly classified multifunction phased-array radar capable of search, automatic detection, transition to track, tracking of air and surface targets, and missile engagement support. It was the most highly sophisticated system Kevin had ever worked with, and he was one of the best with it.

That evening, while on duty, Kevin noticed something odd about a hundred miles north of his position out near Catalina Island. "As the on-watch anti-air warfare coordinator," Kevin explained, "I had asked the electronic warfare supervisor if he held any electronic emissions emanating from the new tracks that I held on SPY radar, giving him the system track number, just east of Catalina Island. He reported back that the system was not detecting any electronic signals originating from the odd formation of five new tracks that I held. I was confident the tracks were actual air contacts because they had the highest possible system track quality. However, the contacts were in a loose formation at 28,000 feet, tracking south at 100 knots. Which was odd. What flies like that? How could something that high travel that slow? Anything lighter-than-air would be traveling in the direction of the prevailing winds, which were from west to east. Not south. It was definitely odd."

With the contacts to the north, Kevin didn't believe it to be too much of a concern from an air defense perspective. He decided to simply track and report, making it apparent to internal and external ship communications. "I thought that maybe it was something entirely civilian related and they didn't even know our strike group was at sea to the south." Kevin continued tracking the group of contacts for about two hours that first evening. "The contacts passed to the east of our ship's position in formation and eventually faded from my radar off the coast of Baja, in the vicinity of Guadalupe Island, Mexico. And with that, I turned over the watch to the next watchstander, and headed below to the chief's mess for the evening."

Whatever had happened was most likely a fluke. Or so Kevin thought. Back on watch the following morning, he detected the objects once again just to the east of Catalina Island. "Now I'm really curious, although not from an air defense perspective," Kevin told me. "Both the *Princeton* and *Nimitz* were at sea to conduct air defense training, but it was not scheduled to take place until November 14, and I was not yet concerned about any potential airspace intrusions presented by the odd formations, which would indeed create safety-of-flight concerns during any would-be air defense exercise taking place in that same airspace."

But over the course of the next few days, the *Princeton* continued to track additional groups of these contacts. The objects seemed to be in loose formation and anywhere from five to ten at a time. They repeated the same tracking over radar coverage. Same altitude and location, traveling from Catalina Island to Guadalupe Island, soon fading from radar. *What the hell is going on?* Kevin remembered thinking. He once again thought it must be something civilian, and surely would not be a problem come time for the actual training exercise.

The day they'd all been waiting for had come. November 14, 2004. Back in the Combat Information Center, Kevin was on watch, preparing for the exercise. He made sure radios and datalinks were working properly. "We were all looking forward to the extremely high-fidelity air defense training with Air Wing Eleven, embarked aboard *Nimitz*, in a couple of hours. The training scenario called for mock-enemy aircraft to launch from Naval Station North Island, Coronado, and attack our strike group located about one hundred miles southwest of San Diego."

Everything seemed normal and the entire crew anticipated a successful exercise by the books. Until the objects returned yet again. No electronic signals, yet there they were populating space on the SPY radar. Kevin was able to brush off the other events. Though curious, they weren't a threat. But this was different. Now he was concerned. "We would be launching exercise aircraft from two directions into the same airspace as the unknown air contacts. I expected them too to track to the east of our position on their slow way south towards Mexico like all of the past groups had done."

The strike group was in position and ready for the exercise. But Kevin knew he couldn't let this exercise happen without voicing his concerns about these unknown objects that had haunted the area and his radar. "I immediately made my way to the front-table area of CIC to brief my concerns to the captain. I told him that we'd been tracking these rather odd formations of unknown air contacts for several days now. With the training exhibition starting soon, I told him I was now gravely concerned about safety of flight. If we launch our aircraft into the same airspace as the unknowns and an air mishap occurs, somebody is going to ask both you and me why we were so damn incurious about the contacts." Kevin briefed the captain on everything he'd tracked, hoping the captain would agree to let him intercept one of these objects. The captain agreed and ordered him to "intercept and VID (visual identification) the object(s)."

Soon, Kevin headed back to his radar console and ordered the air intercept controller to take control of the Fast Eagle 01 flight that had just launched off the carrier. They soon made contact and explained that they indeed had a "real-world tasking" and wanted them to intercept and visually identify the bogey. "The pilot, Commander David Fravor, immediately responded, sounding eager to comply." Soon, Fravor headed toward the inbound unknown group. "Several more voice commands followed with updated vectoring information provided," Kevin explained. "The flight was approaching 'merge plot,' meaning the interceptors would be in the same vertical airspace as the unknowns and on the two dimensional radar displays would look like one contact instead of two."

During this entire exchange, all communication was being fed to an overhead speaker. Kevin patiently waited for any updates, when suddenly the pilot's voice blasted over the speaker, clearly startled. "Oh my God! Oh my God! I'm engaged! I'm engaged!" Fravor reported. "It visibly jolted everyone in Combat. I thought to myself, 'Engaged? What the hell.'" What happened next left Kevin and the team completely dumbfounded. "We watched on radar as the unknown bogey suddenly descended from 28,000 feet in altitude down to the surface of the ocean. We watched as Fast Eagle flight followed it down, attempting to get a clear visual identification. I found out later the next day that the object made the maneuver in .78 seconds! The pilots later all reported there were no sonic booms." Kevin explained to me that anything traveling at that velocity would not only liquify a pilot, but it would most definitely cause a sonic boom of some sort. But this object seemed to defy physics and logic before their very eyes.

The chase continued. "Fast Eagle flight chased it down and again merged with the unknown bogey, this time about fifty feet above the water." Soon, Commander Fravor described what he was seeing, explaining that it was a single object, about forty feet long, no wings or sign of propulsion, and of an oblong shape. He later described it as looking like a "large white Tic Tac." Besides the object itself, Fravor was also mystified as the object, when close to the surface of the ocean, created a disturbance in the water. He watched in amazement as the object soon darted upward at unbelievable speeds again. "We all watched on radar," Kevin explained, "when suddenly, the contact went from the new merge plot position to a point in space called the Combat Air Patrol station, or CAP point. Although well-known to the air defense team, a secret location to everyone else. We all looked in wonder at each other because the contact had somehow went to this CAP point. Latitude, longitude, and altitude. A point then about sixty miles away from the last merge plot position. It had taken the object approximately two seconds to make that maneuver. Now short on fuel, Fast Eagle flight returned to the carrier, the next launch imminent."

Back on the *Nimitz* flight deck, Commander David Fravor instructed the lead pilot of the next launch, Chad Underwood, to be ready to intercept and record the contacts using the Advanced Targeting Forward Looking Infrared Radar (ATFLIR). "I'm gonna go find those things!" Underwood was reported as boasting. But the boasting soon became quite real. Back in the Combat Information Center aboard the *Princeton*, Kevin continued tracking the oblong object as it reconvened with its fellow cluster of unknowns. "As before, the formation continued to track south, 28,000 feet at 100 knots. As if nothing fun or interesting had just happened. The odd contacts acted as though they were simply migrating south like a flock of birds and wanted nothing further to do with us!"

Meanwhile, Underwood was able to get within a twenty-mile proximity of the object and set his infrared gun-pod camera to record. He was able to capture the object. He reported back to the Information Center that the object was behaving exactly like it had when Fravor followed it. "When the interceptors merged with them, the object once again fell from the sky to the ocean's surface in less than a second. At one point, it was raining UFOs. And just like before, when the interceptors chased them down, the bogeys shot straight back up from the ocean's surface, back to 28,000 feet, back to 100 knots tracking south, reforming their group. It was then when I realized that I had just intercepted no-shit UFOs." The objects soon disappeared out of sight, and Underwood returned to base, having just recorded what would soon become one of the most famous UFO videos to ever be made public.

Throughout this entire ordeal, Kevin ran extensive diagnostics on the combat systems to make sure there were no glitches. What they were tracking defied all logic and physics. "In total, about one hundred separate highest-quality radar tracks were held by SPY radar over the course of several days. I had over eighteen years of sea time sitting in front of SPY, with much of that time spent underway right there in Southern California. Not long after, I had orders to transfer off the ship. This was literally my last duty station, when the ship returned to San Diego post-exercise. It was my very last underway while still wearing the uniform. A UFO was also my very last intercept out of the hundreds I'd made during my career as a TOPGUN-trained air intercept controller, including wartime operations. I had never seen anything remotely close to what we'd encountered over those days, much less be in a position to actually intercept a real UFO. But that is exactly what we did."

Any reports of the incident and video footage were handed over through the chain of command and almost immediately died a quick death in terms of further investigation. At least to the knowledge of those involved. As for the attitude on the carriers, word began to spread on the *Princeton* and *Nimitz* about a possible UFO encounter, and then stigma, like it often does with these situations, reared its ugly head. Pilots involved were greeted by members of the intelligence center with tinfoil caps worn on their heads. Anyone involved was ridiculed for weeks after the event. But Kevin was there from the very start and throughout the entire ordeal. The incident, for those who actually experienced it, certainly wasn't a laughing matter. Kevin was nearing the end of his career with the US Navy and understandably didn't want to burn any bridges or risk his highly commendable reputation. And as soon as the event had occurred, it faded into the skies and water of Southern California, for what Kevin believed would be forever.

Kevin retired from the US Navy in 2008. Almost immediately, he went to work for a Defense Department contractor. "My work involved manning and training analysis as well as engineering in support of mostly weapons control systems on naval ships." Things slowed down quite a bit for Kevin as he integrated back into civilian life. And all seemed fine until he began having disturbing dreams of apocalyptic doom and dread. "The dreams themselves did not particularly bother me, but remembering the dreams in the days following did. Dream memories would surface and I would associate some of the more unpleasant memories from my Navy days. I can only describe the experience as flashbacks."

It had been almost four years since the "Tic Tac UFO" encounter, and Kevin found something very troubling about it. "I had retired from the Navy, but my concerns over what we had encountered certainly did *not* retire. Why hadn't big Navy shown any interest over what had happened? What if the same thing happened overseas when the Navy did have live ordnance loaded on our fighters? The shock and awe of encountering a UFO like the ones in 2004 could accidentally end up starting a war nobody planned on or wanted." Kevin attempted to tell his story and express his concerns several times, but it fell on deaf and skeptical ears. "I soon gave up trying, as I could see the blank stares I'd receive in return."

While Kevin didn't fully understand or realize it at the time, burying these concerns deep down began to slowly eat away at him. His nightmares became worse. It seemed as though life was spiraling out of control. The integration back into civilian life, and this highly strange event being so recklessly ignored by the Navy, was dizzying. He couldn't keep silent any longer. "Not knowing what else to do and knowing nobody would likely ever believe my incredible story about intercepting UFOs, I decided to write my story in a semi-fictionalized version of the actual true story. My plan was to hide the story in plain sight, just in case the encounters ever became public." Kevin felt that by putting the story in a fictionalized context, it would at least get the story off his chest and out to the public in some fashion. It would also protect the privacy of those involved who wished to not go public. The incident was written as a short story, "The See'r," which was part of a two-book series Kevin titled *Sailor's Anthology: Books I and II*. It was published in 2008 in the Library of Congress. Little did Kevin know that hiding the story in plain sight would prove beneficial, not only bolstering the entire event, but solidifying his direct involvement when the story would be blown wide open almost a decade later.

While he was able to put the incredible events down in print in the Library of Congress, it didn't change the fact that Kevin, having served in wartime and also being solely responsible for originally tracking the UFOs raining over the coast of Southern California, was suffering greatly. "During these years, my life turned for the worst. I lost several homes during the 2008 housing crisis. My work suffered, too. I ended up quitting my job and moving to Sacramento to attend school. My wife and I separated shortly after. I attended Sacramento State University and attained my master's in education (technology) and a professional certificate in curriculum design for eLearning. Immediately after graduating, I moved back to my home town by myself in Southern Oregon." It was during all of this that Kevin finally went to see Veteran Affairs for help. He was subsequently diagnosed with a complex case of PTSD. "My family, friends, and colleagues were shocked. I had gone from being on track for a nice retirement to living in the Kalmiopsis wilderness, completely broke and disillusioned about my former life."

As time progressed, Kevin felt resentment creeping in. This UFO event, coupled with what seemed like endless other challenges in his life, made him feel quite lost. But slowly he began to rebuild his life. He would eventually purchase a new home, reconnect with his wife, and start volunteering at the local golf course. "My uncle lives three doors down from our place," Kevin happily told me. "My brothers, sisters, many cousins and me had grown up playing capture the flag on the limestone hill behind my uncle's house that forms the east-facing view from our property. We had all somehow come full circle. We were all truly home again." With the remarkable UFO event he'd experienced behind him, Kevin had truly started a new chapter in his life and was finally on a path he'd always wanted. And then a CNN news broadcast would once again change his life, and an entirely new chapter would be written.

After rushing out of the golf course that day in December of 2017, Kevin drove home and immediately hopped online to see just how widespread the news actually was on the "Tic Tac" event he had ostensibly set into motion. His jaw dropped as he clicked through every major news outlet, every one of them reporting on the event. Commander Fravor's face was front and center on every article and video; the *Nimitz* and *Princeton* spanned countless headlines. The story was quickly going viral and it was quite clear that something major was about to happen. Kevin couldn't believe what he was seeing. "I found a YouTube video that was essentially a repost of the earlier live CNN story. I left a comment in the comments section, telling the video's owner, Robert Powell of the Scientific Coalition for UAP studies, that I was the air intercept controller during the event, and that he needed to contact me because I wanted to back up Commander Fravor's story. Robert Powell quickly responded."

Just when he thought he'd left the event behind, it returned in full force. The years of silence, burden, and uncertainty were fading away, and a new world was about to open up for Kevin. He had no choice but to go all in and support Commander Fravor's testimony. "News of my involvement spread like wildfire. It was not long before I was contacted by Dave Beaty, a TV producer. Dave and I collaborated, and I helped him produce his now widely viewed YouTube video called 'The Nimitz Encounters.'" Beaty's video currently has over five million views and continues to grow. But it wasn't only the views that made the video a success. It was the fact that Beaty was able to find other witnesses to the event to come forward. These included even more stunning testimonies from Gary Voorhis, fire controlman on the USS *Princeton*; Patrick Hughes, aviation tech on the USS *Nimitz*; Jason Turner, petty officer 3rd class on the USS *Princeton*; and Ryan Weigelt, leading petty officer and power plant specialist for the SH-60B "Seahawk" helicopter.

Soon, the black-and-white "Tic Tac" UFO video, spanning a little over a minute and a half, now had context and interlocking testimony from witnesses at different vantage points and involvement with the event. The video was one of three videos released alongside a hefty *New York Times* article concerning the Advanced Aerospace Threat Identification Program through the Pentagon.

As the larger story of the program and various other Navy encounters with UFOs were now circulating around the world, Kevin connected with the various other officers and Navy personnel to try to piece this puzzle together. What had they all seen while aboard those carriers in 2004? What had the pilots encountered in the skies? But perhaps most importantly, why was nothing done about it? If the Navy wasn't going to attempt to find answers, or at least make what they knew transparent to the public, then these former shipmates were going to attempt to find answers themselves.

"Over the course of 2018 to 2020, myself and several others formed a tight working group that has now morphed into UAP eXpeditions Group, an Oregon nonprofit." According to the UAP eXpeditions Group mission, the group plans to "provide a free public service, field-testing UAP related technologies. Our top notch team of physicists, research scientists, and trained observers captures and records broad-spectrum evidentiary data from UAP sightings. Partnering with technology developers and entrepreneurs at no direct cost to them, our team tests new equipment and devices featuring multiple data capturing modalities. We hope to provide unassailable scientific evidence that UAP objects are real, UAP objects are findable, and UAP objects are knowable." And what better place to start than where they all had their shared experience? The first expedition will set off for the same location and time period as the 2004 event to see if these phenomena appear with certain frequency and if the phenomena can be observed on our own terms. It's an ambitious undertaking, headed by a passionate team putting their curiosity into an unprecedented experiment. Only time will tell what the UAP eXpedition Group will uncover, but as the world continued to discuss the short video captured that day in 2004, the men who were there were set to embark on finding answers, whether the Navy, Intelligence agencies, or the phenomena itself liked it or not.

In early 2019, I had the immense pleasure and honor of meeting Kevin in California. As my investigative partner, Jennifer, and I were embarking on our own journey to find answers to the Navy UFO videos, we wanted to speak directly with the first person to track the "Tic Tac" UFO. I remember sitting in the hotel lobby before a long day of filming and meeting Kevin for the very first time. I didn't know quite what to expect. I'd interviewed several military officers, officials, and pilots in my years of research, but nothing like this. I was speaking to the man who made history and brought forth one of the most credible and most discussed UFO events of the last seventy-plus years. And while I clearly wanted to save the good stuff for the cameras that day, I couldn't help but excitedly press Kevin the moment I met him. We shook hands, sat in the hotel lobby, and time drifted away as he recounted the entire series of events for me.

After we wrapped the shoot, and the cameras were off, we all celebrated on set with a few beers. I remember clanking bottles with Kevin, a cheer of thanks and appreciation for all he'd done not only for our country, but for the hundreds upon thousands of people all over the world who had looked up in the skies and witnessed something truly unexplainable. And for the silent majority who never spoke a word of their experiences for fear of ridicule or simply a fear of the unknown, Kevin and many others aboard the USS *Princeton* and USS *Nimitz* had brought a level of legitimacy to what a UFO witness was, is, and continues to be: *Me. You. And all of us.* As I packed up my notes and took a moment to breathe, I watched Kevin staring out the large pane-glass window, which provided a beautiful view of the Burbank mountains. It was a moment I'd never forget. What Kevin was thinking or searching for, I left for him and him alone.

The 2004 *Nimitz* encounter was a historic UFO case that helped prompt the US Navy and our government to take the UFO topic more seriously than they ever had before. And that alone continued to drive my work and my passion for this profound mystery. It had changed me, as I'm sure it had changed Kevin. "What if the personal changes that happened to me suddenly happened to seven billion people worldwide?" Kevin asked of us all. "And without any understanding as to why they are changing... suddenly waking up with new abilities, new ambitions, and new questions? Effects on humans from UAP encounters are real. Expect to be changed." Those expectations for each person would be so richly different and personal. And so would the ultimate impact and change on their lives individually, and as human beings collectively. The journey continued, and for Kevin, and all of us, it seemed to have only just begun.

CONCLUSIONS

Many studies on UFO phenomena have come and gone, from lackluster government-funded investigations to independent scientific studies by private and civilian organizations. The results seem to always linger in a frustrating purgatory of mystery. And this goes for the Pentagon UFO program we've learned of as well. The former head of the program, Luis Elizondo, resigned from his position because of the lack of support the program was getting both in funding and being taken seriously. In an exclusive interview with Elizondo conducted by George Knapp on June 27, 2018, Elizondo stated: "There were many, many incidents we looked at. And we looked at them on a continuing basis. And we thought we saw some congruencies throughout these incidents time and time again, some repeated patterns of behavior. And as an intelligence officer, when you see those repeated patterns of behavior, that is key that something's going on. That there is something there—predictability—that you can use then, later on, to figure out how the things work and what the things really are."

So even though the program was making significant progress, because of the bureaucracy of the Defense Department in which the program was housed and the constant stigma attached to the UFO topic, both interest and support for the program began to wane. Elizondo, feeling like more work had to be done outside of the Department to get any answers, resigned. In his official resignation letter, dated October 4, 2017, he stated: "Underestimating or ignoring these potential threats is not in the best interest of the Department, no matter the level of political contention. There remains a vital need to ascertain capability and intent of these phenomena for the benefit of the armed forces and the nation."

Whether Elizondo will find answers outside of the government and inside of his current work with Tom DeLonge and To the Stars Academy, only time will tell. He, like so many others, are on their own journey when it comes to what they want out of this mystery, how they find it, and what they inevitably end up doing with those answers.

We all want those answers. And while I tried to cast my reel far to find them, the true lesson began to take form not in the deep waters of the unknown, but closer to the surface. It was the individual experiencer that was most important. The aftermath upon the witness and experiencer held many more potential answers than the experience itself ever truly could.

Those I'd interviewed recalled some of the most vivid UFO sightings I've come across in my research. The often ordinary circumstances that preceded the sightings, the attention to detail throughout them, and the emotional impacts afterward were powerful, profound, and extremely revelatory. For some, what happened was unexplainable and that was it. The possibilities of what they witnessed are unforgivingly vast, and for most, there is much more in life to ponder than the teasing of such sporadic phenomena. But for other witnesses, it was a challenge to reality, belief, and even for some, spirituality. It was an invitation to reexamine their own lives and what the technology they witnessed could potentially do, positively or negatively, for humanity. It showed us that we could not begin to answer anything fully until all the questions were there. And by the looks of it, there were many, many questions to still be asked.

In terms of exploration, the same could certainly be said for those I interviewed in the scientific and academic fields. The scientific community has not given up on UFOs. Prof. Greg Eghigian showed us the distance between science and UFOs in an extremely logical light, never casting a dark shadow on the possibility of a convergence between fields. Dr. Erol Faruk, Dr. Jeffrey Bennett, and Dr. Robert Davis then gave us hope that scientists are indeed interested in the topic and are willing to speak about their own personal thoughts on what these phenomena could potentially represent.

Marc D'Antonio introduced us to UFOTOG II, which he and Douglas Trumbull are steadily developing. By tracking UFO activity, we could possibly see, for the first time, some of the most detailed photos ever taken of these elusive objects. The same could be said for the work of Dave Cote's CubeSat project, Philippe Ailleris and the team at UFODATA, the work by Christopher O'Brien and the UFO Data Acquisition Project, Robert Powell and the entire research team at the Scientific Coalition of UAP Studies, and the scientific expeditions that would soon take place with the growing team of scientists, former military, and researchers that comprise the UAP eXpedition Group. These ambitious and brave individuals pioneered some of the most sophisticated UFO-tracking systems, technology advancements, and recording of hard data on some of the most elusive phenomena in our lifetime. The argument by many in the scientific community has always been that by the time a UFO sighting is reported, it's already too late to even investigate or apply any type of analysis. With these projects constantly active, we will have exciting new access to uncovering the truth behind the many mysteries, extraterrestrial or not, in our skies.

If the experiences in this book were happening in the reality we can see, smell, hear, and touch, then we are dealing with extremely advanced intelligences that are able to make contact with us in ways we have yet to fully understand, let alone initiate ourselves. They have the ability to appear out of thin air and pierce through the walls of our homes and even our minds. Afterward, they leave almost no trace other than fragmented memories, begging many questions as to why they are doing this and what they may be capable of. Are those who are abducted literally plucked from their lives and dropped back down? Do those who've performed these abductions have any sense of remorse or hesitation on how their actions will affect the individual afterwards? Or, as we've learned from the hypnotherapists and abduction investigators, perhaps there is something special in each of these people that they see vitally important to examine and explore.

That being said, the most important thing to take away from each of the individuals who had abduction experiences is that they confront the experience in a way that they find beneficial. Whether by seeking support with other experiencers or coming forward to those who will hear them out, their stories needed to be heard. Michael Melton, Yvonne Smith, Kathleen Marden, and NK Kranda are out there, waiting to listen. And while I myself am no professional, nor have I studied psychology or psychotherapy, my own observations of those they've worked with are that they are healthy, functioning members of society, contributing in their own ways to the progression of humanity in countless ways. Though I admit that the experiences themselves leave me wondering what actually occurred, I take personal comfort in knowing that even if the experience is alien in some way, the heart of the experience remains *human*, and always will.

The witnesses and experiencers are the key. Without them, we'd have no record of these events. Many will see these stories as just that: nothing more than words. Words either misconstrued, fabricated, or exaggerated. But I refuse to accept that. The words of those I've included in this book are all the proof I need to continue believing there is and remains UFO and possible alien phenomena to continue exploring. Every story has some sort of value in our search, and so does every individual telling them. I hope you'll continue to explore as well. Ask someone if they've ever seen something in the sky they could not identify. Or, if you feel so brave, ask if they've had a brush with something unknown and possibly nonhuman. Hear their voice quiver. See their hands shake. And most importantly, ask them how it changed their life. Perhaps you will experience, just as I have, something vulnerable, beautiful, sometimes scary or traumatic, but inherently human. I wager it may just change your perspective and, possibly, even your beliefs.

While I don't spend every day with these people, nor do I follow up with them each and every night, I most definitely have kept my door open. Some have become close friends, and others have chosen to never speak about the experience again. But their bravery to have their accounts in print has shown me that a shift is occurring in the overall acceptance of these phenomena. And that sense of normalizing the abnormal is a big step in a progressive direction.

As for belief, I never intended to impart my own. But the further I dug into these phenomena, the more I began to realize that I couldn't brush aside my personal involvement. Like a journalist embedded in a war zone, I was unarguably affected by the individuals I met and corresponded with. I could no longer deny the impact their stories had on me. I found myself struggling with my own reality at times. From a simple trip to the grocery store to the most pivotal moments in my life, something always whispers: there's more to all of this. There's more to what you do and do not see. This kept me wanting to hear more stories. I began to realize that perhaps these phenomena weren't preparing us for some grand reveal or the "third act." Perhaps they were touching each individual, one by one, and truly working on our timetable. We just needed a little nudge, as we often do.

My nudge took place as I fished off that dock on the Saint Lawrence River in 1995. After hearing many similar stories to my own throughout my research, I began to question what exactly it was that I'd seen floating over the water that warm summer night. Was it the same craft that Kieran or Shawn spotted? The descriptions were eerily similar. Or could it have been the likes of what Linda or Jennifer had witnessed? Whatever it was, I accepted, just as most of those in this book had, that in the grand scheme of things, it didn't actually matter what the object was. It was how the event touched, shifted, or altogether changed those who'd experienced it. The material I've covered in this book is broad, and it is challenging. With the testimonies of so many, I, as I hope you have, reflect my own life onto those within these pages. What would I have done in their situations? How would I have reacted? What would I take from the experience, and how would I go on with my life having experienced it? Those questions rely solely on your acceptance that there is no singular answer. The fact that you've made it this far shows that you are open to the possibility that the world around us isn't exactly what we perceive it to be.

Being a playwright on the other side of my life, my passion was always in creating the character. The plot itself would eventually manifest through the voices of these characters. And as the plot continues to be written for each and every one of the individuals in this book, I couldn't help but envision each and every one of them standing in a chorus line, stepping forward one by one into a spotlight, and spilling their heart and soul to us, a global audience. They've all presented their monologues in the most primal and vulnerable of ways. They are human beings who have come in contact with something alien, in any and every sense of the word. Within those brief moments when they were granted a view into the heart of these phenomena, they stared into a void of uncertainty, only to discover, perhaps as many of us have, that something will inevitably find a way to stare back.

AFTERWORD

"Bourbon. Neat."

It was April 24, 2015. Almost two years later, to the day. I'd returned to the same bar on the Lower East Side to speak with Tyler in depth about his sighting of the Phoenix Lights incident. I should have known, being a frequent bartender myself, that he'd most likely moved on to another job, or perhaps even another city. Either way, I'd arrived with a notepad in my bag, anticipating an interview that would fill every sheet of paper in my possession. But Tyler had indeed moved on to greener and more prosperous pastures on the Upper East side of Manhattan. In his place to give me this news was Robert. Robert resembled Tyler strikingly, though sporting grey hair and a beard. He was at least a decade older as well. His bourbon pour was conservative, as it should be. He'd never met me before, and my attitude while entering the bar had shifted from excitement to moderate disappointment. But that didn't stop me from taking advantage of the situation and enjoying a drink.

"You a friend of Ty's?" Robert asked.

"We met here two years ago. Told me to stop by any time since..."

"Since he's always working?" Robert laughed. "Yeah, he practically lived here. But we haven't seen him since he sold out to the stroller pushers uptown."

I practically spit my first sip of bourbon in laughter. Apparently tending bar on the lower East Side was the punk version of the trade, and Tyler had signed to a major label.

"I think the bar-back has his phone number, though," Robert told me. "Let me check."

Robert was kind enough to go inquire. As I looked around the bar, I noticed it was noticeably busier than two years prior. And the décor had changed from a dingy dive bar to a hip beer-tasting establishment. Craft beer signs littered the walls alongside flat-screen TVs showing a baseball game. Dubbed the "Subway Series," the New York Yankees and the New York Mets were pitted against one another, the Bronx and Queens battling for supremacy. Living mere miles from Citi Field, I was rooting for the Mets. But my attention veered away from the screen in the bottom of the third inning as the Yankees scored four runs. My mind began to drift as the bar's volume faded into ambient noise.

I reflected back on the conversation I'd had with Tyler. The raw, vulnerable state he'd put himself in as he recalled his sighting the best he could. I'd run into this with every person I talked to about their sighting or experience. They were divulging things they never had before, and I craved that intimacy as each account found its way to me or was personally sought out. My interview skills had hopefully grown since that conversation, and while I didn't write down anything Tyler had told me that night, I remembered distinctly some of the words he'd used to describe the experience: Huge. Bright. Terrifying. Beautiful. Unbelievable. I'd grown accustomed to these words throughout the two-year process of compiling accounts and reports. Yet it was *unbelievable* that always hit me most. Frederik Uldall, our Danish interviewer, had used this word as well. For me, that word had morphed into many different forms throughout those two years. I'd grown comfortable not challenging these phenomena, but embracing them.

I looked around the bar on that unusually cold night as everyone warmed up with spirits and company. They laughed, kissed, debated, cried, and everything in between. The collective guard was down as inebriation slowly eased inhibitions. I couldn't help but smile. For a brief moment, the alien phenomenon had completely detached from my mind. And I sat, more human than ever, absorbing the atmosphere around me.

"You need Ty's number?" The voice snapped me out of the serene moment.

I looked up to see the bar-back, a young guy wearing a Yankees baseball cap. He held a piece of small paper in his hand with a phone number scribbled on it.

"Yeah. Thanks." I folded it once and placed it on the bar.

"How do you know him?"

"He was going to tell me about something that happened to him back in Arizona," I responded, not quite ready to dive into the subject matter in detail.

"The lights."

He said it so matter-of-fact. It completely caught me off guard.

"Yeah. How'd you know?"

He picked up some rogue pint glasses teetering on the edge of the bar. He stacked them one by one into one another like a matryoshka doll, creating a slightly leaning tower of glass. He sensed the nervousness on my face as I was almost positive the glasses would eventually fall.

"Don't worry. I got this. It's all about physics."

A small smirk creeped upward on my mouth as I watched him ambitiously add two more glasses.

"Ty told me that those lights defied physics. How big they were and then how quick they disappeared. It was one of the first things he and I talked about when we met."

"Same here," I responded. It was clear that the phenomenon had not only pulled Tyler and me together, but this young man as well. And just like so many others, it had connected one more dot in and endless game of mystery.

"Well, I hope he answers his phone when you call. He's too good for us now."

His betrayal to the Lower East side had left more wounds than once thought. I looked at the number and began to enter it into my phone. Maybe I could still interview Tyler without this trip downtown being a complete bust in terms of research.

"You know, I don't tell a lot of people about this, but I saw something in the sky once. Didn't look like anything I'd ever seen before."

My eyes shot up toward him. This had become a natural reaction to these types of situations. He appeared hesitant to divulge anything else.

"Really?" I asked. "What do you think it was?"

"I don't know. But it was like this... if I had to... fuck. It was... unbelievable."

I tucked my phone into my pocket. "I'd love to hear about it. Would you be comfortable with that?"

The sound of cheers filled the bar as the Yankees ended the game in the top of the ninth inning, winning six to one. With this victory, I could sense a rush of confidence flood over him.

"I've got a break in, like, twenty minutes. I'll tell you all about it."

I nodded, holding in my excitement. He tipped his brim, grabbed the almost anti-gravitic glasses, and headed back to the kitchen. I took a sip from my glass and reached into my pocket. I took out my notepad and set it on the bar. The empty paper before me would soon be filled with endless possibilities. What those possibilities might entail, I couldn't even pretend to know. But I was ready to listen. And more than anything, I was ready to be changed.

It's now June of 2020 as I add on to this afterword. I

remember that day in 2015 quite fondly. I sat across from the bar-back, Raj as I would soon learn his name, for almost an hour, scribbling notes in my notepad about an event he witnessed in May of 2007 while driving home to Newark, New Jersey, from Manhattan.

According to Raj, it was about 3 a.m. and he was stopped at a red light. The streets were desolate. "I thought about running the red light, because nobody was around. But I traveled this road a lot, and it was known to be a pretty popular speed trap for law enforcement, so I decided to just wait."

As he waited patiently, he looked out his driver-side window to a fenced-off area of open land. He noticed several lights hovering a few feet off the ground in this small field. "They weren't blinking, but almost pulsating. I thought it was weird, so I actually pulled over on the curb to look closer." When he got up to the fence, he noticed that these pulsating lights were in a circular pattern, wrapping around a pitch-black cylindrical structure of some sort. He actually put his face up to the fence bars to try to get a better look, but it was so dark and sleek, it was as if the lights were just floating there. However, he recalled not being able to see the grass behind the lights, so it had to be a structure of some sort. He started laughing nervously and even called to the object that seemed to be floating there. Nobody responded, and he started to get a little scared, so he started backing up. "It wasn't the best neighborhood to be alone in, in the middle of the night, and this thing in the field wasn't helping me feel safe either."

He started backing away to his car, but never taking his eyes off the wraparound lights. Suddenly, the entire structure began to lift slowly into the air, no noise whatsoever, and within the blink of an eye, it darted away. "I can remember the light trace being burned into my eyes. That's how fast it went away." Raj remembered jumping into his car and locking the door immediately, a feeling of danger coming over him. "I don't know why I felt that way. The thing was already gone. But that's how I felt. I can't explain it." He remembers trying to start the car several times, to no avail. It was a classic close encounter scenario, stalled engine and all. He tried several more times, and finally the car started.

I asked Raj what he thought it may have been, and he simply said, "A saucer. It was a fucking flying saucer. Just not silver or metallic. Just black like a dark glass. No noise. Nothing. I don't know who was in it, or who controlled it, but I wanted to get out of there." As soon as Raj was able to start the car again, he noticed the traffic light was red again. "I didn't even hesitate. I said the hell with it, and I gunned it through that red light so fast!"

I asked him if he regretted following the traffic rules the first time, thinking he probably never would have had the experience if he had just driven on. "I don't know. I still can't believe I saw it. I felt sort of lucky, but also I don't know what it was and I don't think I ever will. I sometimes wish the light was green that night. I sometimes wish it was red. All I know is, I didn't get pulled over by the cops, and I saw a flying saucer. So you tell me if that's lucky!"

Raj still works at the bar. I've gone in several times pre-pandemic lockdown (as of writing this in June 2020), and every time he sees me come in, he just yells, "Red light!" My hope is that the bar remains open, that Raj continues working there, and that I can hand him this book and tell him how much his story meant to me. How much every story in this book has meant and continues to mean to me as their journeys and mine continue in this uncertain world we call home. And I hope that many, many more people will take that red light to heart and stop every now and again and look out. Look up. Look within. Every story has value, and as we continue searching for those answers through the words of so many who have experienced the unknown, we can take comfort in keeping our feet on the ground. But in doing so, never stop searching somewhere in the skies.

ABOUT THE AUTHOR

Ryan Sprague is a lead investigator and co-host of the CW television series *Mysteries Decoded* and is also a regular on the Travel Channel series *Mysteries at the Museum*. He is also the creator and host of the *Somewhere in the Skies* podcast. His freelance writing on UFOs found him interviewing witnesses in all walks of life about UFO sightings and close encounters. He's interviewed military and intelligence officials directly on the topic, writing for such news sites as Open Minds Magazine, Rogue Planet TV, and Futurism. Speaking on the UFO topic, he has been featured on ABC News and Fox News, and in the *New York Post*, *Newsweek* magazine, and *VICE*. To learn more, visit: **www.-somewhereintheskies.com**